FIRM FOUNDATIONS

The Development of Professional Accounting in Scotland

Hull University Press

FIRM FOUNDATIONS

The Development of Professional Accounting in Scotland

Moyra J. McI. Kedslie

Lecturer in Accounting
University of Hull

HULL UNIVERSITY PRESS

1990

British Library Cataloguing in Publication Data

Kedslie, M.J.M. (Moyra J.M.)

Firm Foundations
1. Scotland. Accountancy. Organisations.
Institute of Chartered Accountants of Scotland
I. Title
657.060411

ISBN 0-85958-492-5

Phototypeset in 11 on 12 pt Times and printed by the Central Print Unit, Hull University.

For my husband Richard

I hold every man a debtor to his profession; from the which as men of course do seek to receive countenance and profit, so ought they of duty to endeavour themselves, by way of amends, to be a help and ornament thereunto.

From the Preface to Francis Bacon, 'The Maxims of the Law' in *Works* ed. J. Spedding *et al* vol. VII, 1879.

Contents

Preface and Acknowledgements

The professionalization of Scottish accountancy began in Edinburgh in 1853, spread rapidly to Glasgow and then, in 1867, to Aberdeen. Each of these societies confined admission to accountants practising in the respective cities and all quickly required prospective members to complete indentures with a member in public practice, generally on payment of a substantial indenture fee.

This book discusses the development of these Scottish societies from 1850 to 1900 and examines their monopolistic successes in several areas of professional work, the co-operation and competition among them and their fruitless attempts to provide for the registration of accountants.

By 1990, the only Scottish professional accounting society was the Institute of Chartered Accountants of Scotland, whose members voted against a proposed merger with the Institute of Chartered Accountants in England and Wales in 1989, thus ensuring the continuing identity of Scottish CAs.

I believe that this book will be of interest to both young and old accountants and will help instill in the latter a sense of pride in their membership of the Scottish accounting profession.

Over the past few years I have received enormous help from many accountants, historians and others at different stages of this work. My first debt is to Professor Robert Parker, Exeter University, who was responsible for introducing me to accounting history and to this particular area of research. Also to Dr Annette Smith, ex Dundee University, who gave me invaluable advice in the early stages. To Professors Niall Lothian, Heriot-Watt University, and Irvine Lapsley, Stirling University, who examined my PhD and encouraged me to write this book.

Much of my source material came from the Scottish Records Office and from the records of the Institute of Chartered Accountants of Scotland, both of whose staff showed me unfailing courtesy and interest over the years. In particular, Professor Michael Mepham and other members of the Scottish Committee on Accounting History, the staff of the membership records department and Mrs Dorothy Hogg, Librarian and her library staff who spent many dusty hours with me in the Institute archives.

During the final stages, I have been indebted to the indefatigable and meticulous work of Mrs Elizabeth Chilvers, who has cheerfully word processed inumerable drafts and to Miss Jean Smith and Dr Joyce Bellamy, who have painstakingly checked them and whose expert knowledge has been invaluable.

Finally, but by no means least, I must thank my husband Professor Richard Briston, who has been living with this manuscript for rather a long time and without whose support and encouragement this book would never have been completed.

List of Figures

List of Tables

I

Introduction

1. Influences on the Growth of Accounting in the Nineteenth Century

There is ample evidence to suggest that men describing themselves as accountants were common in Britain in the eighteenth century. Although it is impossible to obtain an accurate number of such practitioners, evidence of their existence can be established by using business directories of the period, in advertisements for services being offered and by the fact that there were many teachers of bookkeeping and text books on the subject at that time.

From the beginning of the nineteenth century, the number of people styling themselves as accountants in various business directories grew steadily,[1] suggesting that demand for the services of such persons was correspondingly increasing. Various reasons have been put forward for this increase. Stacey attributed it to the strong economic development of the beginning of the nineteenth century, which 'engendered the need for competent persons with knowledge and ability to practise accountancy',[2] through the necessity to keep proper books of account and to have them audited. Worthington agreed with this contention and, in particular, identified the railway mania of the 1840s as being the principal cause of the extremely rapid growth in the number of accountants listed in the London Post Office Directories during the period from 1840 to 1847, which reveal an increase from 107 accountants in 1840 to 210 in 1845, with a drop to

186 in 1847.[3] Woolf[4] contended that the growth in the number of accountants during the first half of the nineteenth century was due to the general increase in commerce and the expansion of business at that time, citing as additional factors the appointment of accountants as official assignees in bankruptcy[5] and the need for accountants to assist in the preparation of cost estimate information prior to the introduction into Parliament of Private Bills for the construction of railways.

Lee[6] saw the need for persons competent in accounting as having developed in the period up to 1830 when the scale and complexity of industry required more sophisticated accounting, but noted the extreme shortage of properly trained persons: 'Accountants in the true sense hardly existed, there was no body of theory or consistent principles, and the numerous text books (from which the clerks had learnt their bookkeeping) dealt almost wholly with merchants' accounts.' Jones[7] was of the opinion that 'the evolution of the accountancy profession in Britain is inextricably linked with the history of its Industrial Revolution', an opinion which was also expressed in the *History of the Chartered Accountants of Scotland*:

> In the early part of the nineteenth century accountancy work in Scotland must have increased greatly. It was a time of war, when large manufacturing and trading operations were necessary to the survival of the British Isles, and after the war was over in 1815 there ensued a period of what we would now call deflation which led to many commercial failures and widespread depression of trade.[8]

Marwick viewed this area from a different angle when he asserted that the growth of accountancy during this period reflected the increasing complexity of financial organisations.[9] These commentators may be correct in their various assertions. Although very little empirical evidence has been produced to prove that the expansion and impact of the Industrial Revolution was the direct cause of the development of accountancy during the first half of the nineteenth century, there can be no doubt that it was an important factor.

By the middle of the nineteenth century, company legislation was beginning to have some impact on the commercial sector. The repeal of the Bubble Act of 1719[10] in 1825, which allowed an expansion in the size of partnerships by permitting the number of partners to rise from six to twenty, and the joint stock company legislation of 1844-5 relaxed many of the legal constraints upon incorporation, thus encouraging expansion in this area, while at the same time introducing what were seen as safeguards for company shareholders. The Joint Stock Banking Act 1844[11] provided for the publication of a statement of a bank's assets and liabilities at least once a month and for the audit of such accounts. The Joint Stock Companies Act 1844[12] provided for the preparation and audit of such companies' balance sheets. Lee[13] stated that the most significant influence on the development of company law in the early nineteenth century was the railway age between 1830 and 1870. Each new railway company was a statutory company with powers conferred directly by an Act of Parliament authorising the building of railway lines and the raising of funds to meet the costs of construction. Most of the Acts required accounting records to be kept but made no provision for the audit or publication of financial statements.[14] However, the Railway Clauses Consolidation Act 1845[15] provided for the preparation and audit of the balance sheet of such companies.

On the surface, these early Acts would have been thought certain to generate a substantial amount of work for practising accountants. However, this was not the case since none of the legislation required that the preparation or auditing of accounts be undertaken by accountants. Presumably some skill as a bookkeeper was necessary for the proper maintenance of accounting records and for the preparation of statements of account at certain intervals but there is no proof that such work was undertaken by men who devoted themselves entirely to this task or by men who could be described as professional accountants. Nevertheless, Stacey stressed the importance of the Joint Stock Companies Act 1844 as: 'from an accountant's viewpoint, its provisions in regulating accounting safeguards were nothing short of visionary.'[16] This Act was, however, quickly overtaken by the Companies Clauses Consolidation Act 1845[17] which laid down much more specific requirements for company accounts, for the employment of a bookkeeper to enter the accounts in the books and for the appointment of an auditor.

When the area of the audit is considered, doubt must be

expressed as to the quality of the men performing this task. Many of the criticisms of early railway and bank auditing indicate that the audit function was often performed by interested amateurs elected by the shareholders from among themselves.[18] The Companies Clauses Consolidation Act of 1845 did not require that auditors be professional accountants but only required them to hold at least one share in the company. Presumably it was felt that the auditor was more likely to carry out his task properly if he had a vested interest in the company's performance.

In 1855, Parliament passed the Limited Liability Act[19] which automatically provided limited liability to members of companies on registration. This Act did not apply to Scotland but in the following year a consolidation act - The Joint Stock Companies Act 1856[20] - was passed: 'to begin the modern statutory provisions, and to introduce them in their modern form to Scotland.'[21] This Act removed compulsory accounting requirements and compulsory audit for registered companies, apparently for two reasons. First, the provisions in the earlier Acts were so loose as to be ineffective and second the 'strong contemporary feeling that matters of accounting should be dealt with by private contract between shareholders and directors.'[22] However, the Act did introduce a model set of articles of association which included optional accounting and auditing clauses and a standard form of balance sheet.

Without any doubt the nineteenth century Act which had most impact on accounting and accountants was the Joint Stock Companies Act 1862,[23] which was to remain the principal Companies Act until 1908. This Act is often credited with being the reason for the formation of the accountancy profession in England, although Worthington[24] rather exaggerated when he claimed that accountants sprang into being because of this and the Bankruptcy Act 1869[25] since accountants already existed. Stacey's view was nearer the truth, especially when applied to England:

> Perhaps no other professional community, living upon the fruits of trade, commerce and industry, has benefited to the same degree as did accountancy from the enactment of the Companies Act in 1862. Passing of the Act immediately put a living in the hands of an increasing number of accountants.[26]

Carr-Saunders and Wilson[27] had similar views on this but only with regard to the development of the profession in England. As far as Scotland, with its organised accountancy profession, was concerned, Brown had no doubt that the Act was of significance for the Scottish accountant, 'for it provides him with occupation (and incidentally with remuneration) at the inception, during the progress, and in the liquidation of public companies.'[28]

With the exception of Jones who analysed the fee income of the founding firms of Ernst and Whinney,[29] none of the authors substantiated their claims, but they have been repeated often enough to have become generally acceptable. However, one cannot help wondering why, if the Companies Act of 1862 was crucial to the emergence of the profession in England, it was not until 1870 that the first two English accounting societies were formed - the Incorporated Society of Liverpool Accountants in January and the Institute of Accountants in London in November.[30] Perhaps Pixley was correct in his contention that what

> really brought professional Accountants into prominent notice in England was the catastrophe caused by the failures which followed the suspension of the Banking House of Overend, Gurney & Co., in 1866, and which led to perhaps the most serious commercial panic the City of London has ever known.[31]

In Scotland there appears to be general agreement that the emergence of accountants was due to slightly different and more readily identifiable factors, since accountants there were seen to be an offshoot of the legal profession. Green, indeed, went so far as to say that it was lawyers who practised accountancy in Scotland at the end of the eighteenth century[32] and Jones emphasised this difference, stating that English accountants did not have the same degree of involvement in legal matters as their Scottish counterparts.[33] Carr-Saunders and Wilson[34] and Lewis and Maude[35] both referred to accounting as being a development of the legal profession and this was partly confirmed by Thompson's statement that in the 1840s and 1850s Scottish estate accounts were audited by law agents.[36]

Perhaps McClelland exaggerated when he said that the

'import of the word [accountant] in the two countries has quite different significations',[37] but there is no doubt that there were significant differences between them in the early years of the profession. Moreover, Brown argued that Scottish accountants in the mid-nineteenth century did not compose a homogeneous group since Edinburgh accountants were closely associated with lawyers, while Glasgow accountants had loose associations with commerce.[38] Thus, the differences were not limited to those between Scotland and England.

2. Influences on the Formation of the Accounting Profession in the Nineteenth Century

When examining the reasons for the formation of an organised accounting profession, various schools of thought seem to emerge. Stacey attributed this simply to the increasing numbers of accountants and, more particularly in Scotland, to the growth of work in auditing, banking, bankruptcy, financial accounting and cost accounting.[39] Stewart also referred to the growth in the number of people involved in public accountancy work having reached a stage by the middle of the nineteenth century where it encouraged professional formation.[40] Pollard[41] noted the involvement of the legal profession in Scotland with estate administration and claims that it was precisely because of this that accountancy was professionalized in Scotland long before it was in England. *The History of the Institute of Chartered Accountants in England and Wales* (ICAEW) specifically stated that the profession in England and Wales was formed to protect standards of work,[42] a claim reinforced by Millerson, although stated by him in a slightly different way: 'Determined efforts by accountants to reform the profession and reduce malpractice, produced the Institute of Chartered Accountants in England and Wales.'[43]

There is no doubt that the existence of such formal associations of accountants was advantageous in attempts to protect existing areas of practice and to ensure that possible opportunities for expansion were not overlooked. Certainly, after the formation of the ICAEW in 1880, its view was sought on matters of relevance to the profession through representation on government committees. Jeal attributed this representation solely to the existence of professional accounting bodies: 'these national professional organisations provided those men, who had already shown themselves worthy of confidence, with that status which had become overdue.'[44]

Stacey was mistaken when he listed the areas of work undertaken by Scottish accountants at the time of the formation of their professional bodies as being auditing, banking, financial accounting and cost accounting.[45] At that time there was very little banking or auditing work undertaken by professional accountants and cost accounting was certainly considered to be beyond the pale. The history of the Institute of Chartered Accountants of Scotland stated quite clearly that 'the full-time employment of qualified accountants by industry on anything like a large scale is a twentieth century phenomenon.'[46] What Stacey and others appear to confuse is the development of accounting practices with the emergence of professional accounting bodies in the mid-nineteenth century. While it is true to attribute much of the development of accounting as a subject to the growing demands of banking, railways and industry, those accountants who formed the early professional bodies were involved only in public accounting and, in Scotland in particular, were heavily involved in bankruptcy work; they were not employed in any significant numbers or in a full-time capacity by banking companies, insurance companies, railway companies or any industrial undertakings. Indeed, Pollard[47] commented that professional accountants were not equipped to deal with the accounting problems of industry and that manufacturers, during this period of expansion, had to develop their own accounting systems.

The indifference of the Scottish chartered bodies to the needs of industry is illustrated by the fact that when, in the late 1880s, a group of young Glasgow accountants suggested that the examination syllabus should be extended and modernised by the inclusion of Economics and Cost Accounts, their suggestions were rebuffed with the comment that 'Accountants have no concern with the processes of Industry; only with final results.'[48]

When considering the somewhat philanthropic reasons frequently advanced by the early professional bodies to explain their formation, it must be appreciated that they probably present a rather biased view of the picture and that other views are also worthy of consideration. Accountants as a group are, after all, unlikely to have been greatly different from other emerging professions of the mid-nineteenth century and by that time they would have been able to perceive the advantages which other groups had acquired through professional formation.

One theory advanced by Lewis and Maude[49] suggested that, in many cases, professional formation occurred when a group of people found that they were unqualified for the existing professions and determined to remedy this by upgrading their occupation to a new profession. This would imply that the type of work undertaken by members of the new professions was somewhat lower than that undertaken by the older established professions. However, in the case of Scottish accountants such a claim would be difficult to substantiate since much of the work undertaken by them was related to the legal profession and had often been carried out in legal offices. In fact what the Edinburgh accountants did was to form a splinter group composed of people who had a common interest in such work and who, perhaps, had the foresight to see the developments that were bound to come in an era of so much economic change.

Millerson[50] stated that one of the features of professional formation was that influences within the confines of the occupational area were more crucial than any external factors. This is difficult to prove as far as accountancy is concerned but it was possibly correct. Among the external factors that influenced professional formation was changing legislation for all companies, and particularly for railway companies, in the 1840s. As far as Scottish accountants were concerned, the most important influence was the proposed changes in bankruptcy legislation. However, since this last factor only affected accountants already working in that particular area, it is more likely that it ought to be classified as an internal factor.

The other significant internal factor was undoubtedly that of self-interest or protectionism, and the new profession quickly attempted, albeit unsuccessfully, to limit certain areas of work to their own members and also to exclude from membership of the new bodies men who were seen to be working in areas, such as factoring, which were not considered to be appropriate to the new profession. Although the process of protectionism was slow it was steady but after fifty years of existence, Scottish chartered accountants still had no exclusive claim to any one area of practice. They dealt with by far the largest proportion of Scottish bankruptcy work, bank audit and railway company audit but had no monopoly over any of these.

3. The Early Activities of the Scottish Accountancy Bodies

(*a*) *Social Status*

In the relatively small communities of Edinburgh and Glasgow, the existing professions such as law had, by the mid-nineteenth century, acquired significant social status and it was therefore important that the new professional accountancy bodies aimed to achieve a similar status as quickly as possible. The most obvious way to attain this objective was to limit initial and early admittance to accountants who were already seen to have achieved a sufficiently high social status and in the later years, once the profession was established and accepted as having a certain social status, those admitted to the profession would automatically attain this same status. Such a pattern would confirm the views that the professions gave members an enhanced social status[51] and that the primary concerns of a new profession were respectability and status.[52]

An analysis of early Scottish Chartered Accountants tends to confirm these views. In the formative and early stages of the profession the members were of a relatively high social status, although of a lower social mix than Scottish lawyers, and in the developing stages, once the profession was better established, a higher proportion of members came from a slightly lower social background.

There can be little doubt that the early members of the Society of Accountants in Edinburgh inherited some of their initial status from their close involvement with the legal profession. Proof of this involvement can be found in a report prepared in 1834 by a committee of the Society of Writers to the Signet in response to a Bill being presented in Parliament to establish the office of 'Accountant-General in the Court of Session'. In citing the reasons for their rejection of the proposals contained in the Bill the writers stated that 'it excludes a most respectable body of professional gentlemen, who, although they are not incorporated, are perhaps the most fitted for the duty, viz., the Accountants.'[53] However the legal profession was always seen as being more socially desirable than any alternative occupation. In the mid nineteenth century 'it was a good old Scottish custom for younger sons of the lairds to go early into commerce, trade, and the various professions - the bar being generally reserved for the eldest son.'[54] There was also a distinct hierarchy in the Scottish legal profession which, in Edinburgh, meant that 'The Advocates keep the Writers to the Signet at bay, except when these have a fee in their hands. The Writers to the Signet look askanse at the Solicitors before the Supreme Courts, and also at the Accountants; who again will have nothing to do with the Solicitors-at-Law'.[55] Heiton displayed a degree of respect for the advocacy while simultaneously being somewhat disparaging of the origins and abilities of some of its members:

> The Advocates are the highest corporation in Scotland, and their dignity is not merely corporate, for they contain among them individuals drawn from the higher castes, who throw the lustre of ancestry over the society of which they form a part. Yet it is the corporation which for the most part dignifies the individual; and this is the more curious that neither the expense of admission nor the tests of examination are beyond the reach of very humble and very thick-headed people.[56]

The assertion by Heiton that accountancy was ranked lower than most of the branches of the legal profession is confirmed by a study of the population of the new profession which showed that it was rarely the choice of the eldest son in a family, who, certainly in Edinburgh, tended to follow his father's profession or to enter the legal profession.

Such high regard for the legal profession was not found in all parts of Scotland or by all contemporary commentators. In 1873 '*The Baillie*', a Glasgow publication, asserted that: 'It is ten to one that your lawyer is a rogue.'[57] However the same commentator is equally unflattering in his general comment on chartered accountants in 1878 during the aftermath of the closure of the City of Glasgow bank: 'The law-courts were never brisker than now, the corporation of chartered accountants never reaped a richer harvest than that which has fallen to its lot in the autumn of the present year'. He then referred to the chartered accountants as 'the corbie species' - being a Scottish description of a scavenging, hooded, crow.[58] This comment perhaps pinpoints one of the reasons for chartered accountancy failing to achieve equal status with the legal profession as being its preoccupation, at that time, with bankruptcy.

(*b*) *Registration*

'Any attempt to isolate the moment when . . . the profession of accountancy, like Pallas Athene, sprang, fully armed, into the economic arena, remains a difficult task' claims Stacey.[59] In fact the main difficulty is in determining when a profession could be said to be in existence, although Mr Chalmers, addressing the Liverpool Chartered Accountants Students' Association expressed an opinion that 'the profession of accountants took its rise about the middle or end of the last [eighteenth] century.'[60] In Scotland, it is unlikely that the date would be set prior to the formation of the Scottish chartered bodies in 1853 but whether or not such events justified the adoption of the title 'profession' is arguable. Perhaps such status was not achieved until the Census of 1921 admitted accountants to the heading 'professional status.'[61] If professional status cannot be claimed until the occupational group has controlled entry to the group,[62] then accountancy would seem not to have earned the right to be so described in 1895 when Worthington noted that 'the profession of Accountancy is open to any one who chooses to adopt it, and there is nothing to prevent any incompetent person from practising it.'[63]

The problem that is constantly being encountered is that of the failure of the professional bodies or any government to define precisely what is meant by the term 'accountant' and to determine who would or would not be entitled to such designation. Many attempts were made during the late 1800s to remedy this problem by endeavouring to provide registration for accountants which, had any of the attempts been successful, would have limited the use of the term to registered accountants. However, all of the attempts failed because the accounting bodies in existence at that time could not agree on any single definition or set of standards which could be applied through the United Kingdom.

Another possible candidate for the date of formation of the profession in Scotland is 1892 when the three Scottish chartered bodies formed a joint examinations board so that, for the first time, all aspiring chartered accountants faced the same test of professional competence. By the end of the nineteenth century it was generally accepted that a professional accountant was one who was a member of one of the accounting bodies then in existence. However, the practice of those involved in accountancy work adopting the designation 'accountant', although not being members of any professional body, is one that continues to the present time and without the introduction of registration is likely to continue in the future.

(*c*) *Protection and Expansion of Income*

The records of the Scottish Chartered Accountants Societies make it absolutely clear that the reason for the formation of the Edinburgh and Glasgow societies was the proposed changes in bankruptcy legislation which were likely to have an effect on the earning capacity of accountants involved in that particular specialist area. There seems to be little doubt that the professional accounting bodies were formed to protect the interests of accountants involved in bankruptcy work in the mid-nineteenth century and to ensure that this group would be represented in discussions on changes in legislation, which representation would have been most unlikely on an individual basis.

As the second half of the nineteenth century progressed, the work of accountants developed in response to changing needs in the economy and to gradually more complicated forms of business corporations. Bankruptcy work became less important as a whole, although there were various upsurges in this work during the period studied, and what work there was had to be shared between more practitioners. Accountants therefore became involved in new areas of work and more involved in some existing areas of work. One of the effects of the growth in the number of large companies with many shareholders was the necessity for attestation as to the stewardship of the large funds involved by auditors who were properly trained to carry out this function, and research has shown that chartered accountants gradually built up a near monopoly in many specific areas such as railway company audit.[64]

It would appear, however, that the rate of growth in the number of chartered accountants in Scotland, although not particularly spectacular during this period, outpaced the growth in the amount of work available for them. However, Scottish accountants were more fortunate than Scottish lawyers, described as being 'the most unadaptable creature on earth',[65] whose training was limited to the requirements of Scottish law, since they were trained in a discipline that not only had applications in many different kinds of business organisation but also had universal application. The result of these two factors of increasing numbers and a readily marketable service was that, by the end of the nineteenth century, significant numbers of Scottish chartered accountants were practising all over the Empire and were, in many instances, instrumental in helping to establish professional accounting bodies in other countries modelled on those in existence in the United Kingdom.[66]

(*d*) *Monopoly Status*

As accounting developed in the Victorian era, many different matters were of concern to the members of the chartered societies in Scotland. Of these, the records of the three societies indicate that the most important recurring concern was that of protectionism which took various identifiable forms. It can be seen in the way in which the members of the chartered societies endeavoured to retain specific areas of practice exclusively for their members. Indeed, the earliest recorded example of this was the attempt by the Edinburgh society to exclude members of the Glasgow society from obtaining some bankruptcy work.[67]

This attitude continued to prevail and was demonstrated in the continuing attempts to obtain registration for accountants, and thus to exclude from work such as auditing accountants who were not members of the three chartered bodies. Accountants were also interested in proposed changes in legislation which would be likely to affect areas of practice, but they were unsuccessful in having new work designated as being exclusively for them.

The structures of the chartered societies were also of concern to them since by the time of their formation there was fairly generally accepted agreement as to the conditions that had to be fulfilled in order that an 'occupation' might be termed a 'profession'. To this end the societies erected a hierarchical structure of council and sub-committees, carefully monitored the academic and, indirectly, the social qualifications of entrants to indentures, and introduced a detailed system of examination of apprentices.

As the demand for accounting services continued to expand,

the numbers of non-chartered accountants grew and the chartered bodies spent a great deal of time trying to ensure that members of these newer bodies should not receive the same privileges as their own. It was also important that members of a respectable professional group should be seen to be socially aware, and in the case of Scottish chartered accountants, this desire manifested itself in activities such as the formation in Edinburgh of a Volunteer Rifle Company similar to that 'formed by the Faculty of Advocates, the Society of Writers to the Signet, and by other Professional bodies.'[68] On such activities was the image of Victorian professional respectability founded.

II

The Work of Accountants in the Mid-Nineteenth Century

1. The Work Available to Accountants

(*a*) *Merchants' Accounts*

Brown produces ample evidence of the various types of work being undertaken by men styling themselves 'accountants' (in Italy) from the thirteenth century onwards and states that the first recorded association of accountants was founded in Venice in 1581. It is significant that part of the examination for entry to this association was carried out by merchants, indicating the necessity for expertise in merchants' accounts[1] in sixteenth-century Venice. This emphasis on mercantile accounts was also evident in seventeenth-century England where books on this topic were being published and where the influence of those so involved in such accounts led Brown to suggest that 'the profession in England had its origin in this class and was augmented during the early part of the nineteenth century mainly from the ranks of practical book-keepers trained in mercantile or other offices'.[2] Training in mercantile accounts appears to have been recognised as producing men who were held in some esteem by the business community since reference is made to the appointment, in 1849, of two merchants from Liverpool and London as auditors of the Great Western Railway Company.[3]

In Scotland, probably the most famous seventeenth-century

accountant was George Watson of Edinburgh, the son of an Edinburgh merchant, who completed his business education as a merchant by being sent to Holland to learn more about merchandising and to learn bookkeeping.[4] The involvement of accountants in Edinburgh business is indicated in the incorporation of the British Linen Company in 1746 which was established for the encouragement of the linen trade in Scotland and which provided for a bookkeeper and an accountant to be employed in the keeping of the warehouse accounts.[5] This was not an isolated case since Murray states that by the mid-eighteenth century most large mercantile concerns employed an accountant, although the advertisement from the *Glasgow Mercury* which he quotes as evidence of this reveals that men who were skilled at accounts also had to be skilled in business and were more akin to general managers than to the management accountants of the twentieth century.[6]

Since Glasgow was the centre of Scottish commercial activity it is hardly surprising to find records of teachers of subjects which were relevant to young men desirous of embarking on a mercantile career. Indeed Thomas goes so far as to suggest that in the mid-eighteenth century Scotland's educational system was such as to ensure that 'her youth was amply prepared to play a part in the dawning industrial age'.[7]

Many schools in the West of Scotland included bookkeeping in their curricula in the mid-eighteenth century and many of the private teachers of bookkeeping were also authors of books on the subject.[8] Often the titles of such volumes give an interesting insight into the type of accounting education that was considered necessary for young men entering the merchant houses at that time. For example, William Webster's book on *Essays on Bookkeeping*[9] had added to it in 1758 an appendix containing a variety of specimens of company accounts including 'Accounts kept by the Factors in the Sugar Colonies: Accounts kept by the Merchants or Storekeepers in Virginia and Maryland and Shopkeepers Accounts in this country.' It would appear from this and other publications that the emphasis in accounting education at that time was such as to provide trained bookkeepers, clerks and accountants for the large merchant houses both at home and in the colonies, but not to consider the needs of manufacturers.

In examining the links between accounting and management,

Pollard comments that the type of accounting applied in mercantile houses did have something to offer to manufacturing concerns since it was: 'designed to eliminate errors, prevent embezzlement, and establish the value of a business for probate or similar purposes'.[10] However, it failed to provide for the specific needs of industry particularly in the determination of periodic income and in the valuation of capital assets, with the result that each entrepreneur developed a system designed to meet his own specific requirements and no clearly identifiable system of accounting for manufacturing concerns evolved. Since many of these entrepreneurs developed from small family beginnings there was often thought to be no need for an accountant to be employed, and it was not until enterprises became quite large that the value of accounting as an aid to the prevention of theft and embezzlement was recognised. Lacking any substantial literature or training to aid them, many accountants employed in industry were completely inadequate to the task, if not at times also dishonest, and the solution to this problem was perceived to lie, not in an improvement in accounting education nor in the development of better accounting systems, but in the provision of guarantee funds and insurances against the shortfalls of such employees.[11]

Many of the advertisements for services offered by Scottish accountants in the late-eighteenth century include a claim to expertise in the making up of the books and accounts of manufacturers. John Gibson of Glasgow even presumed to strengthen his claims by comparing his skills to those 'practised by the most approved Accountants in Edinburgh'[12] although this probably applied more to his involvement in bankruptcy than to his other work. Such advertisements lead to the conclusion that the employment of accountants in Scottish industry at around the beginning of the nineteenth century was not of any tremendous significance. Stewart was probably correct when he claimed that: 'industry and commerce remained predominantly in the hands of individuals who, if they felt that records were required, kept their own private records and did not recognise any need to employ accountants other than such of their confidential clerks as might be dignified by that title'.[13]

Thus, in spite of the fact that accounting textbooks had proliferated by the mid-nineteenth century and that there was great similarity in the methods expounded in them, there is little proof that such methods were being systematically and uniformly applied in industry[14] or that they were being applied by men suitably qualified so to do. Specific examples of industrial concerns that did keep early accounting records can be found in the Scottish Business Archives. Many of these were kept in the form of journals and ledgers and seem to have been maintained for two main purposes - the costing of different jobs and the prevention of partnership disputes.[15]

Although accounts were prepared by many firms during the early years of the nineteenth century, there was little, if any, practice of publishing them. Shareholders were generally free to examine the books and records of the company concerned and would be most likely to do this when appearing in person to collect dividends.

(*b*) *Canals*

The first widespread development which rendered such a practice inadequate was the building of canals which, particularly in the first half of the nineteenth century, brought together large sums of capital from widely dispersed investors and employed large numbers of manual workers. Generally, canal construction was undertaken in sections, different sections being undertaken at different times and by different contractors.[16] Detailed accounting records were necessary, such as Thomas Telford's elaborate systems of monthly payments and of retention of sums as a guarantee of satisfactory workmanship and punctual completion.[17] But although 'canals in their day reached a far greater pitch of prosperity than the railways have ever attained to'[18] they suffered from a lack of effort to produce a standardised system of management.

The canals were also responsible for producing a new class of investor[19], which Hadfield describes as being largely titled landowners, clergymen, academics, doctors and solicitors.[20] Accountants were generally employed, but would often undertake others tasks within the company or would act as accountant for more than one company. Their job descriptions make it appear that the title of cashier or bookkeeper might have been more appropriate than that of accountant.[21] However, their tasks would have included the preparation of accounts and it is claimed that canal companies were among the first to publish their accounts. This was done because the enormous scale of such operations and the diversity of shareholders meant that the practice of opening the companies' books for inspection by shareholders was not always feasible.[22] This practice was not followed by all canal companies, since only the bigger canals produced printed annual reports and smaller concerns prepared a report to be read at the general meeting.[23]

There were, of course, exceptions to this general rule and from the beginning of 1781 the Forth and Clyde Canal company produced quarterly accounts of revenue and expenditure in response to demands from distant shareholders. On incorporation in 1768 they employed, as oversman/accountant, Alexander Stephen, a former Edinburgh merchant, at a salary of £70 per annum. Stephen's accounting skills seem initially to have been adequate, but he was replaced in 1785 by Richard Smellie, described as an accountant and bookkeeper. One of Smellie's first tasks was to supply books of account covering transactions since 1775, which would suggest that the job had outgrown Stephen's abilities.[24]

Scotland never had anything like the concentration of canals that developed in England. Although individual canals were important, there were never sufficient in existence at any one time in Scotland to make the impact on accounting that the railways were to have. In total, sixteen canals were completed in Scotland, only eight of which were still operating at the time of the formation of the first accounting societies.[25] Only five of them were of any significance and three of these eventually passed into the ownership of railway companies.[26] This meant that there was very little potential employment for accountants in this sector and certainly a lot less than that offered by railway companies. In addition, canal company accounts were very much simpler than railway company accounts since their only significant income came from tolls and sometimes from rents.[27]

None of the post office directories of this time has any listings for canal company accountants, which would suggest that the people filling such roles were not considered to be of as much importance as were bank or railway accountants and that they had little, if any, impact on the development of accounting in Scotland.

(*c*) *Railways*

'Coal made the industrial revolution, and the need for coal built the canals'[28], but after the middle of the nineteenth century the essential role of canals as a means of more efficient transportation of goods was rapidly overtaken by the railway companies. Railways had the additional advantage of being much more suitable for the conveyance of passengers as well as goods. The railway network spread rapidly and involved large numbers of investors and employees and huge capital investment. Returns made as at 1 May 1847 show seventy-four railway lines open for traffic employing 47,218 people, of whom 100 were categorised as 'accountants and cashiers'. At the same date the return for lines and branches under construction showed 256,509 employees, of whom 264 were accountants and cashiers.[29]

These figures would suggest that, from very early in their development, railway companies regarded accountants and cashiers as being essential, both in the construction and operation of railway lines. Perhaps their employment was encouraged by the Railway Clauses Consolidation Act of 1845, which required the preparation of annual accounts of receipts and expenditures and a statement of the balance of the account audited and certified by the directors and auditors of the company. At that stage, however, no uniform accounting requirements were provided and accounts were not kept in a uniform fashion, although certain aspects of the record-keeping did require standardised records.

Railway lines in the 1830s and 1840s were generally rather short but the amount of capital required to finance the building of the lines and the acquisition of the rolling stock was high. During the 1830s, twelve Scottish railway bills were passed authorising the construction of a mere 200 miles of track but authorising the raising of £3 million capital.[30] By the early 1840s, the formation of new railway companies had accelerated rapidly although many of the lines which were authorised by Parliament were never built. Partly because of a lack of availability of other attractive investment opportunities, capital was readily invested in railway companies. In 1846, in Scotland alone, fifty-eight Scottish railway bills were passed followed by, almost inevitably, speculative mania. 'Schemes for constructing hundreds of railways were launched in 1845-6 and a credulous public recklessly invested its money in these impossible ventures, only to realise too late that it had been swindled for the most part'.[31] The resulting chaos undoubtedly provided more employment for lawyers and accountants.

The move from joint ventures and partnerships to increasing

numbers of joint stock companies was so rapid as to be almost revolutionary and the amounts of capital being mobilised were vast. Railway mania had led to such speculation and frauds in the 1830s and 1840s that it became apparent that a *laissez faire* attitude could no longer be allowed to prevail.

> The State itself could not see this growing power of capital without imposing certain restrictions on its exercise and thus there developed during the nineteenth century a great body of Company Law laying down conditions under which companies should work so as to ensure publicity and honesty.[32]

Much of this new company law concerned the regulation of railway company accounts; indeed Stacey[33] goes so far as to claim that 'It was in the first Railways Acts that accountancy made its debut in the modern sense.' Certainly the rules laid down for the maintenance of railway accounts were more detailed and specific than any that had previously been contained in legislation. They provided employment for accountants and bookkeepers within the railway companies and were probably responsible for the development of internal audit since most of the legislation was concerned with internal accounting records and the recording of non-financial items. The requirement to prepare and have audited regular accounts also meant an increase in the work available for the growing body of accountants throughout the country.

The establishment of the clearing house system for traffic in 1841 enabled passengers and freight to be booked through a complete journey regardless of transfers between companies. This necessitated the introduction by the clearing house of standardised forms, generally adopted by member companies by 1844, for daily returns in order to allow the weekly balancing of inter-company transactions.[34] There is no doubt that this gradually introduced a reasonable degree of uniformity in internal accounts and went some way towards removing what Lardner referred to as 'an intolerable chaos of cross accounts'.[35] However, it was not until 1868 that any thorough effort was made to standardise accounts by an Accounts sub-committee of the Railway Companies Association[36], formed to implement the relevant clauses of the Railway Regulation Act 1868.[37]

In 1844 the Board of Trade issued new regulations for railway companies, requiring them to make annual returns of costs of construction, traffic and working expenses, which might well have required the employment of skilled accountants.[38] However, the report on the audit of railway accounts produced in 1849[39] stated that no uniform system of accounting existed[40] and that there was a generally held view that the introduction of a uniform accounting system for railway companies was impractical.[41] The dissatisfaction felt about the work done by railway accountants was strongly expressed in *Herapath's Railway Journal* in 1850: 'the insolent and costly arrogance creeping in amongst accountants. If not checked, we shall presently have accountants with about as much knowledge of railways as the steel pens they write with, becoming the lords and dictators of the whole railway interest.'[42] There were no rules for the preparation of accounts and confusion between the capital and revenue accounts of a company which were often manipulated by the directors and their accountants. It was necessary to charge expenditure against capital before the railway opened but in some cases companies continued to charge some items against capital after opening in order to leave a surplus in the revenue account which could be used for the payment of dividends.[43] However, by 1904 the railways were described as having profited by the experience of canals and having reached a high standard of efficiency.[44]

(i) *Legislation in Private Acts*

Railway companies in the mid 1800s were incorporated under individual Acts of Parliament which contained little in the way of uniform accounting and auditing requirements. In 1811 the Act incorporating the Spittal to Kelso Railway provided that 'proper Books of Account, and other Matters relating to the said Undertaking, shall be kept . . . and every Proprietor at all reasonable Times shall have free Access to the same, for his, her or their Inspection, without Fee or Reward'.[45] This line was obviously planned for horse-drawn wagons since it was constructed prior to the development of Stephenson's 'Rocket' and the company apparently envisaged the possibility of having female shareholders. By 1836, there was still very little detail contained in specific Acts, although generally the requirement was made that accounts be kept and that books be available for inspection[46]. The Act incorporating the Dundee and Arbroath Railway provided that every shareholders' meeting should have the power to call for, audit and settle all accounts of money but two years later in 1838 the Act incorporating the Edinburgh to Glasgow Railway[47] made no such provision. Perhaps this omission in the latter case was because the Treasurer and all receivers, collectors or officers of the company having custody or control of money were required, on appointment, to provide security for such custody of funds.[48] This would be considered to provide sufficient safeguard against fraud and would negate the need to check the accounts through the performance of some sort of audit.

In 1844 a company to make a railway from the city of Edinburgh to the town of Berwick-upon-Tweed was incorporated, with a branch to the town of Haddington. The company would be known as the North British Railway Company and would prove to have a successful place in the annals of Scottish railway history. By 1844 such Acts were providing rather detailed requirements for the keeping and auditing of accounts. This particular Act provided that: 'full and true Accounts shall be kept of all Sums of Money received or expended on account of the Company by the Directors, and all Matters for which such Sums of Money shall have been received or disbursed and paid' and that 'a Book-keeper shall be appointed by the Directors, and such Book-keeper shall enter the Accounts aforesaid in Books to be provided for the Purpose;'. Although there is no definition in the Act as to what constituted a bookkeeper it is significant that the company was endeavouring to ensure that the accounts would be properly maintained by someone with expertise in the area. In addition this Act required the shareholders to elect two auditors one of whom would retire each year but would be eligible for re-election. Since the auditors were elected to look after the interests of the shareholders they were themselves required to hold at least the same number of shares as would be required to qualify as a director and they were debarred from holding any office in the company. The auditors' duties were simply to 'receive from the Directors the half-yearly or other periodical Accounts and Balance Sheet required to be presented to the Shareholders, and to examine the same'[49] but no details of the accounting system were embodied in the Act. There were no accountants in the list of original shareholders of the North British Railway, and although Archibald Horne, an Edinburgh accountant, appears as a director from 1848 onwards[50], it is safe to assume that the original auditors were not accountants but were, nevertheless, considered competent to examine accounts prepared by the company bookkeeper. The shareholding requirement for an auditor was a minimum of twenty shares, each share having a par value of £25[51], i.e. an investment of £500 although not all of this would be payable on application. Professional accountants were employed to audit the accounts of the North British Railway as early as 1854 in the persons of H.G. Watson and R.E. Scott[52] who were, along with Archibald Horne, founder members of the Edinburgh Society of Accountants. The company appears to have been satisfied with the work done by Watson and Scott since they continued to perform this audit until the end of the 1860s. In 1870, the auditors were listed in *Bradshaw*'s as being Walter Mackenzie and J. Wyllie Guild, both of whom were founder members of the Institute of Accountants and Actuaries in Glasgow. By 1900 the audit had been taken over by their sons, R.C. Mackenzie and W.A. Guild, who were also Glasgow chartered accountants.

(ii) *General Legislation*

Companies which were formed after 1844 still required to be incorporated under separate Acts of Parliament and any alterations were required to be dealt with in the same cumbersome way. Nevertheless, the passing of legislation in 1845 made the task of the legal draughtsmen easier since Parliament had passed various Acts to regulate companies and specifically railway companies. From 1845 onwards, all new railway acts incorporated the provisions of this legislation. Some companies increased these basic provisions. In the case of the Deeside Railway there was provision for loan creditors to be entitled to inspect the company's books eight days before and eight days after the company's ordinary meeting.[53] The Caledonian Railway Arrangements Act of 1851 allowed preference shareholders to elect an auditor of the company 'who shall act as Auditor in conjunction with the existing Auditors of the Company'.[54]

The new legislation was designed to introduce some uniformity into the regulations governing the administration and financial matters of railway companies and also to protect members of the public who invested in such companies. Unfortunately, its introduction was accompanied by a flood of railway mania which was at its peak in Scotland in 1845 and burst in 1846 and which was considered to be one of the main causes of the severe financial crisis which the country suffered in 1847.[55] 'While it lasted the pace of railway projection and speculation in the stock of projected railways simply beggared description'.[56] Many of the new companies failed without ever operating and share prices displayed dramatic changes. Two companies which were incorporated in 1845 were the Aberdeen and the Caledonian Railway Companies. The Aberdeen company had a paid-up share value of £10 and during 1845 these shares traded at a premium of £6; by 1846 they were trading at a discount of £9. Similarly the Caledonian had a paid-up share value of £10, traded at a premium of £12 in 1845 and at a discount of £3 5*s*. in 1846. In both cases the disaster was aggravated by the fact that calls were still being made in 1846 when the price had slumped so much.[57] Typically this financial crisis had no great impact on the income of accountants, Frederick Whinney commenting that 'the rail mania of 1845 brought us a very great acquisition of business not only in audits, but also in the winding-up of companies'.[58]

Returns of railway employees were made annually from 1847 to 1860 and listed employees under different categories for lines which were already open and for those under construction. For the first two years accountants and cashiers were listed separately, but from 1849 onwards they were amalgamated. No definition of either position was given, but since clerks were listed separately, it can be presumed that those styled accountants and cashiers were of a reasonably high status in the railway management hierarchy and Reader claims that: 'By the fifties the accountant was distinct from the clerk'.[59] The number of people so employed on lines under construction can be seen from the first nine years' returns for Scottish railway companies (Table 2.1).

Clearly there was not too much stability in employment for accountants and cashiers in the construction sector of the railway industry in Scotland but, with the exception of 1854, there would appear to be a clear correlation between these employees and the number of lines described as open and it would appear that most operating Scottish railway companies did employ a person who might be described as a railway accountant or cashier.

If the status of these railway accountants can be judged by

TABLE 2.1

Accountants and Cashiers employed by Scottish Railway Companies 1847-1855

Bradshaw's Listing of Lines Opened	Year	BPP Reference	Employed on Lines Opened		Employed on Lines under Construction	
			Acc.	**Cash.**	**Acc.**	**Cash.**
-	1847	1847 (579) LXIII, 101	14	5	22	20
28	1848	1849 (249) LI, 141	11	4	14	13
28	1849	1850 (165) LIII, 277	19		12	
28	1850	1851 (102) LI, 255	23		7	
29	1851	1852 (153) XLVIII, 395	24		3	
28	1852	1852-1853 (253) XCVII, 229	22		2	
26	1853	1854 (105) LXII, 559	20		4	
40	1854	1854 (495) LXII, 599	24		8	
30	1855	1854-1855 (511) XLVIII, 631	25		5	

Key
Acc. - Accountants
Cash. - Cashiers

Sources: (i) *Bradshaw's Railway Almanac, Directory, Shareholders' Guide and Manual, 1848, etc.*

(ii) *British Parliamentary Papers*

their inclusion in the post office directories of that time then it would appear to have been rather lower than that accorded to bank and other accountants. Up to 1855 neither the *Edinburgh and Leith Post Office Directory* nor the *Glasgow Post Office Directory* listed a single railway accountant. The first to be so listed was James Stephen, accountant with the Dundee and Newtyle Railway who appeared in the *Dundee Post Office Directory* for 1844-5.[60] In 1850, the Dundee Directory listed James Matthew as accountant for the Dundee and Perth and Aberdeen Junction Company.[61] Neither of these accountants appeared a second time in the directories and neither of them became a chartered accountant. However, the single Aberdonian, William Lunan who was listed in 1854-5[62] as accountant for the Aberdeen Railway went on to become a founder member of the Aberdeen Society.

In the listing of directors of each railway company in *Bradshaw*'s the occupation of individual directors was always given and an examination of the directors of the Scottish railway companies reveals very few chartered accountants. In 1848 three original members of the Edinburgh Society of Accountants were listed: Charles Barstow, Thomas Mansfield and Archibald Horne being directors of the Caledonian, Edinburgh and Northern and North British Railway Companies respectively. All three of these gentlemen were well established in the local business community, having been in practice in the city since 1828, 1825 and 1824 respectively[63] and it is likely that they were appointed directors for this reason with their accounting expertise being a secondary consideration. The shareholding qualification for directors indicates that Horne invested at least £500 in the North British[64] and Barstow at least £1000 in the Caledonian[65], not inconsiderable sums in 1844 and 1845.

Railway companies being launched in the Aberdeen area seem to have been operated originally by a monopoly of advocates, bankers and manufacturers since the boards of directors of the Deeside, Aberdeen, Alford Valley, Great North of Scotland and Great North of Scotland - Eastern extension were, with one exception, identical. Very few of those who became chartered accountants were noted as being involved in the administration of these early railway companies, indeed *Bradshaw*'s listed only two prior to the formation of the first accounting societies. Henry Watson of Edinburgh was the accountant for the Edinburgh, Perth and Dundee Company in 1851 and Walter Mackenzie of Glasgow was the accountant for the Caledonian and Dunbartonshire Company in 1854. Both of them became auditors of these companies within a few years, Watson in 1854 and Mackenzie in 1856. Some directors fulfilled different duties in different railway companies at the same time; for example A.G. Kidston, a Glasgow writer, was a director of both the Caledonian and the Greenock Railway Guarantee Companies in 1852 while also carrying out the duties of joint auditor for the Clydesdale Railway Guarantee Company.[66] James McClelland, a very well respected Glasgow accountant and first president of the Glasgow Institute, was a director of the Glasgow and South Western Company from 1852 to 1870[67], during part of which period he was joint auditor for the Monkland Railways.[68]

Having examined the data provided in the *Bradshaw*'s directories, it would not be unreasonable to conclude that the involvement of early chartered accountants as directors and accountants of early railway companies was slight and was probably, in the case of the former, due to their status in their respective business communities rather than as a direct result of their professional calling.

(*d*) *Banking*

Scottish banks employed people called accountants from the time of their formation but it is difficult to establish exactly what was meant by the term accountant since it seemed to be applied at times to those employed as bookkeepers as well as those employed in a more senior capacity. The Royal Bank of Scotland in 1727, the year in which it was incorporated, employed Thomas Thompson as accountant at a salary of £90 per year;[69] but in 1830 the Union Bank of Scotland only paid its accountant £60 per year.[70]

When the British Linen Company was established in 1746 for the encouragement of the Scottish linen trade, provision was made for the employment in the warehouse of both a bookkeeper and an accountant in addition to two warehousemen and one porter. The total salary bill for these employees was to be £150 per year and the bookkeeper and accountant were not allowed to augment this by receiving gratuities, nor were they allowed to keep public houses or pawnshops.[71] When the British Linen Company gave up its trading and manufacturing operations in 1763 it had achieved the establishment of a payment note system and an agent system throughout Scotland for the linen trade which was easily switched to accommodate branch banking.[72] The other Scottish banks were quick to adopt this branch system of banking which operated through agents rather than through full-time, salaried, branch managers. These agents were generally chosen from the local legal, business or farming community and worked on a commission basis. However, the banks did not entrust the keeping of accounts to their agents: 'The bank required him to employ an accountant, appointed by the bank, who would keep the books, just as his prototype at the head office did. The accountant, like the agent, had his degree of independence: "If the books are well kept, the Accountant is totally independent of the Agent"'.[73]

While it was admirable that the banks should ensure that accountants or bookkeepers were appointed to tend the bank's books, it is doubtful whether such appointees were adequate, at least initially. Certainly the first accountant of the British Linen Bank, James Gordon, was referred to as the 'so-called Accountant'[74] and then on his expertise as an accountant:

> Gordon . . . was steady and painstaking but slow and timid . . . [he] knew nothing of the work of an accountant when he began in 1746, nor did his assistant . . . To remedy this the Directors engaged Mr James Ewart, one of the accountants of the Royal Bank, to instruct them in the 'Art and Practice of Book keeping and Accounts'. Ewart was also requested to 'plan the Company's books and accounts and inspect and direct the same till the first Balance Sheet was made'.[75]

Head office accounts were apparently more onerous than branch accounts if they required a whole year of tuition. At least that is the only impression that can be gained when reading of the work of Alexander Mather, an accountant with the Clydesdale Bank, in the supervision of the opening of new branches in 1842: 'It was Mr Mather's habit to remain for a few days at the new branches to initiate the accountant into the method of book-keeping'.[76] An alternative explanation for this abbreviated form of training might well have been the availability of men for employment in banks who had already gained experience of bookkeeping in other establishment.

Edinburgh was, for many years, the undoubted leader in the field of Scottish banking, particularly in the early 1800s. During the period from 1695 to 1850, 109 banking concerns were created in Scotland but only seventeen of these survived in 1850.[77] Although Glasgow and the West of Scotland had some banks, these were slower to develop and, in particular, slow to adopt the system of branch banking. This led to the situation in 1830 of none of the Glasgow banks having any sort of national coverage within Scotland while Edinburgh and other banks had developed extensive networks and even had the affrontery, in the case of nine of them, to open branches in Glasgow in direct competition to the Glasgow banks.[78] There were two repercussions caused by this underdevelopment by Glasgow banks; first, control of Scottish banking was firmly placed in Edinburgh, but secondly, and probably more importantly, profits from banking activities in the West of Scotland were not staying in that area.

In addition to the banks which operated a branch system, there were a good number of local banks established in various parts of Scotland in the late-eighteenth and early-nineteenth centuries. The first county bank was erected in Aberdeen in 1749 to serve the farming/landowning community and the Dundee Banking Company was formed in 1763.[79] Initially banks employed their accountants from those in practice, sometimes such appointments being at a higher level such as the first manager of the Clydesdale Bank, in 1838, who was Henry Brook, aged forty-two, described as 'a moderate reforming Whig, a leading accountant in Glasgow'.[80] Before long, however, the larger banks had implemented an apprenticeship system, which enabled young men to spend a training period of between four and five years with the bank. In this way the banks soon produced their own generations of accountants.

Prior to 1844, Scottish banks had been fortunate enough to enjoy what Kerr referred to as 'practical immunity from legislative interference'.[81] Effectively, this meant that each bank devised its own systems of accounting and the directors determined how much should be disclosed to shareholders. Generally the directors adopted a policy of extreme secrecy and shareholders were likely only to be told the rate of dividend which was to be paid. Checkland[82] comments that although the new joint-stock bank movement, which began in 1825 after the repeal of the Bubble Act, had been partly a protest against this lack of disclosure by the older banks: 'This fear of disclosure soon infected the directors of the joint-stock banks, so that they, too, dispensed minimal information. None of the Scottish joint-stock banks printed and circulated their annual report.'

In 1836, Parliament appointed a Secret Committee on Joint Stock Banks which met over a period of three years and interviewed many witnesses. There are four main threads running through the various reports periodically produced by this committee. First, whether or not banks should adopt a uniform accounting system; secondly, the degree of disclosure that ought to be applied to bank accounts; thirdly, whether or not the accounts should be audited; and fourthly, who were best equipped to carry out such audits. Many of the witnessses called by the committee were bankers with long experience and a reasonable assessment can be made, from reading their evidence, of the state of bank accounting at that time. According to G. Dundas, ex-manager of the Agricultural and Commercial Bank, Belfast, not only did different banks use different accounting systems, but there was no uniform system of keeping accounts at different branches of some banks.[83] Such a situation was not considered to be at all problematic by J. Amery, general manager of the Stourbridge and Kidderminster Bank who saw no need for uniform accounts: 'The well-established fact that a bank is prudently conducted, will do more to satisfy the public mind than any mere statement of figures, which a number of persons would scarcely understand'.[84] However, the overriding desire for secrecy was held out as the main excuse for non-publication of accounts. P.M. James, a proprietor and manager of the Birmingham Banking Co., expressed his feelings most strongly:

> I think it would be considered exceedingly objectionable on the part of the proprietors, they are exceedingly jealous of having their private accounts laid before even all the directors, although they elect them; and that jealousy would be much increased, and it might tend to break up the banking establishment, if any part of the proprietors were to have the revision of all the accounts of the bank.[85]

Perhaps such bankers were correct in their assertions that the figures produced would be damaging or misunderstood by shareholders but this could no longer be sufficient excuse for continuing to pursue their policy of extreme secrecy.

The committee spent more time on the question of the desirability of the audit of banks' accounts and, in the main, witnesses, albeit grudgingly, admitted that such audit might be useful. In fact some of the banks did have the power to appoint auditors but out of 107 banks who provided information to the Committee only nine had auditors. An additional fourteen were empowered by their Deed of Settlement to appoint auditors but had not done so.[86] The North of England Bank was one such body but its managing director, General Austin, commented that the only time someone proposed the appointment of auditors from among the 200 members present at a public meeting, he failed to get a seconder and the proposal fell. Austin also felt that any audit of the reports and balance sheet should be carried out by auditors, not being directors, appointed annually by the shareholders. However such auditors should not, in his opinion, audit the customers' accounts which should be separately maintained with only the aggregate amount of debts and credits being furnished to the auditors.[87] Hardly satisfactory conditions under which to verify the accounts.

Although some banks purported to carry out an audit, the scope of the audit must at times have been so small as to be practically useless. J.R. Lyle, accountant of the Northern and Central Bank of England described one such audit: 'the directors called together several of the shareholders and submitted the accounts to them previous to going to the meeting'.[88] W. Goodier, manager of the National Provincial Bank of England, Manchester, did not consider that the system at that time in operation in some joint stock banks of producing and verifying a balance sheet was at all satisfactory: 'I think that the public requires more knowledge than is given, and therefore I have thought that auditors ought to be appointed in every case, and those, unbiased, unprejudiced individuals'.[89] Perhaps not surprisingly, the Bank of England had an efficient system of inspection and supervision of its branches: 'By means of an auditor, who goes at any time that he pleases to the branch to audit the whole of the accounts'.[90] This was, however, internal audit or what became bank inspection and not evidence of independent audit.

The Joint Stock Banking Act, 1844, which was founded in the committee set up in 1836 was extended to Scotland by the Joint Stock Banking Act 1846. Among its provisions were those for the publication of the assets and liabilities of the company at least once in every calendar month; the yearly audit of the accounts of the company by two or more auditors chosen at a General Meeting of the shareholders and not being directors at the time; and for the yearly communication of the auditors report, and of a balance sheet and profit and loss account to every shareholder.[91] On the surface this would seem to have been an excellent piece of legislation but it had one fatal flaw - there was no requirement that the auditors be independent, indeed it was almost implied that they ought to be chosen from among the shareholders.

The banking system provided another specialist area of employment for accountants, but the number for the period up to 1855 was probably even smaller than the number of those employed by railway companies. Statutory requirements for banking companies, as contained in the Joint Stock Banking Act 1844, demanded monthly publication of the assets and liabilities of a banking company and yearly publication of a balance sheet and profit and loss account to shareholders, but no requirement to conform to a uniform format. Trade directories for this period listed quite a few bank accountants. For example, the *Aberdeen Post Office Directory* for 1848-9 listed six[92] and that of 1854-5 lists four,[93] each being employed by a different bank. As early as 1787, *Jones' Directory for Glasgow* listed seven bank accountants and three deputy accountants[94] but by 1854-5 only five were so designated.[95] The *Dundee Directory* of 1818 noted two bank accountants,[96] but none appeared in the 1853-4 edition. In Aberdeen, the earliest mention to be found was that of three bank accountants in 1824-5[97] and in 1854-5 there were four.[98] Although the *Edinburgh and Leith Post Office Directory* for 1854-5 listed three bank accountants[99] Brown makes no mention whatsoever of accountants being employed by banks at this time.[100] This would suggest that such accountants were considered insignificant in the development of the accounting profession in Scotland. Nevertheless, as a specialist group they were probably quite important, since by 1848 there were eighteen banks in Scotland, having between them

382 branches[101] and providing some necessity for skilled accountants or bookkeepers.

(*e*) *Estate Management*

Pollard identifies one of the main accounting systems in existence in the second half of the eighteenth century as being that developed in the administration of large landed estates.[102] The person responsible for the production of the accounts of such estates was, however, rarely called an accountant. In England, he was most likely referred to as the steward and in Scotland, as the estate factor or chamberlain. Books were regularly published suggesting ways of keeping estate accounts, but the most common method was some type of charge and discharge system which was claimed to have the effect of concealing 'his real financial situation from the owner even if it served to square the accounts of the steward'.[103] In Scotland, accountants were involved in the administration of estates in certain circumstances. Brown notes the involvement of professional accountants in Edinburgh with estates forfeited after the Jacobite rebellion in 1745.[104] Many of the early Edinburgh accountants had been trained in legal offices and had close links with the legal profession,[105] some continuing to practise accounting as employees of legal firms. However this link with estate administration was not sufficiently strong to justify Pollard's claim that it was the reason for the early professionalization of accountancy in Scotland.[106] Although systems of estate accounting had been in existence for centuries, there is no evidence to prove that those involved with this work constituted an identifiable group or that they had any impact on the development of accountancy or the accounting profession during the nineteenth century.

(*f*) *Local Government*

Very few accountants were employed in government departments or by local authorities and there would appear to have been little uniformity in the accounting systems applied by different departments. Parnell complains about the keeping of unnecessary books and the carrying out of useless, repetitive tasks, and comments that, despite the volume of work carried out, the accounts prepared fail to be of any use in achieving their two main objectives of: 'first, the providing of security against the negligence or dishonesty of accountants; and secondly, the affording of the means of giving, with correctness, facility, and promptness, information upon the several parts of the receipt and expenditure of the public money'.[107]

Although provision had been made for the audit of local authority accounts in England and Wales by the Municipal Corporations Act 1835[108] the requirements were for three auditors who need not have any expertise in accounting matters - described by Stacey as the 'auditing farce of the three lay-auditing musketeers'.[109]

Matters in Scotland would appear to have been no better than those in England and Wales during the eighteenth and early-nineteenth centuries and Smout comments on the imperfections of the administrative machinery for governing cities.[110] Brown notes some of the more important accountants who were involved with the accounts of the City of Edinburgh. Alexander Chalmers held the position of City Accountant from 1717 to 1759, during part of which period he also filled the role of Accountant-General to the Board of Excise in Scotland.[111] James Bruce was City Accountant from 1796 to 1825 at the same time as he carried on a general accounting practice in the City,[112] so the tasks imposed by the office could not have been too arduous. Brown does not recount who was City Accountant in 1833 when Edinburgh went bankrupt[113] and, although it would be unfair to blame such bankruptcy completely on bad accounting practices, this was probably one of the elements desperately needing improvement.

(*g*) *Insurance*

Stewart[114] notes the great expansion of various kinds of insurance business in the middle of the nineteenth century and the involvement of early Scottish accountants in this. But Brown[115] goes even further and claims that:

> The extensive and successful formation of life insurance companies in Scotland during the first half of the nineteenth century was largely organised by accountants. In those days there was no separate profession of actuary, and the accounting profession

appears to have embraced practically all the actuarial skill of the period.

During the early part of the nineteenth century a considerable number of insurance companies were established in Scotland, in addition to which some English insurance companies established offices or agencies in the main cities. By 1840, the *Edinburgh and Leith Post Office Directory*[116] listed thirty-one insurance companies, twenty-one of which had established offices in the city, the remaining ten having Edinburgh agents. The number of companies had risen to eighty-one by 1854[117] with the majority having offices in the city, the number of agencies being very low. The *Glasgow Post Office Directory* for 1853-4 listed 114 different insurance companies with offices or agencies in the city.[118]

The Institute of Actuaries was formed in 1848[119] but the Scottish members seceded in 1856 to form the Faculty of Actuaries in Scotland with an office in Edinburgh.[120] Although the name of this association implied membership throughout Scotland, it appears to have been mainly concerned with Edinburgh members since, in 1881, the Insurance and Actuarial Society of Glasgow was formed 'with the object of affording to those engaged in the various Assurance and Accountants' offices in Glasgow facilities for meeting together to discuss the principles which underlie their business'.[121] Another interesting point to note in the formation of this society is the fact that when the Glasgow accountants began to move towards association in 1854 they determined that the name of their body would be The Institute of Accountants and Actuaries in Glasgow.[122]

The inclusion of actuaries in this title suggests that the founders of the Institute were strongly involved in insurance companies in some way. In fact their influence was significant at that time since at least fifty-two per cent of those accountants who were involved as managers or agents of insurance companies in Glasgow later became Glasgow chartered accountants.[123] Even more significantly, ninety-three per cent of the signatories[124] of the application for the Royal Charter for the Glasgow Institute were involved in this type of insurance work. The formation in 1881 of the Insurance and Actuarial Society of Glasgow required some further investigation into the role of Glasgow chartered accountants as managers and agents. Information in the *Glasgow Post Office*

Directory for 1880-1[125] reveals that involvement in the management aspects of insurance companies had reduced to the point where, although the percentage of accountants involved in insurance had risen from thirty-six per cent in 1853-4 to forty-three per cent in 1880-1, the involvement of chartered accountants had fallen from fifty-two per cent to sixteen per cent. It would appear, therefore, that numbers of non-chartered accountants involved in insurance work had reached a level where it was desirable and feasible to establish a separate identity.

The establishment of a Glasgow Society would suggest either that the calibre of people forming the new society was too low to allow them admission to the Faculty of Actuaries in Scotland, in that their involvement in insurance work was mainly of a non-actuarial nature, or, perhaps, that the Faculty of Actuaries was seen as an Edinburgh association and therefore to be opposed rather than supported.

Although both Brown and Stewart note significant numbers of early chartered accountants involved with insurance companies as directors, managers, actuaries, secretaries, agents or auditors, such employment generally formed only a small part of the workload for any accountant of that period. It is however apparent that these accountants did make a significant contribution to the prosperity of such companies. From an early stage, insurance companies tended to appreciate the need for a proper audit of their work and did not wait for such conditions to be imposed on them. For example the Scottish Union and National Insurance Company had its books audited and balance sheet certified by an independent accountant from its formation in 1824.[126] Insurance companies were quicker than banking companies to realise the importance of audit by professional accountants rather than by amateurs.

(*h*) *Stockbroking*

Another new area of work which became available for accountants in the first half of the nineteenth century was that of share dealing. Although some English cities had stockbrokers in the late-eighteenth century, these did not appear in Edinburgh and Glasgow until the 1820s.[127]

The growth of railway business was considered to play a

significant part in enlarging the London Stock Exchange[128] but it also had a significant impact on the provincial exchanges throughout the United Kingdom. In Scotland, the first recognised share brokers began to appear in Edinburgh and Glasgow in the mid-1820s but exchanges were not established in these cities until December and June of 1844 respectively with Aberdeen following in October 1845. Indeed such was the magnitude of the increase in share dealings at this time that three separate stock exchanges appeared in both Edinburgh and Glasgow during 1845.[129]

The volume of shares being traded on the Scottish exchanges grew steadily but rather slowly,[130] and the attractiveness of this type of business for those carrying on business as accountants varied considerably from city to city. In Edinburgh, where the accounting fraternity had very close links with the legal profession, few accountants became involved in share dealing, an activity which would have involved a loss of status and security.[131] However, in Glasgow, whose stock exchange was formed in 1844, ten of the twenty-eight original members of the stock exchange became Glasgow chartered accountants and very few had any legal connection.[132] This difference from Edinburgh can probably be explained by the mercantile character of Glasgow and the consequent closer links between accountants and industry.

(*i*) *Legal Work*

In spite of the fact that Scottish accountants at the middle of the nineteenth century were being employed by various different types of business enterprises such as banking, insurance and railway companies, the volume of work being generated by such companies was insufficient to provide employment for all of the accountants in practice. By 1850, the post office directories for the principal towns in Scotland, i.e. Edinburgh and Leith, Glasgow, Aberdeen and Dundee, listed 132, 146, twelve and nine accountants respectively. Although a few of these were designated bank accountants or as working with a railway company or utility, the vast majority styled themselves 'public accountants' and the most important area of work being undertaken by them was connected with remits from the Courts.

The development of the Industrial Revolution had led to the introduction of larger and more complicated partnerships which required the application of a great deal of skill when problems arose. During the first half of the nineteenth century the country suffered a series of commercial crises which created business for the professional accountants of that time.[133] It seems that the Court of Session in Scotland very quickly realised that professional accountants were the most suitable people to manage: 'the estates of bankrupts, lunatics, infants, and other persons not regarded as fit to look after their affairs'.[134] Although a few Scottish accountants had been involved in trusteeships from the eighteenth century[135] other professional groups were also involved in particular lawyers and, in Glasgow, merchants.[136]

As the volume of legally related work grew steadily during the first half of the nineteenth century, accountants became involved in an increasing share of the available work so that they thrived on the failures of the new system rather than from its successes.[137] Laird went so far as to claim that, by the middle of the nineteenth century, 'the work of an Accountant at that time consisted principally of court work (that is, remits from the Courts of Law to investigate matters of accounting) and the winding up of bankrupt estates'.[138] Although Laird purported to be speaking of Scottish accountants in general, his remarks would have been more correctly addressed to describe the work of Edinburgh accountants who were more heavily involved in this work than were Glasgow accountants. However, from the evidence given in 1836 by Kirkman Finlay of Glasgow to the Select Committee on Joint Stock Companies, it is quite clear that, in both Edinburgh and Glasgow, professional accountants had convinced the Courts that they were one of a small group of professional men who had the particular skills required for this type of court work.[139]

2. Importance of Bankruptcy during the First Half of the Nineteenth Century

There is evidence to prove that bankruptcy work was extremely important to eighteenth-century Scottish accountants. In intimating his commencement of business in 1778, John Gibson of Glasgow offered many services, including that as an accountant in 'Settling of Copartnery or Other Disputes, Making Out Accounts of the Rankings of Creditors, and the Division of Subjects,'.[140] Gibson widened the scope of his work in 1784, on entering into partnership with Richard Smellie, to include acting 'as Factors on Estates and Subjects, under the management of Executors or Creditors'.[141] Other advertisements appeared around the same period, although some were hardly likely to instil much confidence in prospective customers such as: William Hattridge 'Being at present out of employment, begs leave to offer his services to the public as a FACTOR or ACCOUNTANT'.[142]

Particularly in Edinburgh, the ties between accountants and the legal profession were very strong and: 'In Scotland during the latter part of the eighteenth century it was not uncommon to find lawyers practising accounting as a proper part of their professional activities'.[143] In addition, many of the early members of the Edinburgh Institute were trained in legal offices[144] and in the *Edinburgh and Leith Post Office Directory* from 1847-8 onwards, accountants ceased to be listed under Professions and Principal Trades and appeared in the Law Directory section.

It is not difficult to appreciate the need to employ accountants to act as trustees on sequestrated estates during the mid-nineteenth century, since the provisions of the Act for Regulating the Sequestration of the Estates of Bankrupts in Scotland required that

> the Trustee shall keep a Sederunt Book in which he shall record all Minutes of Creditors and of Commissioners, State of Accounts, Reports, and all the Proceedings necessary to give a correct View of the Management of the Estate; and he shall also keep regular Accounts of the Affairs of the Estate, and transmit to the Bill Chamber Clerks, before each of the Periods herein assigned for Payment of a Dividend, a Copy, certified by himself, of such Accounts, . . . '.[145]

For very small and straightforward sequestrations there was, perhaps, little knowledge of accounting needed, but for the more complicated and lengthy cases a considerable depth of specific knowledge was necessary, and the appointment of an accountant was almost inevitable.

Unfortunately, the data relating to bankruptcy work prior to 1856 is of very poor quality, being fragmented and incomplete.

However, an indication of the occupation and income of those who were appointed trustees on sequestrated estates in Scotland in the mid-eighteenth century has been obtained from an analysis of a directory published in 1851.[146] This claimed to comprise 'almost all the information which any Creditor can require in regard to the affairs of a Scotch Bankrupt, who is his Debtor.' The book listed 1,155 sequestrations which were either completed in 1851 or were still outstanding at the end of that year, and deals with total trustees commission of just over £89,000. Since much of the accounting work on such estates was, at that time, dealt with by accountants employed in legal offices, it is interesting to note that legal expenses on these same estates totalled just over £91,000.

An analysis of these trustees, by occupation and by income, is shown in Figure 2.1. This chart shows, quite clearly, that people designated as 'accountants' were the most important single occupational group dealing with sequestration work prior to 1851. They were appointed trustees in fifty-five per cent of the total number of sequestrated estates and took seventy-eight per cent of the total fee income. A further analysis of the figures for accountants as a whole reveals that more than two-thirds of the cases undertaken by them were administered by accountants who later became members of one of the bodies of chartered accountants in Scotland. Perhaps of greater interest is the fact that these future chartered accountants were dealing with thirty-eight per cent of the total cases, but were earning sixty-three per cent of the total fee income from this source, thus suggesting that they administered the most remunerative estates; while the accountants who did not later join one of the chartered bodies dealt with seventeen per cent of the cases and received fifteen per cent of the total fee income.

Other professional groups, dealing with smaller numbers of sequestrations, were members of the legal and banking professions. Those included in the miscellaneous group, who dealt with twenty-seven per cent of the cases and earned eleven per cent of the fee income, came from a wide variety of occupations ranging from farmers and axle-makers to tanners, with more than one third of them being described as 'merchants'. This term could apply to anyone from a small shopkeeper or salesman to a large businessman, so that its exact meaning is impossible to determine. In smaller towns it would appear that there was often a single person who was regarded

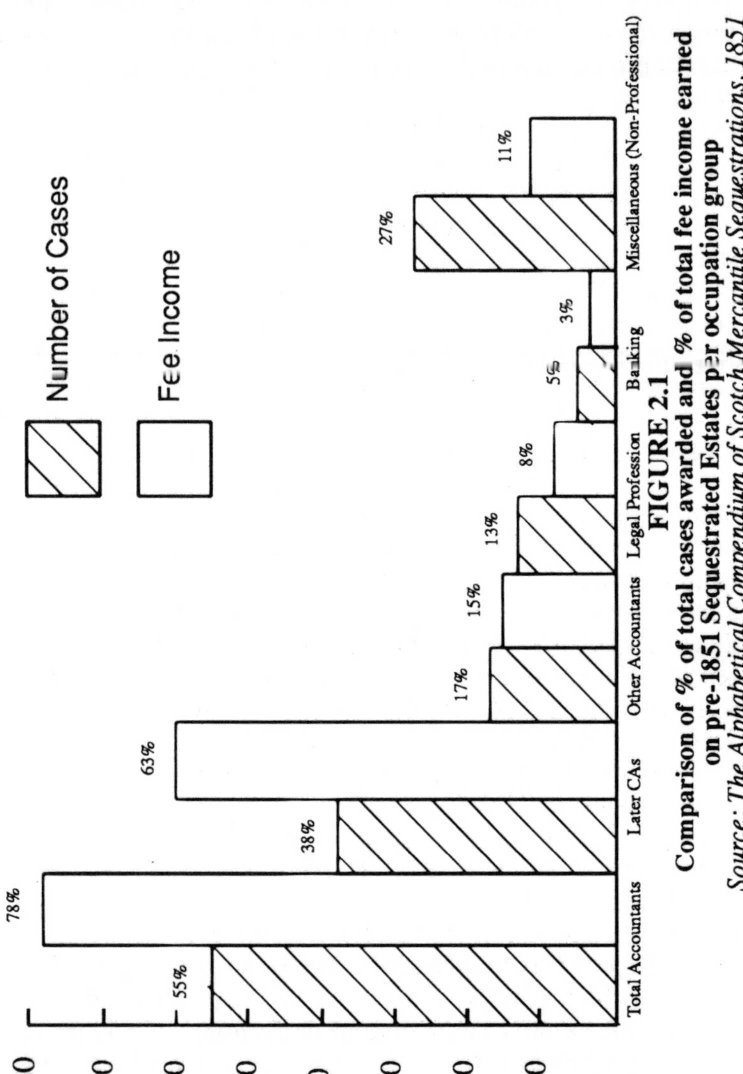

FIGURE 2.1

Comparison of % of total cases awarded and % of total fee income earned on pre-1851 Sequestrated Estates per occupation group

Source: The Alphabetical Compendium of Scotch Mercantile Sequestrations, 1851

as having the expertise to act as a trustee on a sequestrated estate. For example, in St. Andrews, all cases were administered by Peter Steele, described as a merchant.

Looking at the complete picture portrayed by the chart there are two significant features:

> during this period, accountants dealt with fifty-five per cent of all sequestrations and the most important occupational group to be involved in this work consisted of those accountants who later became chartered accountants;
>
> from all the occupational groups identified, those who later became chartered accountants dealt with the most lucrative, and presumably the most complicated, cases, since, although they only dealt with thirty-eight per cent of the total cases, they collected sixty-three per cent of the total fee income. Indeed, the largest fee during this period amounted to £12,420 11*s* 8*d* and was paid to Donald Lindsay, later to be a founder member of the Society of Accountants in Edinburgh, for his work as trustee on the Marquis of Huntly's estate, which was sequestrated in 1839.

Since Edinburgh was the first city to have a Society of Chartered Accountants, closely followed by Glasgow and later by Aberdeen, the geographical dispersion of accountants (both those who later became chartered accountants and those who did not) acting as trustees on sequestrated estates was examined, with interesting results, as shown in Figure 2.2.

The analysis of the geographical dispersion of accountants acting as trustees on sequestrated estates shows little difference in numbers between Edinburgh and Glasgow accountants. In the case of those who later became chartered accountants they were forty-five per cent and fifty per cent respectively and, in the case of the non-chartered accountant group, thirty-four per cent as compared to forty per cent. The total percentages for non-chartered accountants were lower, because of the twenty-four per cent of the total who were widely distributed throughout Scotland, with representatives in Paisley, Perth, Inverness, Greenock, Tain, Elgin, Wick, Hamilton,

Sanquhar and Hawick, but with very few cases being handled in these centres.

When the number of cases dealt with by these groups of accountants is examined in Figure 2.3, a significant difference can be seen. As the chart shows, in both groups, Glasgow accountants dealt with a far larger proportion of cases than did Edinburgh accountants; seventy per cent to twenty-seven per cent in the case of the chartered accountant group and sixty-three per cent to sixteen per cent in the case of the non-chartered accountant group.

Further comparison based on Table 2.2 shows that each Glasgow chartered accountant dealt with an average of 8.7 cases and earned an average of £624, while each Edinburgh chartered accountant averaged 3.8 cases and earnings of £1044. This implies that, although Glasgow chartered accountants dealt with more cases, the more lucrative cases were dealt with by the Edinburgh chartered accountants.

It is not surprising to find a larger proportion of cases being dealt with by Glasgow accountants, both CA and non-CA. The Bankruptcy (Scotland) Act of 1839[147] gave extensive bankruptcy jurisdiction to the Sheriff Courts which resulted, in most cases, in the sequestration being dealt with in the county where the bankrupt traded. Glasgow was a much larger centre of population and trade and therefore gave rise to more sequestrations. The higher average income of Edinburgh chartered accountants might perhaps have been explained by the fact that some sequestrations were referred to the Court of Session because of special factors and such cases were almost always awarded to Edinburgh accountants, but, in fact, if we exclude from the calculation of average income the £12,410 11*s* 8*d* previously mentioned as having being paid to Donald Lindsay for one sequestration, we find that this reduces the average income arising from this type of work to £658 per Edinburgh chartered accountant, though their average fee per sequestration was still higher than in Glasgow.

Perhaps the essential difference in the importance of this work to the accountants who later became chartered accountants and those who did not can be seen from Tables 2.3 and 2.4. These show quite clearly that sequestration work was of more importance to the group who later became chartered accountants than to those who did not, and, looking at the dispersion of this work throughout the main

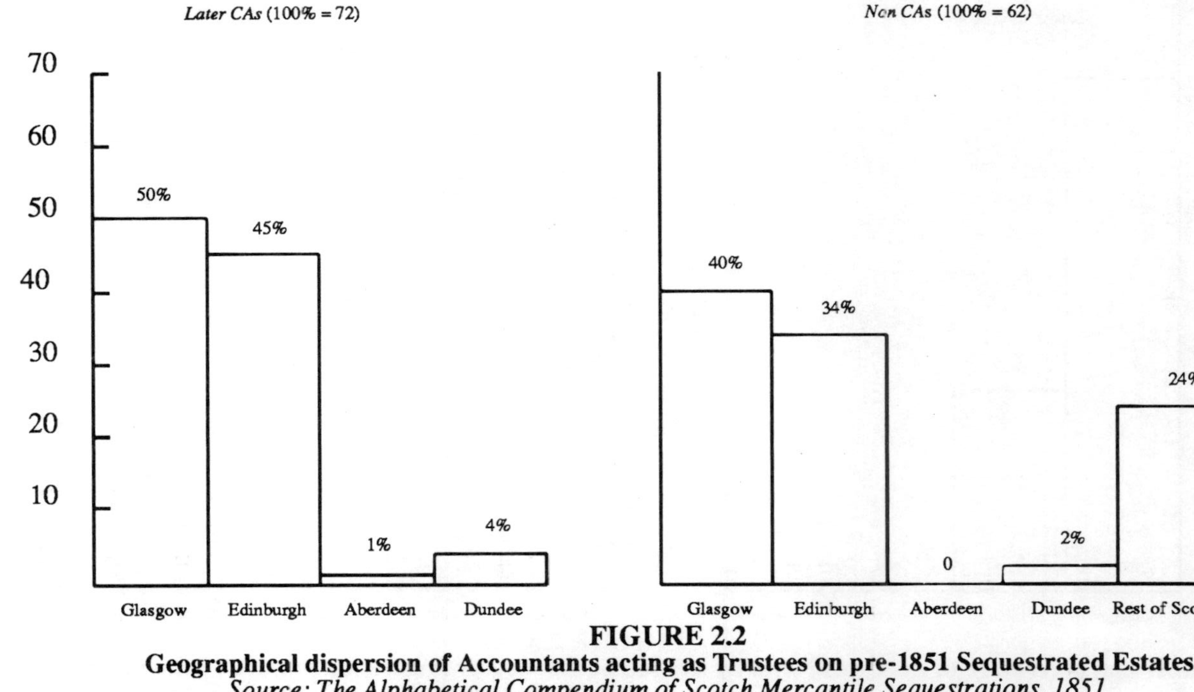

FIGURE 2.2
Geographical dispersion of Accountants acting as Trustees on pre-1851 Sequestrated Estates
Source: The Alphabetical Compendium of Scotch Mercantile Sequestrations, 1851

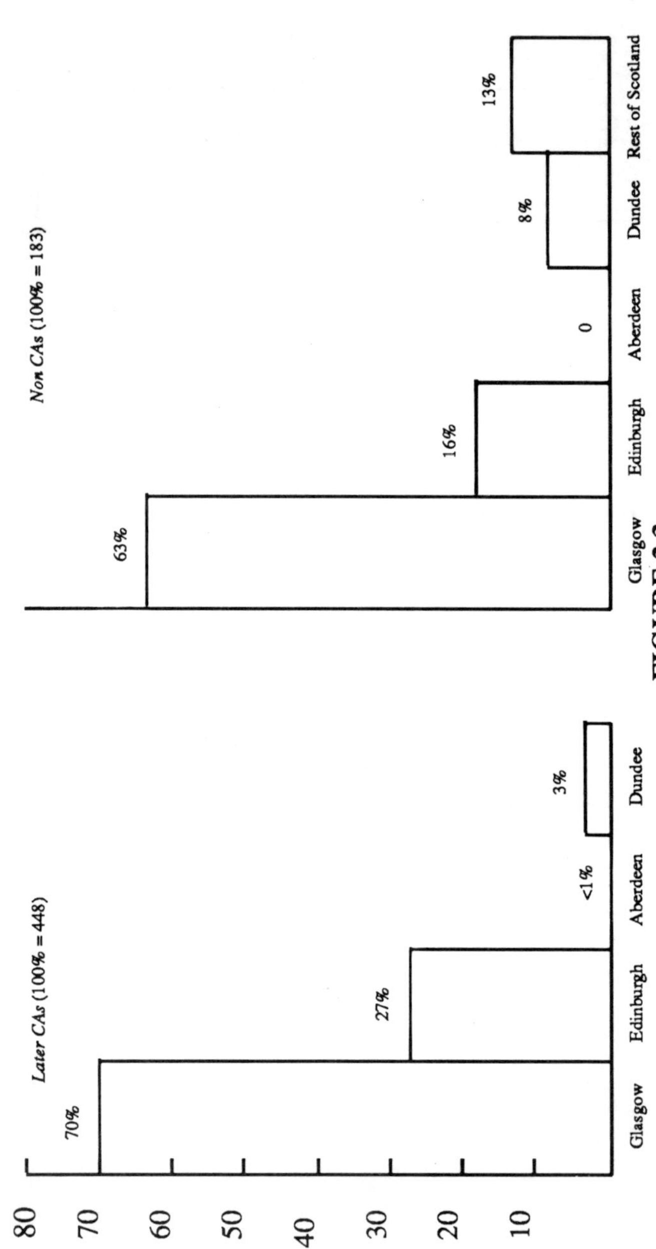

FIGURE 2.3

Number and percentage of cases dealt with by Accountants acting as Trustees on pre-1851 Sequestrated Estates

Source: The Alphabetical Compendium of Scotch Mercantile Sequestrations, 1851

TABLE 2.2

Fees received by accountants becoming chartered accountants

	Number of Accs	Number of Cases	Total Fees Recorded	Average Number of Cases	Average Fees per Case
			£ s d		*£ s d*
Aberdeen	1	1	928:14:7	1	928:14:7
Dundee	3	13	Not Stated	4.3	-
Edinburgh	32	121	33,412:9:3	3.78	276:14:0
Glasgow	36	313	22,469:9:9	8.69	71:15:9
Total	72	448	56,810:13:7	6.2	126:16:0

Source: *The Alphabetical Compendium of Scotch Mercantile Sequestrations, 1851*

TABLE 2.3

Fees received by accountants not becoming chartered accountants

	Number of Accs	Number of Cases	Total Fees Recorded	Average Number of Cases	Average Fees per Case
			£ s d		*£ s d*
Aberdeen	0	0	-	-	-
Dundee	4	16	907:5:10	4	56:14:1
Edinburgh	21	32	875:15:9	1.52	27:7:1
Glasgow	25	123	9,844:4:7	4.92	80:0:8
Others	16	25	1,442:2:10	1.56	57:13:9
Total	66	196	13,069:9:0	2.97	66:13:8

Source: *The Alphabetical Compendium of Scotch Mercantile Sequestrations, 1851*

TABLE 2.4

Relative fee income of chartered and non-chartered accountants

	No. of CAs Non-CAs	**Cases Dealt With**	**Total Fee Income to Nearest £**	**Average Number of Cases**	**Average Income per Trustee**
			£		£
chartered accountants	72	448	56,810	6.2	789
non-chartered accountants	66	196	13,070	2.97	198

Source: *The Alphabetical Compendium of Scotch Mercantile Sequestrations, 1851*

cities in Scotland, it is easy to appreciate the later concern of Edinburgh and Glasgow accountants with regard to bankruptcy work.

Dundee had approximately seventy sequestrations during the period covered by the directory and trustees on sequestrated estates were divided approximately twenty-three per cent to accountants, twenty-five per cent to the legal profession, five per cent to bankers, and forty-seven per cent to a miscellaneous group, mainly merchants. Aberdeen had only forty-four cases in the same period and an entirely different dispersion of work among different trustee groups. Fifty-five per cent of cases were dealt with by the legal profession, twenty-four per cent by bankers, nineteen per cent by a miscellaneous group and only one case by an accountant who later became a member of the Aberdeen Society of Accountants.

3. Summary

This chapter has examined the various areas of work which provided employment for men styling themselves accountants up to the middle of the nineteenth century. Although the contribution of accountants in most of these areas was probably significant in itself, the volume of work in each was not particularly large and provided relatively few jobs. In addition, it would appear that many people so employed who enjoyed the title 'accountant' were in fact more akin to bookkeepers.

The exception was in the group of accountants which specialised in bankruptcy work. Here the volume of work was such as to require the involvement of a significant number of men specialising in this area and also to provide an adequate income for these men. This specialisation would inevitably have led to the situation where such a man would: 'increasingly identify with and share the values and behaviours of his fellow specialists. An occupational community will develop, fostering solidarity among its members'.[148]

The following chapter will examine whether or not this was the pattern for the formation of the first Scottish Accounting Societies.

III

Scottish Bankruptcy Legislation and the Formation of Professional Accounting Bodies in Scotland

1. Scottish Bankruptcy Legislation in the Nineteenth Century

In 1814 an attempt was made to improve the efficiency of dealing with bankruptcy in Scotland by the passing of 'An Act for rendering the Payment of Creditors more equal and expeditious in Scotland.'[1] This Act required creditors within three weeks of sequestration to appoint an Interim Factor to take over custody of a bankrupt estate and within a further two to four weeks to choose a Trustee whose task it would be to settle the estate. If the creditors failed to appoint an Interim Factor, then the care and custody of the estate would devolve upon the sheriff clerk of the county where the business was carried on. In addition, the creditors would appoint three of their number to act as Commissioners who would, among other duties, audit the Trustee's accounts.

The Trustee was required to verify all claims from creditors and to keep 'a regular Book of Accounts with the Bankrupt's Estate'; thus for all but the simplest of sequestrations, he would have required some competence in bookkeeping. Although the majority of those appointed as Commissioners probably had little experience in the field of audit, their mere presence was designed to ensure that the Trustee carried out his task more carefully and the provisions for an audit to be carried out ten months from the date of the first deliverance on the petition for sequestration and at six-monthly intervals until the sequestration was completed,[2] must have encouraged a more orderly approach to the task.

The 'Act for Regulating the Sequestration of the Estates of Bankrupts in Scotland' 1839, hastened the election of the Interim Factor to within one and two weeks of the award of sequestration and the election of a Trustee to within a further two to four weeks. Three Commissioners were still elected by the creditors from among themselves and charged with superintending the Trustee's proceedings and auditing his accounts.[3] In addition, an attempt was made to monitor the progress of all sequestrations by requiring every Trustee to make an annual return on 31 October, to the Sheriff Clerk of the appropriate sheriffdom, of all the sequestrations in which he was involved. These returns were remitted to the Bill Chambers Clerk to allow the compilation of a total return. In this way a statement of the position of all current sequestrations could be produced for the use of any interested parties. Perhaps, too, it was considered that the need to make such public returns would encourage the speedier settlement of bankrupt estates.

Subsequent legislation suggests that the 1839 Act made no appreciable difference to the speed of settlement, since the 'Bill to Amend the Laws relating to Bankruptcy in Scotland' described one of its main objectives as being the 'more speedy Distribution of the Estates of Bankrupts under Sequestration in Scotland' and suggested that one way of achieving this would be the abolition of the office of Interim Factor and the immediate possession of the bankrupt's estate by the Sheriff Clerk.[4] This proposal was soon amended in Committee[5] to a requirement that the Interim Factor be appointed by the Lord Ordinary by whom the sequestration was awarded or by the Sheriff of the County in which the bankrupt traded, rather than being elected by the creditors and this provision was included in the subsequent Act of 1853.[6] For the first time, the Interim Factor was required to find caution, the amount to be determined by the Lord Ordinary or Sheriff. The inclusion of this requirement would suggest some degree of concern as to the quality of the work being done by some Trustees and would have had the effect of precluding some people from undertaking such work in the future. The Act contained no specific requirement for the preparation of periodic accounts, although it must have been necessary to prepare some sort of charge and discharge accounts in order to establish dividend payments and there was still a requirement that the Commissioners should audit the Trustee's accounts. In addition to this, the final accounts had to be submitted for taxation by the Auditor of the Court of Session or the Auditor of the appropriate Sheriff Court.[7]

This new legislation was apparently not very satisfactory since, before two years had elapsed, a 'Bill to Consolidate and amend the Laws of Scotland regarding Insolvency and Bankruptcy' was being discussed[8] to consolidate and replace the Acts of 1814, 1839 and 1853. Although the Bill was further discussed and amended in committee in July 1855, February 1856 and April 1856[9], the provisions affecting the Trustee remained unchanged. The various Bills passed into Law in the Bankruptcy (Scotland) Act 1856[10] which came into effect on 1 November 1856 and laid down more detailed requirements for the Trustee with regard to his management of bankrupt estates. For the first time, the Trustee had to be confirmed in his appointment by the Sheriff or Sheriff Substitute under whom the sequestration was being awarded, and in addition the three Commissioners elected at the same meeting could be either creditors or mandatories of creditors.[11] This opened the way for the involvement of people with specialist knowledge to be introduced in sequestrations where creditors had no specific investigatory or accounting skills and gave the Sheriff the right to refuse confirmation to persons whom he considered unsuitable as Trustees. One of the most important changes contained in the new legislation regarding accounting was the establishment of the Accountant in Bankruptcy,[12] who would be 'a Person versant in Law and Accounts', appointed to oversee all sequestration work in Scotland. This official was to have no other professional connection with the courts, was to command a yearly salary not exceeding £850 and was to be allowed to appoint three clerks to assist him in his duties, each of whom was to be allowed a salary not exceeding £450 per annum.

The Trustee was required to keep such books and accounts as were necessary to give a correct view of the management of the estate and to produce regular accounts for transmission to the Accountant in Bankruptcy.[13] Although the original Bill suggested that the Trustee's accounts should continue to be audited by the Commissioners,[14] the Act only provided that the Commissioners would superintend the proceedings of the Trustee[15] and contained no requirement for them to audit his accounts.

Each Trustee had to prepare an annual statement of each sequestration in which he was acting, authenticated by the Accountant in Bankruptcy. The Accountant, in turn, would present an annual report to the Court of Session showing the state of each current sequestration, which the Court could direct to be published in the *Gazetter* or otherwise. The fact that the person appointed to monitor the progress of sequestrations was required to be knowledgeable in law and accounts was significant. What was even more significant was that the position was always held by an accountant, each one occupying the post for a considerable period of time. The first holder of the office was George Auldjo Esson CA who was Accountant in Bankruptcy from 1856 until 1885.[16] Esson was a founder member of the Edinburgh Institute and one of those invited to the first meeting for its formation. When he resigned at the age of seventy-two, his place was taken by John Stuart who acted as Interim Accountant in Bankruptcy from 1886 until 1888.[17] In 1889 the Judicial Factors (Scotland) Act[18] came into power and, among other things, united the offices of the Accountant of the Court of Session and the Accountant in Bankruptcy in Scotland into the office of Accountant of Court. This office was filled in 1889 by Joseph Campbell Penney CA,[19] who continued to hold the office until his death in 1920. Prior to his appointment, bankruptcy records show that Penney had been involved in some sequestration work.

The annual reports produced showed in some detail the number of sequestrations awarded and settled in the year, the value of estates settled and the amount of various expenses on such estates.[20] In order for these to be compiled, it must have been necessary for the Trustees to submit similarly detailed accounts of the individual sequestrations in their charge and for them to maintain reasonable accounting records for each one.

The professionalization of accountancy in Scotland began on 17 January 1853[21] between the introduction of the Bill to Amend the Laws relating to Bankruptcy in Scotland and the subsequent Act which came into force on 4 August 1853. Because of the involvement of a number of accountants in this area of work it is not surprising to find them expressing a group interest in the outcome of the new legislation which might well have some impact on their future income. Brown comments that the Edinburgh Institute considered these proposed changes in Scottish bankruptcy legislation as soon as it was formed since it was apparent that the Bill had been introduced into Parliament by the Lord Advocate and was scheduled for its second reading on 12 May 1853. He refers to the 1853 Act as 'being only of a limited and tentative nature', as indeed it was proved to be, as evidenced by its speedy replacement in 1856, and comments on the involvement of both the Glasgow and Edinburgh accounting societies in the structuring of the 1856 Act, which he describes as 'being generally recognised as having established an excellent bankruptcy system'.[22] No doubt Brown considered that this was largely due to the contribution made by the respective accounting societies, and his claim can be supported by the fact that the 1856 legislation remained largely unchanged for more than fifty years.

2. Formation of the Institute of Accountants in Edinburgh

(*a*) *Process of Formation*

The first successful attempt to form a recognised association of accountants in the United Kingdom was that instigated in Edinburgh on 17 January 1853 by Alexander Weir Robertson when he circulated fourteen practising accountants in Edinburgh as follows:

> Several gentlemen connected with our profession have resolved to bring about some definite arrangement for uniting the professional Accountants in Edinburgh and should you be favourable thereto I have to request your attendance in my chambers here on Thursday next the 20th Inst at 2 o'clock.[23]

Robertson's chambers were situated at 15 Dundas Street,[24] an area which was central to the business life of the city and around which many other accounting and legal offices were clustered. The accountants to whom the circular was sent were: J.J. Dickson, T.G. Dickson, A. Horne, K. Mackenzie, A. Borthwick, W. Moncreiff, T. Martin, G. Meldrum, J. Scott-Moncreiff, S. Raleigh, T. Scott, W. Wood, C. Pearson and G.A. Esson, but of those, only Mackenzie, Borthwick, Martin, Meldrum, Scott-Moncreiff, Raleigh and Wood attended the meeting; Pearson sent his apologies.[25] Borthwick was asked to take the chair and, if the minutes of the meeting are a true record of the proceedings, it would seem that a substantial amount of preparation had been done before the meeting, since he is reported as saying that:

> the Meeting was aware that various attempts had from time to time been made to incorporate the Accountants in Edinburgh but that such attempts had hitherto proved fruitless. That the failure was to be attributed to several causes but that it had appeared to him and other gentlemen, that means might be followed now, whereby this very desirable object might be accomplished. With this view, therefore, it had been resolved to use every effort to form a Society of those gentlemen who were recognised by the profession generally, as carrying on the business exclusively of Accountancy in Edinburgh, and for this purpose there had been prepared and would now be read for the consideration of the Meeting a sketch of a Constitution and Rules for the formation and regulation of such an Association.

The Law Directory of the *Edinburgh and Leith Post Office Directory* for 1853-4 listed 132 accountants,[26] yet Robertson only invited fourteen to meet with him to discuss his idea. Perhaps the fact that there had already been several unsuccessful attempts to form an association had led Robertson to believe that a small group of like-minded people was more likely to succeed than a large group with more diverse ideas. If some accountants had been discussing the formation of a society for some time then they would undoubtedly have noted the formation of other professional bodies around that time, such as the Royal College of Veterinary Surgeons which was chartered in 1857.[27] Living in Edinburgh and having close links with the legal profession, as most of this group did, they could not have failed to be influenced by the clear identity of this profession which had been largely gained from its formal association.[28] But, however much the move towards professionalization by other institutions may have affected the accountants, there can be no doubt that the final catalyst was the proposed alterations to bankruptcy law in Scotland, which were being discussed by Parliament at that time. Since the management of bankrupt estates was largely intrusted to accountants, they were, naturally, concerned that any proposed changes would interfere with their livelihood. It is also interesting to note that, from the beginning, the Society set out to limit membership to those exclusively involved in accountancy in Edinburgh, immediately establishing two professional parameters, namely the type of business undertaken and the geographical location of practitioners.

Of course, it is entirely possible that these requirements for membership were introduced in order to limit the new society to manageable numbers and to give it immediately a very clear identity. However, it is also likely that the accountants were like other groups identified by Lewis and Maude:

> Though the adoption of professional organization is advocated on the grounds that the ruling body will be better able to regulate the conduct and qualifications of members, to improve the service to the public, the prime motives are generally the desire to raise status and increase remuneration by some measure of restriction.[29]

Events moved rapidly in those early days and a second meeting, attended by Robertson, J.J. Dickson, Mackenzie, Borthwick, Moncreiff, Martin, Meldrum, Scott, Wood, Ogilvy, Macandrew and Gordon was held two days later on 22 January 1853 - the last three accountants having been approached after the first meeting. 'At this Meeting the proof print of the Constitution was fully considered and amended'.[30] Those present discussed the proposed rules and regulations and took it upon themselves to encourage other practising accountants in the city to join with them in their venture.[31]

They were reasonably successful in this recruitment campaign, since forty-seven accountants attended the next meeting on 31 January 1853 in Gibbs Royal Hotel, Edinburgh.[32] Interestingly, the meeting was unanimous in calling James Brown to the chair, although he had not been a recipient of Robertson's original letter; nor had he been present at either of the preliminary meetings, but had presumably been canvassed for support by one of the men present at the second meeting, or by his partner Pearson, who had been invited to the initial meeting. Since he was a prominent Edinburgh accountant,[33] it is conceivable that it was felt that his support was necessary in order to succeed in forming the new society and in having it accepted by the public. Also, he was, at the age of sixty-six, one of the elder statesmen among the Edinburgh accountants and, therefore, likely to lend the new society added respectability.

At this much larger meeting, Borthwick reminded those attending that the idea of an association was not new, but that in the past, attempts to join together had not been successful -

> After referring to the various important duties which the Accountants practising in Edinburgh were called upon to discharge, he said he presumed there could be no difference of opinion as to the expediency of endeavouring by such an Association as that now proposed, to have those important duties intrusted only to those who were qualified by their education and business acquirements to fulfil them with credit.[34]

Admissions to membership of the new Institute closed at this meeting and subsequent applicants had to apply according to its regulations so that those who were undecided had little time to make up their minds.

Although a large number attended this meeting, more than sixty per cent of the accountants listed in the 1853-4 *Edinburgh and Leith Post Office Directory* were not present. This could have been because they could see no benefits to be gained from professional assocation and deliberately chose to remain outside the Society, though their decision may have been different had they realised that the newly-formed Society would attempt to impose a closed shop on much of the work undertaken by its members.

Those who did attend the meeting clearly considered themselves to be fully trained and respectable as befitted a professional body and wished to reinforce this image by keeping out those whom they viewed as being untrained and less respectable.[35] Any prospective member had to be proposed by one member, seconded by another and elected by three-quarters of the members present at any General Meeting voting in their favour,[36] a system that ensured the exclusion of any undesirable accountant.

At this early stage in its development, the Society was a voluntary association called the Institute of Accountants, although there were tentative plans to apply for a Royal Charter of Incorporation.[37] Initially membership consisted of two different categories, being Ordinary Members who were in practice as accountants in Edinburgh and Honorary Members who had formerly been in practice as accountants but who now held positions as managers of Life Assurance Companies or had appointments from the Courts.[38]

The category of Honorary Member disappeared at the time of the receipt of the Royal Charter of Incorporation in October 1854 at which time it was stated that, since the petition for the Charter had proceeded on the assumption that all petitioners were practising accountants, it would be necessary for Honorary Members who wished to become members of the Society of Accountants in Edinburgh, as it became on receiving its Royal Charter, to pay arrears of membership fees and to become Ordinary Members.[39] This was rather an interesting decision and the offer was taken up by seven honorary members but declined by six who thus ceased to be members. Of the seven who became ordinary members, four were involved in insurance, one was manager of the Edinburgh Savings Bank, one was Deputy Clerk of Tiends and one was the Accountant of Court. Presumably they and the Council of the Society felt that there was sufficient contact with accounting in their career to justify extending full membership to them.

(*b*) *Actions to Preserve Fees from Bankruptcies and Other Work of a Legal Nature*

Immediately the members had settled the matters of eligibility for and cost of membership of the Institute, they moved to a discussion of the matter that was of prime consideration to them. At a meeting of the Council of 8 April 1853 Archibald Borthwick had drawn the attention of those present to the fact that:

> various meetings had recently been held with a view of considering the alterations that ought to be made on the Bankruptcy Law, and that a report by a General Committee on that subject was now ready; that he

> thought it would be desirable that the opinion of the Institute should be taken as to the proposed alterations; and that as the Lord Advocate had a Bill in proof it would if deemed advisable be necessary that the matter be taken up without loss of time.[40]

By 11 May 1853 the Council was ready to discuss the Bill along with a report by the Edinburgh Committee on Bankruptcy Law Reform.[41] Clause I of the Bill proposed that the office of Interim Factor be abolished and that his powers and duties be devolved upon the Sheriff Clerk of the County in which the bankrupt traded[42] and the committee were most strongly against this proposal on the grounds that 'the extent of laborious and onerous duties thus imposed by the Bill on a single official' was highly inexpedient.[43] Of course, it must also be recognised that they were undoubtedly perturbed at the thought of a legal official taking over a job that had formerly been commonly undertaken by accountants, and by the subsequent loss of a steady source of fee income and a high status position. The accountants strengthened their criticism by further stating that:

> It appeared to the Meeting to be very desirable that any amendments on the present Bankrupt Act should be carefully considered by them on the part of the Institute, and the more so, because, by the annual returns made under that Act, it is shown that nearly five-sixths of the whole Bankrupt Estates in Scotland are intrusted to Accountants.[44]

The analysis in the previous chapter would indicate that this claim was exaggerated in terms of the numbers of cases dealt with by accountants but that it was only slightly exaggerated in terms of the percentage of reported fee income earned by accountants and this latter criterion was probably the more important of the two. Certainly, Stewart claimed that: 'the fees in the more important bankruptcy cases, though few in number, could be very substantial in amount'.[45] In any event the involvement in bankruptcy work by these accountants is clearly indicated in Table 3.1 which shows that, of those practising accountants invited to discuss the formation of the Institute, only two of the fifteen had no known involvement

TABLE 3.1

Edinburgh Accountants involved in formation of Institute of Accountants in Edinburgh

	Invited to First Meeting	Attended First Meeting	Attended Second Meeting	Involved in Pre 1854 Bankruptcy Work
A. Borthwick	*	*	*	*
J.J. Dickson	*		*	*
T.G. Dickson	*			
G.A. Esson	*			*
R. Gordon			*	*
A. Horne	*			*
T. Martin	*	*	*	*
G. Meldrum	*	*	*	*
W. Moncrieff	*		*	*
J. Macandrew			*	*
K. Mackenzie	*	*	*	*
J. Ogilvy			*	
C. Pearson	*	Apologised		*
S. Raleigh	*	*		
A. Robertson	Organiser	*	*	*
T. Scott	*			
J. Scott Moncrieff	*	*		
W. Wood	*	*	*	*

Sources: (i) *Institute of Accountants in Edinburgh, Sederunt Book, Council Minutes, No. 1.*

(ii) *The Alphabetical Compendium of Scotch Mercantile Sequestrations, 1851*

in bankruptcy work.

The representations of the Institute of Accountants must have been taken into account since the Bill was amended in Committee[46] by the removal of the offending clause and its replacement with the provision that the Interim Factor would be appointed by the Lord Ordinary or Sheriff as opposed to being elected by the creditors. Perhaps the legal authorities were unhappy as to the quality of some of the men being elected to this role and foresaw that controlling the appointment could lead to a more professional approach to the task and more efficient completion of sequestrations. In an event, it was this amended proposal that came into power with the passing of the Bankruptcy Act on 4 August 1853.

It would appear from the records that the members of the Edinburgh Institute determined to protect their interests in those sequestrations administered by the Lord Ordinary by placing a list of Edinburgh accountants, skilled in such work, in the hands of the Bill Chambers Clerk, which presumably contained only the names of accountants who were members of the new Institute. The discovery of the existence of this list caused consternation in the ranks of the Institute of Accountants in Glasgow whose Council requested a meeting with their Edinburgh counterparts to discuss this matter. At the meeting on 9 April 1854, they complained of the:

> exclusive nature of appointments of Interim Factors on Sequestrated Estates made by the Lord Ordinary on the Bills in terms of the recent amendment act that he understood that the appointments were made from a list in the hands of the Bill Chambers Clerks which did not contain the names of the principal Accountants in Glasgow and altho' it was not known how that list was made up, it was evident from the appointments made that the Court were not aware that there were gentlemen in Glasgow whose respectability and standing fully entitled them to consideration.[47]

The eventual outcome of the discussions between the two groups of accountants was that the Secretaries of both Institutes were asked to prepare lists of their members and present them to the Head of the Court in order that the appointments could be shared in a more equitable fashion between the Edinburgh and Glasgow accountants. The members of the Edinburgh Institute had perhaps been of the opinion that their proximity to the High Court entitled them to the exclusive right to these appointments, but the fact that approximately two-thirds of all bankruptcies at that time occurred in the West of Scotland and had formerly been largely administered by Glasgow accountants countered this attempt at restriction.

At the next meeting of the Edinburgh Council the main subject for discussion was the application for a Royal Charter, which had been raised at the first Annual Meeting of the Institute on 1 February 1854. The granting of a charter would certainly increase the status of the new Institute and lend weight to its opinions on changes in legislation. The petition described the business of an Edinburgh accountant as encompassing all the knowledge required by an actuary and a considerable amount of legal knowledge: 'an intimate acquaintance with the general principles of law, particularly of the Law of Scotland; and more especially with those branches of it which have relation to the law of merchant, to insolvency and bankruptcy, and to all rights connected with property'. It draws attention to the employment of accountants by the Court of Session in various matters of accounting which require professional assistance and most specifically to the employment of accountants:

> in Judicial Remits, in cases which are peculiar to the practice of Scotland, as, for instance, in Rankings and Sales, in processes of Court and Reckoning, Multiplepoinding, and others of a similar description: That they are also most commonly selected to be Trustees on Sequestrated Estates, and under Voluntary Trusts, and in these capacities they have duties to perform, not only of the highest responsibility, and involving large pecuniary interests, but which require, in those who undertake them, great experience in business, very considerable knowledge of law, and other qualifications.

It also describes those who have formed themselves into the Institute of Accountants as being 'those at present practising the profession'[48] but the petition was only signed by fifty-four of the 129 accountants listed in Edinburgh at that time.[49] Clearly too, the petition indicates that: 'when boiled down it may be said that the work of an Accountant at that time consists principally of Court work (that is, remits from the Courts of Law to investigate matters of accounting) and the winding up of bankrupt estates'.[50]

On 23 October 1854, the Royal Warrant was given for the incorporation of the Institute of Accountants in Edinburgh under the name of The Society of Accountants in Edinburgh.[51] The Charter which had been obtained at a cost of £204 9*s* 6*d*, was presented to the President and Council of the Society on 18 December 1854[52] and to a General Meeting of the Society on 29 December 1854.[53] At this same General Meeting the Secretary read a circular which he had received from the Crown Agent: 'requesting the Society to furnish the Lord Advocate with their views on the report by the Faculty of Advocates on Bankruptcy Law'. A committee was appointed to consider this and at a meeting of Council on 26 January 1855 a communication was read from the Lord Advocate requesting a meeting with a deputation on the subject. James Brown and Archibald Borthwick were the two council members appointed to this task[54] and the importance of the matter can be judged by the calling of a Special General Meeting on 30 January 1855 where the report on Bankruptcy Law reform was placed at the top of the agenda.[55] No further mention was made of this matter, therefore the assumption must be that it met with the approval of the Society.

Further proof of the Society's endeavours to protect certain areas of work for their members can be found in the Minute Books. At a meeting of the Council of 16 December 1863, the members' attention was drawn to Clause 125 of the Court of Session Bill in which powers were to be given to the Courts to remit matters connected with accounts to 'Accountants or other qualified persons'. The Society requested the Lord Advocate to insert the word Chartered before accountant in order to debar non-members but were unsuccessful in this effort.[56] Once again the new Society displayed the main characteristics of a new professional body in this attempt at restriction and at debarring those they considered to be unsuitable for the task.

The continuing importance of Court work to the Edinburgh Society is indicated by the concern expressed by them in 1867 as to the role of the Accountant of Court of Session.[57] At that time the

Office was separate from that of Accountant in Bankruptcy, although both were held by members of the Edinburgh Society. The Society's concern covered various aspects of this Office, the first being the limiting of the salary to £600 per annum which was said to be insufficient and resulted in the incumbent continuing to practise privately as well as holding office, a practice of which they clearly disapproved. Their suggestion was that the holder should be debarred from all private practice and that to compensate, the salary should be increased to approximately £1500 per annum - a change which it was claimed would attract professional men of the highest standing. The money to pay for this increased salary could be met from extending the Accountant's powers to cover Judicial Factors, with a resulting increase in fee income from that source. No change was made at that time and the matter was not discussed again until December 1873[58] when the Edinburgh Society co-operated with the Glasgow Institute in applying to the Lord Advocate to place Judicial Factors under the surveillance of the Accountant of Court. A further attempt to increase their Court work was made in June 1874 when the Council unanimously requested the President to write to the Lord Advocate suggesting that a Bill be introduced into Parliament providing for the regular audit of the Accounts of Judicial Factors.[59]

It was not until the passing of the Judicial Factors (Scotland) Act 1889 that these suggestions were implemented. Under the Act, the Accountant was not allowed to engage in any other business for profit and all Judicial Factors were brought under the supervision of the Accountant. The duties of audit were greatly increased in that all cases coming under the supervision of the Accountant for the first time were to be audited unless he thought it unnecessary on the production 'of reports of a professional or official auditor'. In addition he had the power to remit the audits to 'such duly qualified persons as he may with the approval of the Lord Advocate select to audit'.[60]

The legislation did not restrict any of this new work to members of the Chartered bodies but the office of Accountant of Court had been held from its inception in 1850 to his death in 1865 by John Maitland and from 1865 to 1889 by William Moncreiff,[61] both original members of the Edinburgh Society. Under the Act the office of Accountant was amalgamated with that of Accountant in Bankruptcy and Moncreiff resigned, at the age of seventy-six, when the new office was filled by Joseph Campbell Penney, aged thirty-eight, also a member of the Edinburgh Society and like Moncreiff from a legal background. This continuation of chartered accountants in these influential offices cannot have had anything other than a beneficial effect on the awarding of such Court work to fellow members.

Although chartered accountants were not given a monopoly of bankruptcy work there can be no doubt that it was of great importance to them, particularly during the early years of the Society's existence. Several factors strengthen this claim. Bankruptcy statistics for the periods before and after the formation of the Edinburgh Society show the strong involvement of its members in this area; Stewart comments on various early members who were trained in legal offices and who specialised in bankruptcy work; the wording of the Petition for a Charter of Incorporation gives prominence to various aspects of legal work and the Minute Books of the Society reveal how much time was devoted to discussing means of protecting the interests of chartered accountants in it.

3. Formation of the Institute of Accountants and Actuaries in Glasgow

Many of the group of accountants who formed the Glasgow Institute were also involved in bankruptcy work, although not to the same extent as the corresponding group in Edinburgh. However, they were more obviously employed in other areas than were the Edinburgh accountants. The *Post Office Glasgow Directory* for 1853-4 shows a considerable number of them being involved in insurance work, particularly as agents[62] and the records of the Glasgow Stock Exchange Association which had been founded in 1844 show that many of them were also actively involved in stockbroking in the city.[63] In addition to this, there is a suggestion that they were often involved in accounting work for clients unlike the group in Edinburgh.[64]

The successful formation of the Institute of Accountants and Actuaries in Glasgow arose from a requisition signed in September 1853 by twenty-seven accountants, who had begun practising in Glasgow between 1841 and 1853, being sent to fifteen accountants who had been in practice in the city at 1 January 1841, suggesting the formation of a Society. This was apparently not the first attempt to form such a Society since the requisition stated clearly that:

> It has long been felt by gentlemen practising as Professional Accountants in Glasgow, that the formation of a Society or Institute of Accountants is in every way desirable by means of which they may be enabled to advance those objects in which they have a common professional interest.
> Many suggestions have been made and plans proposed for carrying this into effect, but from various causes the attempt has always been delayed.[65]

If previous attempts had come to nothing there must have been special factors which led these accountants to believe that this attempt might succeed. One factor might have been the example of the formation of the Society of Accountants in Edinburgh which had been accomplished earlier that same year. However, the stated reason was the same catalyst which had been responsible for the earlier formation of the Edinburgh Society, the new bankruptcy legislation which had been introduced on 4 August 1853.

> The late changes and contemplated alterations in the Bankrupt Law of Scotland, point out, in a marked degree, the necessity and importance of now carrying the proposal into execution, in order that the practical experience of those parties who have hitherto been entrusted with the management of Bankrupt Estates in the West of Scotland may be properly represented, and have due weight in determining what changes require to be made upon the existing Bankrupt Law.[66]

This minute also suggests[67] that the younger members who proposed the formation of the Society recognised that a society had little chance of successful recognition without having the support of these senior accountants.

Comparison of accountants listed in the *Post Office Glasgow Directories* for 1840-1 and 1853-4 shows that twenty-one accountants were listed in both. Therefore, since only fifteen of these were approached, the younger members must have considered some of them to be too elderly or of insufficient status to be approached to form the society. In addition, neither James Gourlay nor Walter Mackenzie were listed as being in practice in the 1840-1 directory, but they were both recipients of the original requisition. Gourlay's omission from the 1840-1 directory was probably due to the fact that he only set up as an accountant in Glasgow in 1841, having previously been a commercial traveller.[68] Mackenzie was only assumed as a partner by James McClelland in 1841 and was listed in later directories.[69]

Although the main reason for the formation of the society was the protection of bankruptcy work, the group of Glasgow accountants who signed or received the requisition had a slightly weaker involvement in bankruptcy work than had their counterparts in Edinburgh. Twenty of the twenty-seven signatories and nine of the fifteen recipients of the requisition are known to have been involved in bankruptcy work at that time, i.e. seventy per cent compared with eighty-three per cent of those involved in the early stages of the formation of the Edinburgh Society. However, the *Post Office Glasgow Directory* for 1853-4 lists 150 accountants known to be practising in the city,[70] of whom only one-third are known to have been involved in bankruptcy work; thus those who formed the Glasgow Institute had a much stronger than average interest in that particular area.

Of the recipients of the requisition, A. Cuthbertson, T.G. Buchanan, A. McEwan, D. Dreghorn, P. White, W. Anderson, J.C. Foulds and W. Mackenzie met with J. McClelland on 3 October 1853 and, having discussed: 'the advantages and objects of such an Association as that contemplated, it was resolved that the meeting should cordially accede to the wish expressed in the Requisition and that a Society of Accountants be hereby formed'.[71] McClelland was appointed President and a Committee of Elder Members was formed, consisting of McEwan, White, and Mackenzie. In fact, none of the members of the Committee was particularly elderly, McClelland being fifty-four and McEwan, White, and Mackenzie being forty-one, forty-three, and thirty-seven respectively, so the title must have been one of respect for experience.

Once formed, the Society proceeded rapidly towards proper

organisation and within six weeks of the first meeting the members had agreed on rules for the admission of new members, including the level of entry money and annual subscriptions, and Council members had signed the constitution and admitted the first new members.[72]

At the first Council meeting subsequent to that at which the constitution was signed, the main topic of discussion was the new bankruptcy legislation and a decision was taken that, given the seriousness of this subject, a Special General Meeting of the Institute would be called at which a committee might be appointed to investigate this fully. This meeting was held in the following week and attended by twenty-three members and the committee of nine members was given responsibility 'to watch the present movement for the alteration of the existing Law for Scotland to draw up suggestions for its judicious amendment and to co-operate with other bodies for that object'.[73] One of the first things that the Council realised was that any recommendations that they might make would have little impact on the proposed changes if people were not aware of the existence of the Institute, as the Society had now become called. They therefore resolved to publicise their existence before writing to the authorities in bankruptcy in Edinburgh.[74] It is interesting to note to whom the Institute addressed its publicity: the Lord Advocate, Solicitor General, Judges, Sheriffs, Directors of Merchants House and of Chambers of Commerce and the Dean and Council of the Faculty of Procurators. Although most of these were members of the legal profession, it is significant that they considered it prudent to communicate with industry through the media of the Merchants House and Chambers of Commerce. These publicity efforts were relatively unsuccessful since in 1867, by which time the Institute was well established, the Lord Advocate expressed ignorance of the existence of a Chartered Institute in Glasgow.[75] Probably this ignorance illustrated the gulf which existed between the professional bodies of Glasgow and Edinburgh.

The sections of the amendment Act which concerned accountants were Section I, which provided for the appointment of the Interim Factor on a bankrupt estate by the Lord Ordinary or Sheriff as opposed to his previous election, and Section II, which provided for the election of Trustees by creditors.

By the time that the new Act had been in operation for eight months the Glasgow accountants expressed their concern over its impact on their involvement in bankruptcy work by calling a Special General Meeting on 21 March 1854 to consider the working of the Act with regard to the sections on Interim Factors and Trustees.

The meeting also discussed what steps should be taken with regard to Lord Brougham's Bankruptcy Bill, 'the purpose of which was to import into Scotland, in a great measure, the English system, with its Bankruptcy Court, Judges, Registrars, official Assignees, and other officers'[76] which had been read for the first time in the House of Lords and which would have removed much bankruptcy work from accountants. It was decided to form a petition against the Bill but before determining a course of action on the other matter it was agreed to seek advice from the Edinburgh accountants.[77] Perhaps they chose this course of action because they felt that a united approach by the two bodies would carry more weight or perhaps they were of the opinion that the Edinburgh accountants' closer relationship with the legal profession would give them a clearer understanding of how best to approach this matter. In the event, the advice from Edinburgh, which was reported at the reconvened meeting on 29 March 1854, was that, rather than endeavouring to persuade the Lords Ordinary that creditors be allowed to recommend someone for appointment as Interim Factor, the best course of action would be for both bodies to bring before the Lords Ordinary the names of the members of both institutes: 'as parties, all eligible for the office of Interim Factors'.[78] This list was prepared but appears to have gone astray between the Glasgow Institute and the Bill Chambers Clerks since within a few weeks the Glasgow accountants were complaining that they were not being included in those appointed as Interim Factors.[79]

The provision of a list of members available to undertake sequestration work was clearly designed to remove this lucrative area of work from the sphere of a variety of people who had claimed an ability in this area under the old legislation and to endeavour to make it the exclusive domain of the members of the two accounting societies. This did not immediately come about, but by the end of the nineteenth century there could be no doubt that, in most parts of Scotland, chartered accountants dominated this area of work.

The complaint that the Institute had about Lord Brougham's Bill was that there was at that time a Commission of Enquiry into the improvement of certain points of Mercantile Law, including

Bankruptcy. Since the Commission had not yet completed its investigations it was felt that:

> it would be injurious to the interests of the Mercantile Community in Scotland to proceed with the consideration of the Bill until the Commission referred to has had an opportunity of reporting to Parliament the result of its enquiries on this important and difficult Branch of Mercantile Jurisprudence.[80]

In making this complaint, the Institute was following the example of the Merchants House of Glasgow who had first discussed the Lord Advocate's amendment Act on 25 May 1853 and described it as being 'objectionable in many particulars'.[81] On 15 November 1853 they had gone to discuss Lord Brougham's Bill and unanimously agreed to oppose it and decided to invite Mr MacEwan, accountant, and another accountant to join in their deliberations.[82] At their meeting on 14 March 1854, the petition was finalised, the main complaint being that the Bill: 'seems to be founded exclusively on the Law and Practice of England, embracing all its cumbersome, complicated, and expensive machinery and totally overlooking the more simple and less expensive Practice of Scotland'. They also sent a deputation to London to put their case more strongly to the parties concerned.[83] The Bill was withdrawn, although perhaps not because of these petitions, and the Commission on Mercantile Law reported in the following two sessions of Parliament, resulting in the Bankruptcy (Scotland) Act 1856.

Another issue which was discussed at the meeting on 29 March 1854 was the approach to be adopted with regard to the appointment of Interim Factor and Trustee. Generally, it would appear that these two offices were filled by the same person, there certainly being nothing in the legislation to prevent this. It was suggested by Peter White, who was active in bankruptcy work in Scotland, that the appointment of an Interim Factor should not preclude others from canvassing creditors for support for the office of Trustee. Similarly, someone appointed Interim Factor should feel free to offer himself as Trustee unless this would mean displacing another member of the Institute who had previously been involved with the Insolvent's affairs.

This particular suggestion did not meet with any favour in the Edinburgh Institute since in Edinburgh there was 'very seldom . . . . any previous employment of an Accountant prior to sequestration'.[84] However, the fact that the matter had been of concern to the Glasgow accountants does imply that at that time they were actively involved in providing services to industry and commerce and would, through being known to creditors, be quite likely to be appointed as Trustee in the event of a sequestration taking place.

Having dealt with the topic which had determined their formation into an Institute, the Glasgow accountants then turned their attention to the need for a Royal Charter, which would place them on the same footing as their colleagues in Edinburgh. The Council of the Glasgow Institute met on 4 July 1854 and resolved to proceed to apply for a Charter expressing the conviction 'that a Charter would greatly improve the position of the Institute, and promote the objects it had in view'.[85] This action on the part of the Glasgow Institute followed closely on similar action that had been taken by the Edinburgh Society, who had finalised their application arrangements in June 1854.[86]

The petition emphasised the rapid growth in Scotland in the number of people practising accountancy and the high respect in which the profession in Glasgow was held.[87] Accountants listed in the *Post Office Glasgow Directory* had increased from forty-eight in 1840-1 to 151 in 1854-5, a significant increase in the number of men who considered that they were eligible to be called accountants. However the petition was only signed by forty-nine accountants,[88] so the majority of Glasgow accountants were considered unsuitable for membership of the new society at the time of its formation.

The petition for the grant of a Royal Charter which was prepared by the Glasgow Institute was a little shorter and less detailed than that prepared by the Edinburgh Society, but its essence was similar. In particular, it noted the necessity to have a knowledge of the Law of Scotland because of the amount of work arising from legal proceedings, specifically:

> that they are also most commonly selected to be Trustees on Sequestrated Estates, and to act as Trustees under private Deeds of Trust on large landed Estates, and that in these capacities they have often to

> consider and determine, in the first instance, important questions of law relating to property;.[89]

Clearly these accountants viewed their contact with the legal profession as central to their prosperity and were determined to protect it as far as possible. Since the granting of a Royal Charter would have been most unlikely on the grounds of protectionism, the case had to be made on more reasonable grounds and the Glasgow accountants followed the same arguments as had those in Edinburgh, namely that the quality of professional performance could only be protected through ensuring that members had been properly educated and trained and that, for this reason alone, it was necessary to have formal recognition of their status.

The objects of the new Association were, at this time, stated to be 'to elevate the attainments and status of the Accountants of Glasgow, to promote their efficiency and usefulness and to give concentrated expression to their opinions upon all questions and laws bearing upon, or incident to, the business of their profession'.[90] Thus, along with the intention of enhancing the professional status of those who were admitted to this newly-formed closed shop, the members were also involved in protecting their professional sphere from other professional groups by convincing others that there were certain professional tasks which could only be satisfactorily performed by those accountants who were considered suitable for membership of the chartered body.

In common with the petition for the Edinburgh Charter, the Glasgow petition refers to the requirement for an accountant to be skilled in actuarial work. An examination of the *Post Office Glasgow Directory* for 1853-4 reveals that almost seventy per cent of the accountants signing the Glasgow Charter were involved in insurance in some way, mainly as agents. This compares with thirty-six per cent of all Glasgow accountants listed also being listed under insurance so, as was also the case in the area of bankruptcy, those accountants who formed the new society had a much stronger than average representation in the field of insurance; indeed almost fifty per cent were known to be involved in both of these areas. Another factor which confirms this involvement in actuarial work is in the choice of the name for the new Society: The Institute of Accountants and Actuaries in Glasgow. This could be seen as an indication that although the members wished to pursue any advantages that might be gained from forming a society of accountants similar to that formed in Edinburgh, they were anxious not to exclude themselves, through their choice of society title, from insurance work.

The Glasgow Charter was granted on 15 March 1855[91] approximately five months after the granting of the Edinburgh Charter.

In December 1854, the Bankruptcy Committee of the Institute met to discuss a letter from the Crown Agent in Edinburgh written on behalf of the Lord Advocate. This stated that the Lord Advocate was anxious to know the society's views on the Faculty of Advocates' report on bankruptcy law and asked for these to be sent to him for communication to the Lord Advocate.[92] In October 1855, the minutes of the Quarterly Meeting reveal the Institute's representation on a general committee formed in Glasgow to monitor the progress of the Bankruptcy Bill along with representatives from the Town Council, Merchants House, the Chamber of Commerce, the Faculty of Procurators, and the West of Scotland Guardian Society for the Protection of Trade and Bankers,[93] a sign of the early acceptance of the new Institute by the older, well-established bodies in the city and also, perhaps, of the closer links felt to exist with the city institutions than with the Edinburgh accountants.

The only other bankruptcy matter of interest that is minuted after the passing of the Bankruptcy (Scotland) Act 1856 is a report on a meeting with George Esson, Accountant in Bankruptcy, presented to the Annual General Meeting on 23 January 1857 in which it was stated that Esson was preparing notes on the new legislation and the role of Trustees, presumably to dispel confusion as to the workings of the new Act. It was also noted that it was intended to reach agreement on a uniform form of Accounts of Intromission for adoption by Trustees.[94]

Mann referred to the work done by Glasgow Accountants at the time of the formation of the Glasgow Institute as 'a kind of clamjamfry or gallimaufry', meaning a mixture of many different things. Among these were balancing books and preparing accounts, some income tax work, estate management, directorships, stockbroking and insurance work but no auditing.[95] These interests are also periodically mentioned in the early records of the Glasgow Institute. However, in spite of the fact that these were more varied interests than those of the Edinburgh Chartered Accountants, their prime concern was exactly the same, the preservation of their involvement in bankruptcy work.

4. Formation of the Society of Accountants in Aberdeen

Practising accountants in Aberdeen did not see any need to form themselves into a proper society until 1866. One possible reason for this was that the number of accountants was not of sufficient significance to warrant a society. The *Aberdeen Post Office Directory* for 1824-5 only listed three bank accountants and the *Aberdeen Directory* of 1828-9 did not list any. From 1846-7 onwards the post office directories show a slight increase and in that for 1854-5, when the Edinburgh and Glasgow Societies were in the midst of obtaining charters, eighteen men were designated as accountants, though only seven of these subsequently became chartered accountants. In 1866-7 twenty-five accountants were listed, of whom five were described as employed by banks, three by railway companies, and one each by a shipping company and insurance company respectively, leaving fifteen undesignated and presumed to be public accountants.

Another reason for the lateness of societal formation in Aberdeen could have been the complete lack of involvement of Aberdeen accountants in bankruptcy work and their subsequent lack of interest in pending legislation changes in the mid-1850s. Just over half of the bankruptcy work in Aberdeen at that time was undertaken by the legal profession, with the other half split evenly between a variety of merchants and the banking fraternity. By 1867, sequestration work was still only averaging twenty cases a year in Aberdeen and trusteeships were dealt with mainly by the legal profession and by an assortment of merchants and tradesmen.

In the absence of any conflicting evidence, the probable reason for the formation of the society was that, having seen the successful establishment of the Edinburgh and Glasgow chartered accounting bodies, Aberdeen accountants felt that it was time that they were on a par with them. So in 1866 the practising accountants formed themselves into a formal society.[96] Since only twelve accountants were involved they proceeded directly to petition for their charter without first adopting a constitution as the other societies had done.[97]

Much of the wording in the petition was an exact replica of that set forth in the successful petition for the Edinburgh Charter and the business of accountant as practised in Aberdeen was described as being:

> varied and extensive, embracing all matters of Account, and requiring for its proper execution an acquaintance with the general principles of law, particularly of the Law of Scotland, and more especially with those branches of it which have relation to the law of Merchant, to Insolvency, and Bankruptcy, and to all rights connected with property: That they are also frequently selected to take the charge of landed properties and of bankrupt, insolvent, and other trust estates, and in that capacity they have duties to perform, not only of the highest responsibility and involving large pecuniary interest, but which require in those who undertake them, great experience in business, very considerable knowledge of law, and other qualifications which can only be attained by a liberal education.[98]

It is noticeable that the Aberdeen petition omits any reference to actuarial work and to work directly involved with suits before the Court of Session, but what is also noticeable is that up to and including the year of the formation of the Society there had never been any more than one sequestration case per year in which an accountant had been involved.

The person who is always credited with having been the main force behind the formation of the Society of Accountants in Aberdeen was James Meston, who was not known to have any connection with bankruptcy. However, three of the twelve original members were known to have such an involvement, John Crombie, Robert Fletcher and John Smith, the first President of the Society at the age of seventy. Smith had originally practised as an advocate, and at least six of the twelve original members had contacts with the legal profession. Crombie, Meston, Milne and Smith[99] are known to have received their early training in legal offices; Leslie became Sheriff

Clerk Depute of Aberdeen and Kincardine and Steele was an advocate's managing clerk. It can also be assumed that the legal and business community in Aberdeen in 1866 was closely knit and that the fact that most of the original members of the Aberdeen Society would be known to one another explains the absence of formation details in the Minute Books.

The original Rules and Regulations of the Aberdeen Society were also closely modelled on those in force in the Edinburgh Society in 1866. Although the application for a Royal Charter of incorporation for the Aberdeen Society did not mention actuarial work, Paragraph 40 is identical to Paragraph 39 of the Edinburgh Society and identifies subjects for examination as being:

> algebra, including the use of logarithms - annuities - life assurances - life rents - reversions - book-keeping - framing of States under sequestrations, trusts, factories executries - the Law of Scotland, especially that relating to bankruptcy, private trust and arbitration, and rights and preferences of creditors in rankings.[100]

This would suggest that, although at its formation, members of the Aberdeen Society were not greatly involved in either actuarial work or bankruptcy, they felt that it would be prudent to extend the possible boundaries of their work to cover the same areas as those likely to be covered by the Edinburgh Society.

On receiving the petition for a Charter of Incorporation from the Aberdeen accountants, the Lord Advocate contacted the Edinburgh Society and suggested that a more sensible idea would be to grant a supplementary charter to the Edinburgh Society so as to allow it to grant diplomas to accountants in the provincial towns of Scotland.[101] One can imagine the reaction that such an act would have had in the city of Aberdeen which almost certainly was not considered by its inhabitants to be a provincial town and whose accountants would have been appalled at an attempt to make them inferior members of the Edinburgh Society. However this was avoided through the existence of the chartered body in Glasgow, which set a precedent for charters other than that granted to the Edinburgh Society. Thus the Society of Accountants in Aberdeen was chartered in 1867,[102] but since the rules and regulations of all three accounting bodies limited membership to accountants practising in the three respective cities, accountants living in provincial towns were still denied the advantages of society membership.

5. Summary

This chapter has discussed the mechanics of the formation of the Scottish Chartered Accounting societies and the reasons for their formation. It was particularly important that they all received Royal Charters of Incorporation since this had become established as the status symbol of the new professional bodies and was seen to be a sign of their maturity and of public recognition of their value to society.[103] The importance of bankruptcy work to the Edinburgh and Glasgow members has been stressed along with the fact that, without any doubt, the catalyst for the formation of these two societies was the proposed changes in Scottish bankruptcy legislation.

By the end of 1867, Scotland had three bodies of chartered accountants, before any accounting societies had been formed in England and this earlier organisation can only be attributable to the earlier reformation, in Scotland, of bankruptcy legislation. However, these societies did not form themselves but were the product of a great deal of effort by their founders. 'The history of every association is the record of one or more devoted individuals, whose spark ignited a movement, or revived a decaying structure. Without these individuals, there could be no organization'.[104] The accountancy profession was no exception to this and the following chapter proceeds to examine the social background of those who formed the three societies and those who were members during the first fifty years of their development.

IV

Social Background

1. Introduction

In the initial stages of professional formation one might argue that the social status of the founding and early members is transferred to the new profession, while in the developing years membership of the profession earns social status for the members, and accountants would seem to be no different from other new professional groupings in this respect. The petitions for Charters for both the Edinburgh and Glasgow societies make reference to the fact that the profession of accountancy had long existed in Scotland and was very respectable.[1]

In the eighteenth and early-nineteenth centuries, the three liberal professions were identified as the Church, medicine and the law, and these served as examples for the new professions which were formalised from the mid-nineteenth century onwards.[2] Accountancy in Scotland had been regarded for many years as a specialised occupation which was largely, particularly in Edinburgh, a branch of the legal profession, so that when separate accounting societies were formed the members were very conscious that, once detached from the legal profession, they would probably lack social prestige.[3] In addition, the definition of the title 'accountant' was so wide as to encompass all sorts of people, from those acting as house factors and auctioneers to those engaged in highly specialised work such as the administration of bankrupt estates, and there was understandable concern that the admission to the new societies of men operating on the fringes of accountancy work would immediately devalue the new profession.

When the first two Scottish accounting societies were formed, care was taken to ensure that 'accountants' working in the less specialised and less acceptable areas of accounting were not invited to become members. In particular, great efforts were made to ensure that members were fully occupied as public accountants and were not involved in trade, since there was undoubtedly a feeling in the mid-Victorian era, as reflected in the words of Trollope's Mrs Marrable: 'that when a man touched trade or commerce in any way he was doing that which was not the work of a gentleman.'[4]

By limiting original membership of the new societies to those who were already perceived to be eminent in the field of accounting, the originators removed the problems that divisions of social class might initially have caused in the new profession.[5] There were, of course, differences in the social origins of the early members of the accounting bodies but all of the original members had already achieved a certain status in the profession through experience over a period of years. In the developing years, membership of the profession imputed a certain social status to its members[6] and there were interesting changes in the social mix of members over this period.

2. Father's Occupation

(*a*) *Introduction*

'In Great Britain, occupation is probably the most important single criterion of status'[7] therefore an examination of the occupations of the antecedents of chartered accountants should indicate the social status which they held on becoming members. One advantage of choosing parental occupation is that, in Scotland, most of the stated occupations can be confirmed from primary sources such as certificates of birth, marriage or death and from Census records.

Fifty per cent of those admitted to membership originated in professional or privileged families and, with a further seventeen per cent coming from a mercantile background, this would suggest that two-thirds of such accountants came from upper-or middle-

TABLE 4.1

Social Origins of Admissions to Membership: Formation - 1904.

	Edinburgh		Glasgow		Aberdeen		Total	
Father's Occupation	No.	%	No.	%	No.	%	No.	%
CA	33	6.0	40	7.0	-	-	73	6.1
Accountants and Related Occupations	17	3.1	36	6.3	4	5.7	57	4.8
	50	9.1	76	13.3	4	5.7	130	10.9
Legal Profession	72	13.0	32	5.6	3	4.3	107	9.0
Financial Institutions and Insurance	34	6.1	23	4.0	2	2.9	59	4.9
Church	40	7.2	42	7.4	7	10.0	89	7.4
Government and Armed Services	33	5.9	6	1.0	1	1.4	40	3.3
Landowner	45	8.1	38	6.7	7	10.0	90	7.5
Other Professions	45	8.1	38	6.7	4	5.7	87	7.3
	319	56.5	255	44.7	28	40.0	602	50.3
Businessman	33	5.9	16	2.8	4	5.7	53	4.4
Merchant	51	9.2	94	16.5	6	8.6	151	12.6
	403	72.6	365	64.0	38	54.3	806	67.3
Manufacturer	11	2.0	41	7.2	3	4.3	55	4.6
Craftsman/Tradesman	40	7.2	33	5.8	8	11.4	81	6.8
Miscellaneous: Post of Responsibility	23	4.1	37	6.5	12	17.1	72	6.1
Miscellaneous: Others	7	1.3	5	0.9	2	2.9	14	1.2
Unknown	71	12.8	89	15.9	7	10.0	167	14.0
TOTAL	555	100.0	570	100.0	70	100.0	1195	100.0

Source: Scottish Records Office

class families. During this period fewer than twenty per cent of chartered accountants admitted to membership are known to have come from the lower social classes. It would seem, therefore, that chartered accountancy had no difficulty in achieving a recognisable social status since its membership was largely from the higher social classes. Only eleven per cent of the members came from an accounting background and, of that proportion, only fifty-five per cent were sons of chartered accountants (Table 4.1). This proportion was inevitably one which would grow slowly, since initially the numbers of chartered accountants were small and openings in the new profession were limited. In addition, a fifty-year study can really only claim to provide adequate analysis of two generations but further analysis of the population would seem to suggest that this particular percentage showed an upward trend.

The profession in Scotland was originally organised in three separate chartered societies, and there were significant differences between their membership. Without any doubt, the members of the Edinburgh Society were of higher social origins than were members of the other two societies and in particular, showed a much higher percentage of men from a legal, financial and government background. Glasgow had a considerably higher proportion of members from a commercial background and Aberdeen much higher percentages of craftsmen, tradesmen and those in lower-class occupations but in positions of responsibility. This suggests that there were significant differences in the social origins of men being admitted to the three societies which might be a reflection of the area from which members were drawn. In addition to the difference between the three societies there were changes in the background of the members of each of the societies over the period examined.

(*b*) *Changing Patterns: Edinburgh*

The strong foundations on which Scottish chartered accountancy has flourished were laid in Edinburgh where the first society was formed. Those who determined the composition of the steering committee are unknown but Alexander Robertson acted on their behalf when he circulated fourteen accountants in Edinburgh with the suggestion that a society ought to be formed.[8] At that time the *Edinburgh and Leith Post Office Directory* listed 123 accountants[9]

TABLE 4.2

Changing Social Origins of Edinburgh Chartered Accountants

Father's Occupation	Recipients of Original letter 1853 %	Signatories of Charter 1854 %	Admitted as Members 1853-79 %	Admitted as Members 1880-1904 %
CA	-	1.6	5.0	6.4
Accountants and Related Occupations	6.7	4.9	2.8	3.2
	6.7	6.5	7.8	9.6
Legal Profession	26.7	18.1	19.6	9.9
Financial Institutions and Insurance	6.7	8.2	6.1	6.1
Church	13.3	16.4	10.1	5.9
Government and Armed Services	13.3	8.2	6.7	5.6
Landowner	13.3	11.5	7.8	8.3
Other Professions	-	4.9	6.7	8.8
	80.0	73.8	64.8	54.2
Businessman	-	1.6	-	8.8
Merchant	-	-	3.9	11.7
	80.0	75.4	68.7	74.7
Manufacturer	-	1.6	1.1	2.4
Craftsman/Tradesman	6.7	3.3	5.6	8.0
Miscellaneous: Posts of Responsibility	-	-	5.0	3.7
Miscellaneous: Others	-	-	0.6	1.6
Unknown	13.3	19.7	19.0	9.6
	100.0	100.0	100.0	100.0
Number	15	61	180	375

Source: Scottish Records Office

TABLE 4.3

Background of Sample of Writers to the Signet

	Period in which writers qualified		
	1690-1749	1750-89	1790-1829
Father's Standing	%	%	%
Legal Profession	22	20	30
Landowner	49	41	25
Minister	9	10	3
Army Officer, Colonial Adventurer or Civil Office-Holder	3	1	10
Physician, Teacher or Architect	2	10	8
Tenant-Farmer	1	3	9
Merchant	12	13	13
Tradesman	2	1	2
Unskilled Labourer	-	1	-
	100.0	100.0	100.0

Source: T.C. Smout, *A History of the Scottish People 1560-1830*, (London: Collins, 1969) p. 375

and presumably the chosen few were considered to be the most senior and influential accountants then in the city (Table 4.2). The occupation of fathers of two of these fifteen were unknown, and one was described as a builder without any qualification as to the scale of undertaking with which he might have been involved. The remaining twelve were members of the legal profession, the Church, banking, government service, landowners and one was an accountant. None of the fifteen was the son of a manufacturer and eighty per cent were from upper-class backgrounds. The largest grouping was that from the legal profession, being four out of fifteen. Perhaps this was a reflection of the fact that Robertson himself came from a family of lawyers[10] but it was also in keeping with Smout's observations that:

> The real leaders of Edinburgh society, however, were not to be found among merchants and tradesmen but among professional men: and among the professions there were none, in numbers, wealth or prestige, to equal the lawyers.[11]

Smout analysed a sample of 300 Writers to the Signet for the period 1690 to 1829 which showed that ninety-eight per cent of them came from upper- or upper-middle-class backgrounds (Table 4.3).

The most significant differences between his 1790-1829 figures and the 1853 Edinburgh chartered accountants are in the classification of landowner, the Church, other professions and merchants. The writers showed twenty-five per cent with landowning fathers compared with thirteen per cent for accountants. Ministers were fathers to only three per cent of writers but to thirteen per cent of accountants; none of the accountants had fathers in other newer professions and none was from a merchant background, while thirteen per cent of writers were. Perhaps these differences indicate that the newer professions such as accountancy attracted, to some extent, those who were ineligible for entry to the established professions.[12]

Carr-Saunders and Caradog Jones[13] discuss the difficulties of establishing social class by reference to occupation, but it is still possible to obtain an idea of the background of early chartered accountants in comparison to other groups.

Some of the trends revealed by the analyses of those who signed the Charter; those admitted between 1853 and 1879 and those admitted between 1880 and 1904 can be quite easily explained, in particular the increasing incidence of 'other professions' which grew as more professions became recognised. Those members with fathers who were chartered accountants grew steadily, showing that there was an increasing degree of self-recruitment into the accountancy profession similar to that which has been said to exist in teaching, medicine, the Church and the law.[14] At the same time the numbers coming from other accounting backgrounds only rose very slightly suggesting that perhaps in Edinburgh there were quite distinct divisions in the work being undertaken by chartered and non-chartered accountants.

Although financial institutions and insurance remained reasonably steady over the period examined, the influence of the legal profession, the Church and the government and armed services declined steadily and there could have been several reasons for such changes. It is conceivable, for example, that in the early days of the profession the close relationship with legally related work, in particular with bankruptcy work, and therefore with the legal profession in Edinburgh, encouraged lawyers to view accountancy as a suitable profession for sons who were not attracted to the legal profession. In addition, the decline in some professional groups was counterbalanced by an increase in others. The incidence of landowner fathers may have fallen because fewer men could afford to be landowners without following some other occupation and they could, therefore, be included under some other occupational category.

Despite any rationalisation that might be suggested for the changes in social background that occurred over the first fifty years of the accountancy profession, the figures suggest that, in Edinburgh, accountancy became less attractive to certain upper- and upper-middle-class groups. By the end of the first fifty years of its existence the Edinburgh Society of Accountants was drawing twenty per cent of its members from a commercial background but still taking a very small percentage from a manufacturing background. This can be explained by the fact that Edinburgh, apart from the importance of brewing to the city, was not a manufacturing centre to the same extent as was Glasgow. For the remaining members a steady proportion of lower-middle- to lower- class backgrounds emerged which was significant enough to enforce the traditional Scottish view that, although privilege was no deterrent to acceptability in a profession, neither was it an essential prerequisite for admission.

(*c*) *Changing Patterns: Glasgow*

The first analysis of those who received a letter suggesting the formation of a society in Glasgow indicates that there was a strong influence from trade and commerce among those practising accountancy in the city (Table 4.4). Occupations of fathers included two general merchants, one merchant, one clothier, a hatter and a master wright. There was only one member of the legal profession, one banker and two ministers and the most significant group was that from a commercial background. The trends revealed by the periodic analysis show a slight drop in those with chartered accountant fathers, but a steady proportion coming from other accounting backgrounds. A survey of social origins of Glasgow chartered accountants carried out by Cairncross for the period 1931-7 revealed only five per cent of accountancy apprentices with chartered accountant fathers which perhaps indicates a continuing drop in this group, although he claims that one in five of the sons of accountants becomes an accountant.[15] Of the upper- to upper-middle-class groups only 'other professions' shows a significant rise and can probably be explained by the increased availability of such occupations particularly in a heavy industrialised area. The proportion of members from an upper- and upper-middle-class background declined steadily over the period while businessmen and merchants displayed reasonable growth. Considering the fact that Glasgow was a major industrial centre it is surprising to see this slow growth in the manufacturing and craftsmen categories, but perhaps young men from such backgrounds were attracted to other new professions such as engineering, which would be seen as being more prestigious than learning a trade.

(*d*) *Changing Patterns: Aberdeen*

The population of chartered accountants in Aberdeen for the period to 1904 was very small when compared with those of Edinburgh and Glasgow, and the highest number of chartered accountants to be listed in the *Aberdeen Directory* during the period studied was twenty-six in 1904. Because the Aberdeen Society was not formed until 1867, the comparison in the last two columns of Table 4.5 is

TABLE 4.4

Changing Social Origins of Glasgow Chartered Accountants

Father's Occupation	Recipients of Original Letter 1853 %	Signatories of Letter 1853 %	Signatories of Charter 1855 %	Admitted as Members 1853-79 %	Admitted as Members 1880-1904 %
CA	-	-	-	7.6	6.8
Accountants and Related Occupations	14.3	7.7	4.1	6.2	6.3
	14.3	7.7	4.1	13.8	13.1
Legal Profession	7.1	11.5	8.2	6.9	5.2
Financial Institutions and Insurance	7.1	3.8	4.1	5.6	3.5
Church	14.3	7.7	8.2	8.3	7.0
Government and Armed Services	-	-	-	0.7	1.2
Landowner	7.1	19.3	12.2	11.1	5.2
Other Professions	-	7.7	2.0	4.9	7.3
	49.9	57.7	30.6	51.3	42.5
Businessman	-	-	2.0	1.4	3.3
Merchant	28.7	7.7	18.4	15.3	16.9
	78.6	65.4	51.0	68.0	62.7
Manufacturer	-	11.5	6.1	6.2	7.5
Craftsman/Tradesman	14.3	-	8.2	4.9	6.1
Miscellaneous: Posts of Responsibility	-	3.8	2.0	3.5	7.5
Miscellaneous: Others	-	-	-	1.4	0.7
Unknown	7.1	19.3	24.5	16.0	15.5
	100.0	100.0	100.0	100.0	100.0
Number	14	26	49	144	426

Source: Scottish Records Office

TABLE 4.5

Changing Social Origins of Aberdeen Chartered Accountants

Father's Occupation	**Original Members 1867 %**	**Admitted as Members 1867-79 %**	**Admitted as Members 1880-1904 %**
CA	-	-	-
Accountants and Related Occupations	-	-	8.3
	-	-	8.3
Legal Profession	-	-	6.3
Financial Institutions and Insurance	-	-	2.1
Church	8.3	4.5	12.5
Government and Armed Services	16.7	9.1	-
Landowner	8.3	13.6	8.3
Other Professions	-	-	16.6
	33.3	27.2	54.1
Businessman	8.3	4.5	-
Merchant	8.3	9.1	14.6
	49.9	40.8	68.7
Manufacturer	8.3	9.1	2.1
Craftsman/Tradesman	-	9.1	14.6
Miscellaneous: Posts of Responsibility	25.0	27.4	8.3
Miscellaneous: Others	8.3	4.5	4.2
Unknown	8.5	9.1	2.1
	100.0	100.0	100.0
Number	12	22	48

Source: Scottish Records Office

slightly different from that in the cases of Edinburgh and Glasgow; nevertheless, identifiable trends can still be seen for the period from 1867 to 1904. Of most significance is the fact that, prior to 1880, none of the Aberdeen chartered accountants came from an accounting, legal or financial family background. Perhaps the lack of accounting parentage was due to there having been very few accountants in Aberdeen in the early nineteenth century; certainly the *Aberdeen Directories* for the period from 1824 never listed more than twenty-five persons so designated.

It would appear that much of the accounting work was carried out by the legal profession in Aberdeen and the majority of the original members of the Aberdeen Society received their early training in legal offices in the city.[16] The driving force behind the formation of the Aberdeen Society was James Meston described after his death as:

> a self-made man who rose from a comparatively humble station in life to a first place in the ranks of the professional men of the country.[17]

His father was the road toll-keeper in Kintore, a position which undoubtedly carried a great deal of prestige in that community and which perhaps exposed Meston, during his formative years, to the elements of accounting. George Marquis was the son of the postmaster at Fochabers and was at different times in partnership with William Lunan, son of a minister, and William Milne, son of a merchant tailor, who were also founder members of the society. James Augustus Sinclair came from an army background and became 16th Earl of Caithness in 1889, the first chartered accountant to become a peer. William Steele provides another example of the self made man having been the son of a mailguard in the days of stage-coaches. Over the period examined, Aberdeen displayed an increase from twenty-seven to fifty-four per cent in the proportion of its accountants who came from a professional background. Although businessmen disappeared by 1880 this loss was counterbalanced by an increase in those designated as merchants. Manufacturers decreased but the Aberdeen Society became more easily accessible to young men from an artisan background. The fall

TABLE 4.6

Comparison of Social Origins of Charter Members

Father's Occupation	Edinburgh %	Glasgow %	Aberdeen %
CA	1.6	-	-
Accountants and Related Occupations	4.9	4.1	-
	6.5	4.1	-
Legal Profession	18.1	8.2	-
Financial Institutions and Insurance	8.2	4.1	-
Church	16.2	8.2	8.3
Government and Armed Services	8.2	-	16.7
Landowner	11.5	12.2	8.3
Other Professions	4.9	2.0	-
	73.8	30.6	33.3
Businessman	1.6	2.0	8.3
Merchant	-	18.4	8.3
	74.5	51.0	49.9
Manufacturer	1.6	6.1	8.3
Craftsman/Tradesman	3.3	8.2	-
Miscellaneous: Posts of Responsibility	-	2.0	25.0
Miscellaneous: Others	-	-	8.3
Unknown	19.7	24.5	8.5
	100.0	100.0	100.0
Number	61	49	12

Source: Scottish Records Office

in those classified as holding miscellaneous posts of responsibility reflects the fact that positions such as toll-keepers and mail-coach guards had disappeared by 1880 and also that more people were moving into the recognised professions.

(*e*) (*i*) *Comparison of Charter Members*

This comparison in Table 4.6 shows quite clearly the wide differences that existed in the backgrounds of the founder members of the accounting societies, and particularly the differences between the Edinburgh and Glasgow Societies which were formed within months of each other. Edinburgh members show a stronger background in two of the liberal professions, the law and the Church[18] and a total upper-class background that was more than double that of the other two societies.

Both Glasgow and Aberdeen show a significant background in trade which is almost non-existent in Edinburgh. This is almost certainly a reflection of the different activities carried on in these cities and is indicative of the much closer ties between accounting and commerce in the West of Scotland.

(*ii*) *Comparison of Admissions from Formation to 1879*

The professional classes formed a much higher proportion of the population in Edinburgh than they did in Glasgow or Aberdeen, which showed an extremely small proportion in this class (Table 4.7). Once the businessmen and merchants were included, the proportions of upper- and upper-middle-class origins in Edinburgh and Glasgow were practically identical at sixty-eight per cent but that for Aberdeen was only forty per cent. The differences between the Edinburgh and Glasgow professional and business grouping was similar to that discovered by Smout in his comparison of late eighteenth-century populations of the two cities[19] and it is conceivable that the low proportion of these classes in Aberdeen reflects the lower social status which the profession in that city held.

TABLE 4.7

Social Origins of Admissions to Membership: Formation to 1879.

Father's Occupation	**Edinburgh** %	**Glasgow** %	**Aberdeen** %
CA	1.0	7.6	-
Accountants and Related Occupations	2.8	6.2	-
	7.8	13.8	-
Legal Profession	19.6	6.9	-
Financial Institutions and Insurance	6.1	5.6	-
Church	10.1	8.3	4.5
Government and Armed Services	6.7	0.7	9.1
Landowner	7.8	11.1	13.6
Other Professions	6.7	4.9	-
	64.8	51.3	27.2
Businessman	-	1.4	4.5
Merchant	3.9	15.3	9.1
	68.7	68.0	40.8
Manufacturer	1.1	6.2	9.1
Craftsman/Tradesman	5.6	4.9	9.1
Miscellaneous: Posts of Responsibility	5.0	3.5	27.4
Miscellaneous: Others	0.6	1.4	4.5
Unknown	19.0	16.0	9.1
	100.0	100.0	100.0

Source: Scottish Records Office

TABLE 4.8

Social Origins of Admissions to Membership: 1880-1904.

Father's Occupation	Edinburgh %	Glasgow %	Aberdeen %
CA	6.4	6.8	-
Accountants and Related Occupations	3.2	6.3	8.3
	9.6	13.1	8.3
Legal Profession	9.9	5.2	6.3
Financial Institutions and Insurance	6.1	3.5	2.1
Church	5.9	7.0	12.5
Government and Armed Services	5.6	1.2	-
Landowner	8.3	5.2	8.3
Other Professions	8.8	7.3	16.6
	54.2	42.5	54.1
Businessman	8.8	3.3	-
Merchant	11.7	16.9	14.6
	74.7	62.7	68.7
Manufacturer	2.4	7.5	2.1
Craftsman/Tradesman	8.0	6.1	14.6
Miscellaneous: Posts of Responsibility	3.7	7.5	8.3
Miscellaneous: Others	1.6	0.7	4.2
Unknown	9.6	15.5	2.1
	100.0	100.0	100.0

Source: Scottish Records Office

(*iii*) *Comparison of Admissions from 1880 to 1904*

During the period from 1880 to 1904, admission to the three Scottish societies was at a higher level than in the earlier period examined and the consequent larger numbers lend themselves to more meaningful analysis (Table 4.8). The first interesting point is the significantly higher rate of recruitment into the profession from an accounting background in Glasgow, although the reason lay not in recruitment from a chartered accountancy background, but in the relatively higher proportion from non-chartered accountancy origins in Glasgow as compared with Edinburgh. The legal profession, the financial institutions and insurance and the government and armed services continued to have more influence on accountants in Edinburgh than in Glasgow and Aberdeen, but the Church and other professions were significantly higher in Aberdeen than in the other two societies. When businessmen and merchants were included, the Edinburgh Society's proportion of upper- and upper-middle-class origins rose to seventy-five per cent while that of both Glasgow and Aberdeen was less than seventy per cent. Glasgow continued to show the highest proportion of the three in manufacturing and Aberdeen the highest proportion in the craftsmen/tradesmen bracket. These figures reinforce the view that Glasgow was much more of an industrial city than either Edinburgh or Aberdeen, and might also suggest that in Aberdeen, craftsmen and tradesmen were held in much higher esteem than in the other two cities. Despite the differences that still existed in the second period analysed, the general picture that emerged was one of a more uniform social stratification among those admitted to membership of the three societies in this later period with the most significant difference appearing to be the continuing higher proportion of merchants and manufacturers in Glasgow.

(*f*) *Grandfather's Occupation*

For all three societies it was possible to establish the occupation of the paternal and maternal grandfathers of approximately fifty per cent of the members (Table 4.9). Since civil registration did not begin in Scotland until 1855 and records prior to that were kept on a parish basis and were of very varied quality, it was easier to find this

TABLE 4.9

Comparison of Occupation of Paternal and Maternal Grandfathers of Members of Three Scottish Societies: Formation to 1904.

	Edinburgh				Glasgow				Aberdeen			
	Paternal		Maternal		Paternal		Maternal		Paternal		Maternal	
Occupation	No.	%	No.	%	No.	%	No.	%	No.	%	No.	%
Accountants and Related Occuaptions	10	1.8	3	0.5	9	1.6	8	1.4	1	1.4	-	-
Legal Profession	34	6.1	23	4.2	6	1.1	7	1.2	-	-	-	-
Financial Institutions and Insurance	7	1.3	8	1.4	10	1.8	10	1.7	1	1.4	1	1.4
Church	26	4.7	15	2.7	11	2.0	12	2.1	1	1.4	-	-
Government and Armed Services	11	2.0	16	2.9	3	0.5	5	0.9	1	1.4	-	-
Landowner	41	7.4	46	8.3	47	8.3	40	7.0	12	17.1	11	15.7
Other Professions	19	3.4	15	2.7	16	2.8	14	2.5	1	1.4	3	4.3
	148	26.7	126	22.7	102	18.1	96	16.8	17	24.1	15	21.4
Businessmen	12	2.2	11	2.0	20	3.5	7	1.2	1	1.4	1	1.4
Merchants	36	6.5	33	6.0	59	10.4	58	10.2	2	2.9	6	8.6
	196	35.4	170	30.7	181	32.0	161	28.2	20	28.4	22	31.4
Manufacturer	8	1.4	17	3.1	24	4.2	25	4.4	-	-	-	-
Craftsman/Tradesman	40	7.2	31	5.6	43	7.4	44	7.7	9	12.9	3	4.3
Miscellaneous: Posts of Responsibility	12	2.2	12	2.2	28	4.9	31	5.4	2	2.9	5	7.1
Miscellaneous: Others	19	3.4	21	3.8	19	3.3	18	3.2	3	4.3	-	-
Unknown	280	50.4	304	54.6	275	48.2	219	51.1	36	51.5	40	57.2
TOTAL	555	100.0	555	100.0	570	100.0	570	100.0	70	100.0	70	100.0

Source: Scottish Records Office

information for later entrants to the profession.

Because accountancy was less well developed in the early-nineteenth century, and was commonly carried on in conjunction with another occupation, very few of this population were designated accountants. In all three groups the most significant designation was that of landowner. Edinburgh, as in the case of father's occupation, revealed a stronger background in the legal profession and in government and armed services. The most significant background in Glasgow was again that of merchant and it was also the group with the lowest number of professionals. Of those for whom this information could be ascertained the background was largely from the higher social classes

3. Education

(*a*) *General*

Education in Scotland was much more widely available at the beginning of the nineteenth century than in England. This was largely as a result of the passing of the Scottish Education Acts of 1641[20] and 1696[21] which required schools to be established in every parish, and during the eighteenth century school attendance was compulsory in most places.[22] At that time, compulsory education was at a primary level but the demand for secondary education grew during the eighteenth century, and much of the education provided in the new academies or private grammar schools was of a commercial nature. In addition, there were many private teachers of bookkeeping and accounting in Scotland at that time[23] who were involved in preparing young men for employment with large commercial concerns both at home and in the colonies.

An advertisement which appeared in the *Edinburgh Courant* in November 1705 indicates the importance imputed to the knowledge of bookkeeping by Edinburgh City Council:

> The Council of Edinburgh considering how necessary the Science of Book-holding is for the Advantage of Trade and Commerce, especially when the same is carried on in Co-partnery, have therefore

> thought it convenient to establish a publick Profession of the said Science within this City; An having several Years Experience of the Ability and Capacity of John Dickson Merchant (present Book-keeper and Accomptant to the Good Town of Edinburgh) to teach the said Science; Do therefore nominat and Authorize the said John Dickson to be Master and Professor thereof within this City. . . .[24]

By the middle of the Victorian era in Scotland, one child in 205 was receiving secondary education as compared with one in 1300 in England and the ratio of university students to population in Scotland was six times that of England.[25] The comparative ease of acquiring an education in Scotland at that time led to there being more educated men than there were openings for them, which resulted in a regular export of educated and talented people to England and to the colonies.[26]

To the aspiring middle classes in Victorian Scotland, education became seen as a passport to success and, particularly in the West of Scotland, the path to success and improved social status led to commerce:

> In Anderston, the shipping quarter of Glasgow, the educated boys went mostly to offices instead of following their fathers' occupations, this being looked on as a rise in social position.[27]

The development and growth of the professions during the mid-nineteenth century created a need for young men of a certain academic standard and the improved social status seen to exist through acceptance into a profession led to an increased awareness of the need for education. This led to an increase in the number of public schools as:

> the social ambition of the middle classes increased . . . and as it became increasingly necessary to pass examinations to enter the professions.[28]

There is no doubt that the pursuit of knowledge was very

characteristic of the Victorian middle class, who viewed knowledge as power.[29]

Despite the steps taken to improve education in Scotland, the general level of education which was available at the beginning of the nineteenth century was far from satisfactory, though it showed considerable improvement during the century. Much of this improvement came through the influence of wealthier members of the community, who ensured the proper education of their sons either through the foundation of new schools or by 'turning charitable institutions for the poor into fee-paying institutions for the offspring of the middle classes.'[30] Universities in Victorian Scotland were viewed largely as establishments for the development of intellect rather than for the provision of a suitable cadre of men for the new professions, professional training being gained through the system of apprenticeship and so: 'Public school education, far more than university education, became the hallmark of the later Victorian professional man.'[31]

In this respect, accountancy seems to have been no different from the other merging professions. All three petitions for charters stress the need for a liberal education as a prerequisite for apprenticeship, and this view was also expressed by James McClelland who described a typical apprentice as being: 'a youth fresh from the public schools'[32] and records suggest that the public schools were significant in the education of early Scottish chartered accountants. The universities also played an important role in that all apprentices were required to attend law classes in order to enable them to cope with the large proportion of accountancy work that was related to legal work, in particular to insolvency work.

(*b*) *Teaching of Bookkeeping in Scottish Schools*

It was not uncommon for Scottish schools to offer bookkeeping as a subject in the nineteenth century; indeed it was taught in Aberdeen Grammar School in the middle of the eighteenth century.[33] The study of bookkeeping at school was not required for would-be accountants and the petitions for charters for the Scottish societies all stated the need for a 'liberal education' rather than a commercial one. Perhaps this apparent anomaly can be better understood by examining the evidence given in the *Report of the School Inquiry Commission of*

1867/8, which included in Part 1 a general conclusion that there should be no attempt to make school a substitute for apprenticeship, and referring specifically to bookkeeping:

> though it was often taught in schools, and with some success, yet was not generally recommended. It was said that a boy who had learnt it often found that the particular system which he had learnt was not that which he afterwards had to practise; while, on the other hand, a boy who had a thorough mastery of arithmetic could learn any system of book-keeping in a very short time.[34]

Despite this comment, the Commission found that in 1866 bookkeeping was taught in thirty-four out of fifty-six secondary schools in Scotland and attracted more students than Greek.

The Committee sent out one of HM Inspectors of Schools to sixteen Scottish schools, among them Edinburgh Royal High, Aberdeen Grammar School and Glasgow High School, and some interesting facts emerge from the reports prepared by the Inspector. As well as considering the cost of education, subjects on offer and quality of teachers, the report analysed the social class of the pupils at each school based on a classification of their father's occupation.

This pattern in Table 4.10 is similar to that in Table 4.1 with Edinburgh High School showing a much higher proportion of parents in the professional groups and Glasgow reflecting a larger proportion in the manufacturing and retailing categories. All three schools taught bookkeeping, Edinburgh High School charging half a guinea per quarter for its tuition and Glasgow High School one guinea per six months. The report on the teaching of the subject at Glasgow High School indicated that about forty-five pupils enrolled for the course every half year and that the teaching was comparatively good:

> I was particularly pleased by the teaching of book-keeping . . . at Glasgow High School the subject is really taught with much intelligence, and in a lively and interesting manner . . . they were not merely learning by rote, but were receiving intelligent instruction in some of the financial principles of trade

TABLE 4.10

Occupation of Fathers as Indication of Social Class of Pupils:

	Aberdeen Grammar School %	**Edinburgh Royal High School %**	**Glasgow High School %**
Landed Proprietors and Country Gentlemen	2.9	7.1	2.5
Professional: Clerical, medical, legal	22.4	30.4	6.2
Merchants, wholesale traders, manufacturers	16.9	12.5	25.0
Farmers, overseers, managers, secretaries	13.6	-	18.8
Superior retail traders, larger shopkeepers	12.3	35.7	42.5
Small shopkeepers, clerks and farmers with income £150-£250 p. a.	15.5	14.3	5.0
Labourers, artisans	16.6	-	-
	100.0	100.0	100.0

Source: School Inquiry Commission, *Report* BPP 1867-8 Vol. XXVIII, Part 5.

> and commerce. I think the subject taught in this way may be made of real use to youths who are going into business, and, indeed, that the subject is one of which no man ought to be entirely ignorant.[35]

This was an unusual view in that most of the references to the desirability of teaching bookkeeping in schools are unfavourable. The general opinion of the committee was that it was better taught in an accountant's office because each office tended to use different methods and any boy who had studied bookkeeping at school would have to be re-educated on employment.[36]

Apparently in some areas of Britain the teaching of bookkeeping was far from satisfactory:

> It is only in town schools, and chiefly in private schools, that this subject is taught: and the teaching is of so slovenly a character that it might almost as well be expunged.[37]

In Scotland, however, the schools accepted that adapting to the needs of commerce was one way to success.

(*c*) *Schooling of Early Chartered Accountants*

If attendance at fee-paying school can be safely used as an indicator of social status, then the chartered accountants of Edinburgh would appear to have been somewhat superior, socially, to those in the other two Scottish societies (Table 4.11). However the apparent difference between the figures for the different cities, and in particular the low recorded percentage for Glasgow, is almost certainly partly due to the fact that Edinburgh fee-paying schools were in the habit of producing registers of their past pupils, a good number of which were published in the early twentieth century, while Glasgow schools did not produce such publications. Although some attendance ledgers still survive in one or two of the Glasgow schools, they only list the name of the pupil.

One other difference between Edinburgh and Glasgow is disclosed in the indenture records for the two societies. The records for Glasgow are unusual in that they show a considerable number of young men being indentured as apprentices after having completed some years as clerks in accountant's offices. This would suggest that some clerks from a lower social background, having proved their aptitude for the profession and being able to raise their indenture fee, were given the opportunity to embark on a full apprenticeship, unlike

TABLE 4.11

Education of Scottish Chartered Accountants

	Edinburgh %	**Glasgow** %	**Aberdeen** %
Known to have attended fee paying schools	47.0	20.2	40.0
Known to have university attendance	17.3	5.1	18.6

Source: School registers and obituaries

the situation in Edinburgh where, generally, articles were entered on straight from school.

In Edinburgh by far the most popular school was Edinburgh Academy where almost forty per cent of those attending named schools were educated. The only other Edinburgh schools attended by significant numbers of future chartered accountants were George Watsons and the Royal High. In Glasgow, the popular schools were Glasgow Academy, Glasgow High School and Kelvinside Academy. Stewart claimed that the lower attendance of Glasgow accountants at such schools was an indication of their lack of social status. Certainly very few are known to have attended Glasgow Academy, which was described in its prospectus as being for 'the sons of gentlemen'.[38] In Aberdeen, the choice of school was much narrower and the only one of any significance to accountants was Aberdeen Grammar School, which was attended by over eighty per cent of those known to have been at fee-paying schools.

(*d*) *Role of University Education in Chartered Accountancy*

In the mid-nineteenth century it was not unusual for young men to attend some university classes without any intention of studying for a degree.[39] This opportunity was only practically available to those who lived in the university towns of Scotland, Aberdeen, Edinburgh, Glasgow and St. Andrews. Much of the work of early chartered accountants was involved with bankruptcy or other court work for which a knowledge of Scots Law and Mercantile Law were necessary. In order to obtain this knowledge the trainee accountant often attended law classes at his local university.

The Royal Charter for the Society of Accountants in Edinburgh noted particularly the need for 'an intimate acquaintance with the general principles of law, particularly of the law of Scotland.' Stacey claimed that from the time that the Scottish Chartered Accountancy bodies came into being, one of the requirements for apprentices being admitted to membership was attendance at law classes at university, saying that this:

> was the result of enlightened professional educators stemming from social causes which at once placed accountancy in Scotland on a different plane from what later the organised profession secured for itself in England.[40]

Early membership records for the admission of apprentices to the Institute of Accountants and Actuaries in Glasgow frequently referred to the fact that the candidate had attended Scots Law classes at the University or that he intended so to do, this being seen as a desirable pre-requisite for entry.

The Minute Books of the Edinburgh Society noted a suggestion in December 1861 that the society should found a lectureship in the University on subjects like Commercial Law and Bankruptcy at an annual salary of £105.[41] However, this suggestion was not taken any further.

Brown stated that the societies: 'required the attendance of apprentices at University Law Classes, a rule which undoubtedly has had its effect in maintaining a high standard among those becoming members.'[42] However, despite Stacey's statement and Brown's implication, attendance at University Law classes was not compulsory from the time of the formation of the societies. Although it may have been unofficially suggested that this was desirable, the first requirement to attend such classes in Edinburgh and Glasgow was not imposed until ten years after the founding of the respective societies. In January 1855, the Glasgow Institute agreed to introduce the examination of applicants for admission in subjects including the elementary principles of Bankruptcy Law, and the practical working of Bankruptcies, Trust Estates and Voluntary and Judicial Factories,[43] but there was no compulsion to attend law classes, although it was perhaps felt unnecessary to make such a ruling if the majority of apprentices already attended such classes. It would appear that apprentices needed to be encouraged in their law studies, since, in January 1868, the Glasgow Institute established an annual prize for the best accounting student in the Scotch Law Class in the University 'with a view of encouraging young men training for the profession.'[44] The University Law class was apparently not wholly satisfactory for the requirements of apprentices since, by the end of 1871, they were complaining that they could: 'but cursorily touch upon the subjects more immediately connected with our profession'[45] and requesting that special lectures be provided by the Institute.

In Aberdeen, presumably because the original rules and regulations of 1867 were closely modelled on those of the Edinburgh Society, all apprentices were from the beginning required to attend two sessions of Scots Law lectures in Aberdeen University.[46]

In spite of this early requirement to attend university classes, the three accounting societies remained unimpressed by men possessing university degrees and consistently refused to reduce apprenticeship periods or conditions for graduates.[47] In 1893 the Edinburgh Society allowed graduates exemption from the preliminary examination and this was also implemented in Glasgow in 1896.[48] In 1899 the Glasgow Institute increased the normal period of apprenticeship to five years with a one year reduction for graduates[49] and at the same time the Edinburgh Society allowed the period of apprenticeship for graduates to be four years.[50]

Thus the role of the Universities in Scotland in relation to the accounting profession was not the provision of better educated entrants to apprenticeship, but the training of apprentices in the specialist area of law, which the profession felt it was not equipped to do itself.

(*e*) *Attendance of Chartered Accountants at University*

Although most of the population of accountants being studied would be required to attend university classes and, prior to that requirement, some of them had done so, surprisingly few of them are known to have become graduates.

In Edinburgh, so far as can be ascertained, only twelve out of a total population of 555 chartered accountants gained degrees, seven of them having an MA from Edinburgh University. However, Edinburgh chartered accountants, unlike their counterparts in Glasgow, appear to have developed strong links with Edinburgh University and Heriot-Watt College. In 1920, at the age of sixty, Thomas Laird was appointed to be the first Professor of Accounting and Business Method at the University of Edinburgh.[51] This was twenty years after the first UK Professor of Accounting had been appointed at Birmingham in 1900.[52] Laird held this position until his death in 1927, when he was succeeded by William Annan, a fellow member of the Edinburgh Society. Annan held the Chair until he retired in 1947 at the age of seventy one.[53]

Robert Millar was the first lecturer on the Practice of Commerce at Heriot-Watt College, being appointed in 1886[54] and was succeeded in this position by his brother Thomas Millar, also a member of the Edinburgh Society, in 1904.[55] Other members of the Edinburgh Society who lectured on bookkeeping at Heriot-Watt College were William Brown,[56] George Lisle[57] and William Middleton.[58] Four Edinburgh members made their marks in the educational fields of other countries. David Park lectured on banking at King's College, London;[59] Arthur Muir was the first lecturer in accounting in the Faculty of Commerce of Queens University of Belfast; William Leslie lectured in accounting at Teacher's College, New York City from 1908,[60] and in 1914 James Findlay became Professor of Accounting at the South African School of Mines and Technology, Johannesburg.[61]

The population of Glasgow chartered accountants for the period contained twelve university graduates, ten graduating from Glasgow University; however, there are no records of any involvement by the members of the Glasgow Society in teaching at the University.

Among the Aberdeen members, Henry Davidson began

lecturing on accounting and business method at the University of Aberdeen in 1919[62] and was joined by John Reid in 1923;[63] both Davidson and Reid were graduates of Aberdeen University and Davidson, by the time of his appointment, practiced as a law agent not as an accountant.

None of these positions was filled on a full-time basis, nor did they pay particularly well, the part-time position at Aberdeen being advertised at £300 per annum.[64] Of course, there was little need for lecturers in accounting in the Scottish Universities at that time since accounting was one of the professions listed by Carr-Saunders and Wilson as remaining at that time (1933) 'largely outside the university ambit'. Now accountancy has followed the path laid down by other professions in encouraging the provision in universities and colleges of 'facilities for theoretical training in the subjects of the examinations.'[65]

4. Geographical Origins

Because membership of the three chartered societies was limited to those practising in the city in which the society had been formed, most of the members came from one of these three cities. The vast majority of members were born in Scotland, with a few coming from England and very few from Ireland or having been born abroad. It is not surprising to find such a small percentage coming from outside Scotland since, particularly in the early years, the profession was built around bankruptcy work and bankruptcy legislation differed in Scotland and in the other parts of the United Kingdom.

What is perhaps surprising is the percentage of members coming from parts of Scotland other than the immediate environs of the city wherein the society operated (Table 4.12). With the exception of Aberdeen, where numbers were very small, this percentage shows a significant drop in the period from 1880 to 1904 compared with the period up to 1879 and the figures for members born in their city of membership show an even greater increase. This means that, during the first fifty years of its existence, as far as recruitment of members was concerned, the new profession became increasingly a localised

TABLE 4.12

Place of Birth of Admissions to Membership

	Edinburgh 1853-79 %	**Glasgow 1853-79 %**	**Aberdeen 1867-79 %**
Edinburgh and district	55.0	3.5	8.7
Glasgow and district	1.6	62.5	-
Aberdeen and district	0.6	-	74.0
Dundee and district	1.6	1.4	4.3
Other Scottish locations	20.6	14.6	-
Total Scotland	79.4	82.0	87.0
England	2.8	0.7	-
Ireland	1.1	0.7	-
Abroad	1.1	0.7	4.3
Not Known	15.6	15.9	8.7
	100.0	100.0	100.0
Number	180	144	23

	Edinburgh 1880-1904 %	**Glasgow 1880-1904 %**	**Aberdeen 1880-1904 %**
Edinburgh and district	69.9	1.9	-
Glasgow and district	3.7	72.5	-
Aberdeen and district	1.1	0.5	65.3
Dundee and district	0.5	4.5	-
Other Scottish locations	12.3	8.5	4.3
Total Scotland	87.5	87.9	69.9
England	3.2	1.2	8.7
Ireland	0.8	1.2	-
Abroad	2.7	2.3	4.3
Not Known	5.8	7.4	17.4
	100.0	100.0	100.0
Number	375	426	47

Source: Scottish Records Office: Registers of birth, marriage and death

profession despite the fact that figures for the corresponding period show increasing numbers of Scottish chartered accountants practising outwith those three cities.

Perhaps the reason for this trend lay in the apprenticeship system. During the early years of the profession 'masters' were limited as to the number of apprentices that they could take, on the grounds that one master could not adequately train a large number of apprentices. With the exception of attendance at university law classes, all of the early training was carried out under the system of 'learning by doing'[66] and so quality was maintained at the cost of quantity. There can be little doubt that there was also some benefit to be gained from this slow growth in the profession in that the available work was limited and any rapid expansion in membership would have been economically harmful to the existing members. Another factor could be that, since apprenticeships were scarce, they went in the first instance to those who had some contact with the tight communities in the three cities and anyone without an entrance to these groups would find it almost impossible to get a foot on the ladder. Therefore it is conceivable that the increasing numbers of local young men desiring to fill the limited numbers of apprenticeships resulted in the societies becoming more limited in their ability to employ apprentices from outwith these three main locations.

The first Scottish census was in 1841 and a search of that and subsequent records served to confirm the earlier findings on the social status of these Victorian accountants. In Edinburgh, the early accountants lived in the New Town, among lawyers, doctors and civil servants. Residences contained from ten to twenty-three rooms, some even larger, and the number of resident servants varied from three to seven. When considering this last factor, one must remember that the census records only list servants who were there at the date of the census and so this figure, if anything, will be conservative. As the city expanded, some accountants moved out to the newer, high-class suburbs such as the Grange and Dean, but up to 1891 the largest concentration remained within the New Town, showing that accounting was sufficiently lucrative to enable such a standard of living and also that the members of the Edinburgh Society were seen as being of a similar social standing to their neighbours in other professions.

In Glasgow there seems to have been much the same pattern. The earlier members occupied large houses in the city centre in Bath Street and St Vincent Street, consisting of up to twenty rooms and employing up to five servants. There was a move out to Blythswood when it was developed and, as the nineteenth century progressed there was a complete exodus from the city centre when areas that had been residential became commercial. Those who moved went out to the new suburbs and for members of the Glasgow Institute the most popular of these were the Hillhead and Kelvinside areas of the city with their stately terraced homes and large parks. Some of the members chose to live in the Pollock and Langside areas on the other side of the city and certainly, by the end of the period being studied, all of the Glasgow accountants were commuting from the suburbs or from towns within easy reach of Glasgow, to their offices in the centre of the city.

Aberdeen accountants, in general, appear to have lived in slightly more modest accommodation occupying houses of around ten rooms, although with some being larger. They chose to live in quite close proximity to the city centre in Albyn Place and Albert Street with a few moving out at a later stage to Rubislaw and Ferryhill. They were also more modest in their employment of resident servants, showing an average of two and in many cases only one. It is impossible to say why they lived on an apparently more modest scale but we could hypothesise that the members considered unnecessarily grand living to be unimportant to their social standing in the community or perhaps they were just more thrifty than their counterparts in Glasgow and Edinburgh.

Of the three groups, the members of the Edinburgh Society displayed a greater tendency to live near the office and to group together in a small geographical area, while Glasgow members displayed the greatest tendency to decentralise. This latter trend has been explained by the fact that industrialisation in Glasgow quickly encroached on the centre of Glasgow and also that 'changes in fashion and improvements in transportation provided the upper middle class with more positive inducement to leave the central business districts.'[67]

5. Other Characteristics

(*a*) *Involvement in Public Life*

The involvement of members of the three societies in the public life of their respective cities varied considerably. An analysis of death certificates and obituaries in the *Accountants' Magazine* shows that out of a total population of seventy accountants, Aberdeen produced one magistrate and one JP. Edinburgh produced four JPs, one Lord Provost, three members of the Merchants Company or Chamber of Commerce and four Deputy Lieutenants of the Counties of the City of Edinburgh, Glasgow and Moray and one Lieutenant of the City of London. The Members of the Glasgow society appear to have been much more deeply involved in the life of the community, since they are known to have produced forty-two JPs, two Lord Provosts, of Glasgow and Troon, and one Provost of Kilmarnock, sixteen members of the Merchants House and two Deputy Lieutenants, one of Glasgow and Lanark and one of Middlesex.

One of the most prestigious groups to which one could belong in Scotland was the Royal Company of Archers and few chartered accountants were invited into this group. The Edinburgh Society is known to have had seven members and the Glasgow society only two. If the award of honours can be taken as an indication of the involvement of chartered accountants in public life, then the members of the Glasgow society did considerably better than those of the Edinburgh Society with both outshining the nil return from the Aberdeen Society. As far as can be ascertained, the Glasgow chartered accountants collected four baronetcies, five knighthoods, one MBE, eight OBEs and one CBE while those from Edinburgh collected one baronetcy, one knighthood, one MBE and one OBE.

One area where Edinburgh members certainly outshone Glasgow members was in producing Members of Parliament. The Glasgow society is only known to have produced one, Sir Reginald Blair, Conservative MP for Bow and Bromley 1912-22 and for Hendon, Middlesex 1935-45, but the Edinburgh Society is known to have produced five, George Currie, Unionist MP for Leith Burghs 1914-18; David Erskine, Liberal MP for West Perthshire 1906-10; John Hope, Liberal MP for West Fife 1900-10, Haddingtonshire 1911-18 and Berwickshire and Haddingtonshire 1918-22; John

Macleod, Conservative MP for Glasgow, Central Division 1915-8 and Glasgow, Kelvinside 1918-22 and George Touche, Conservative MP for North Islington 1910-8.

Involvement in sport at national level was not shunned, and the Glasgow society produced one Scottish Football International, four Scottish Rugby Internationals, one five times West of Scotland singles tennis champion and one amateur golf champion for India and the East. The Edinburgh Society could boast two Rugby Internationals, and one member whose claim to fame seems to have been the ability to tear in two a complete pack of playing cards. More worthy of remembrance was Leonard Dickson of the Edinburgh Society who died as a result of severe head injuries when attempting to stop a runaway horse in George Street, Edinburgh.[68]

(*b*) *Individual interests and contributions*

There is little doubt that the Victorian professionals viewed public service as being a duty which accompanied social status. An area where many chartered accountants were involved was in giving service as church treasurers and elders, but various members were also known for their contribution to specific causes.

John Mann of Glasgow was involved in the Workers' Educational Movement, was instrumental in the purchase of Jordanhill for the training of teachers and was also very active in the introduction of cremation in Glasgow.[69] Hugh Brechin was one of the founders of the Boy Scout movement in Glasgow[70] and James Grahame[71] was responsible for setting up the first Scottish Society for the Prevention of Cruelty to Children. Edinburgh accountants were also involved in such work; Mowbray Douglas was for many years treasurer of the Church of Scotland magazine *Life and Work*[72] and Thomas Whitson was instrumental in the foundation of Edinburgh Zoo.[73] William Walker bought Clermiston Tower which had been built by William Macfie of Clermiston in 1871 to celebrate the centenary of Walter Scott's birth, and presented it to the City of Edinburgh as a tribute to Sir Walter Scott during the Scott centenary in 1932.[74] Archibald Bryson was responsible for the erection of the clock at Canonmills, Edinburgh.[75]

In the sphere of education two Aberdeen accountants made notable contributions. Walter Reid founded the Reid Library and

Rowett Institute for Animal Nutrition in Aberdeen.[76] James Milne, during his period as President in 1907, gave a prize of £50 as a fund for prizes for Aberdeen apprentices who passed their Final Examinations with distinction[77] and the James Milne prize is still awarded by the Institute of Chartered Accountants of Scotland. Robert Fletcher, a founder member of the Aberdeen Society who moved to London in 1868, also instituted a prize. Strangely, although Fletcher continued to have a close association with Aberdeen and was President of the Aberdeen Society from 1875-7 he instituted his prize with the Institute of Chartered Accountants in England and Wales. This was probably because of his involvement in 1870 in the formation of the Institute of Accountants in London[78] which then combined with the Incorporated Society of Liverpool Accountants to form the nucleus of the English Institute. The Robert Fletcher Prize of £60 is still awarded to the candidates gaining third place in order of merit for Part 2 of the professional examinations of the English Institute.

However, it was the Glasgow Society that had as members one of the most generous accountants and one who would have a continuing effect on the education of accountants. David Myles of Dundee, who joined the Glasgow Society in 1891 under the change of rules which opened admission to accountants living outside Glasgow, on his death in 1898 bequeathed £10,000 to University College Dundee for the provision of bursaries which are still being awarded.[79] David Johnstone Smith was responsible for the founding of the Johnstone Smith chair of accountancy at the University of Glasgow which is still held by a practising accountant. The chair was founded in 1925 after Smith's period as President of the Glasgow Institute from 1922-4. He continued to be Treasurer of the Institute until 1935 when he was seventy-seven years of age.[80]

6. Summary

The early members of the three Scottish Chartered societies displayed social backgrounds which were noticeably different. However, these differences, in particular those between the members of the Edinburgh and Glasgow societies, reflected the different characters of the two cities. It was claimed that Edinburgh had a disproportionately large middle class[81] but the comparison that is most obvious is of the different types of middle-class occupations followed in the two cities, Edinburgh with its legal and banking interests and Glasgow with its manufacturing and trading strengths.

> Edinburgh and Glasgow represented in their different ways the quintessence of two streams of middle class life, Edinburgh dominated by the professional classes, and Glasgow by the triumph of the commercial and manufacturing interests.[82]

This middle-class domination in Scottish accountancy extended until at least 1937 when Cairncross calculated that a minimum of seventy per cent of entrants to chartered accountancy in Glasgow were from a middle class background.

Glasgow accountants were more actively involved in philanthropic activities than were those from Edinburgh and this is considered to be a reflection of their backgrounds, Glasgow being the commercial centre and Edinburgh being mainly a professional city with a strong Church presence. As Checkland commented:

> Perhaps the ruling classes of Edinburgh, confident after a long period of power and influence, were less willing to involve themselves charitably. For in Edinburgh charitable initiatives could fail for lack of support . . . Glasgow, the commercial capital of Scotland, had few contacts with the traditional landed class. The initiative for ameliorative social action there rested squarely upon the commercial, merchant and industrial classes.[83]

Having examined the factors significant to the formal organisation of accountancy in Scotland and the social background of the founder and early members of those groups, the following two chapters will examine some of the factors responsible for the development of the profession in Scotland during the second half of the nineteenth century.

V

Importance of Bankruptcy Work to the New Professional Bodies

1. Introduction

The association which early Scottish accountants had with legal work and which formed the catalyst for the formation of the first Scottish accounting societies continued long thereafter. The first committees of the Edinburgh and Glasgow societies were formed to discuss the proposed changes in Bankruptcy law although other legislation affecting companies was dealt with sporadically.[1] It was claimed that representations made by the societies did influence the Bankruptcy Act of 1856 which was to be the main Act in Scotland for most of the period studied and the continuing interest shown in the various Minute books suggests that bankruptcy must have been a very remunerative branch of an accountant's work.[2]

Specific references were made to the importance of bankruptcy work in individual firms of accountants. Thomson McLintock, who became a member of the Glasgow Institute in 1891, noted bankruptcy work as being one of the main sources of his firm's income and was said to have gained his reputation as an accountant in Glasgow through his involvement in the many cases arising after the City of Glasgow Bank crash in 1878.[3] John Wilson who joined the Glasgow Institute in 1868, and was a founder partner in Wilson, Stirling and Co., later to become part of Touche Ross and Co., 'became recognised as an expert in bankruptcy and it was on that foundation that this thriving business was built.'[4] Indeed Touche Ross and Co. derived most of their income from the two areas of accountancy services and sequestration until the end of the nineteenth century.[5]

In 1881, immediately after the formation of the English Institute, the President of the Manchester Society recognised that the public associated the members with 'the position of receivers and trustees in the estates of bankrupts and liquidating debtors'[6] although he insisted that their duties were much more varied than these. Jones, too, referred to the importance of bankruptcy work for the founder firms of Ernst and Whinney and noted the period of years over which complicated bankruptcies could provide fee income.[7] He analysed the fee income of Whinney, Smith and Whinney from 1848 until 1900 (Table 5.1), and proved the importance of this source of income to that firm until around 1890,[8] when the passing of the Companies Winding-up Act curtailed the employment of accountants in England in this area of work. However, Brown was still of the opinion in 1904 that liquidation would continue to bring steady and remunerative employment to accountants in Scotland.[9]

Pixley commented on the appointment of chartered accountants as arbitrators, trustees and liquidators in 1897, saying that their knowledge of accounts was necessary in order to carry out these tasks properly.[10] Also in 1897, Mr John Baird of the Scottish Institute of Accountants made passing reference to the services 'which accountants render to the community as trustees under the Bankruptcy Acts, and as voluntary trustees, as receivers, judicial factors, curators, factors *loco tutoris*, and as liquidators. Accountants most commonly are, and in every case should be, the persons appointed to discharge these duties.'[11] The contents of early issues of accountancy periodicals also give an indication of the importance of bankruptcy through the preponderance of articles and comments on the subject.

After the Bankruptcy (Scotland) Act came into operation on 1 November 1856, returns by trustees on sequestrated estates were required to be made annually to the Accountant in Bankruptcy and reports were prepared by him for the Court of Session, which meant that records were more accurately kept than before. This chapter analyses the *Annual Reports* from 1857 to 1904 to discover the

TABLE 5.1

Composition of Fee Income of Whinney, Smith and Whinney

YEAR	Insolvency		Accounting		Auditing		Trustee and Executorship		Special Work		TOTAL
	%	£	%	£	%	£	%	£	%	£	£
1848 (6 months)	73.2	153	1.9	4	-		17.2	36	7.7	16	209
1849	74.6	600	8.2	66	-		11.9	96	5.2	42	804
1853	76.9	1,861	17.2	410	-		4.2	101	1.8	44	2,416
1854	69.4	2,488	27.0	970	-		1.3	45	2.1	76	3,579
1855	80.6	3,937	13.3	648	-		6.1	298		-	4,883
1858	93.2	13,478	6.2	1,091	-		0.6	106		-	14,675
1860	85.8	7,610	7.6	672	2.4	220	3.6	319	0.6	52	8,873
1865	93.9	22,814	3.3	808	1.1	255	1.6	387	0.04	10	24,274
1867	85.3	25,447	10.8	3,221	2.1	637	1.7	501	0.1	39	29.845
1870	93.6	17,751	2.4	451	2.2	413	1.7	329	0.07	14	18,958
1875					4.3	617	Only Category Positively Identified				
1880	72.3	9,965	11.2	1,544	10.9	1,506	3.5	478	2.2	297	13,790
1884	66.2	9,773	8.6	1,281	19.8	2,920	3.7	548	1.7	244	14,766
1885	60.0	7,420	8.7	1,073	26.0	3,217	4.6	573	0.7	84	12,367
1890	45.6	6,490	10.0	1,436	36.8	5,237	4.3	606	3.3	468	14,237
1895	15.1	1,464	22.7	2,193	54.3	5,244	2.1	204	5.7	549	9,654
1900	19.9	2,844	16.9	2,421	52.9	7,544	5.6	794	4.7	671	14,274

Source: E. Jones, *Accountancy and the British Economy 1840-1980* (London 1981) p. 47.

trends in sequestrations and further to establish how much of this work was being undertaken by chartered accountants during this period.

2. Analysis of Sequestrations Awarded 1856-1904

(*a*) *Number of sequestrations awarded - 1856-1904*

The graph illustrates the fluctuations in the number of sequestrations awarded over the period 1856 to 1904, indicating that the volume of work varied considerably. Peaks in activity can be traced to periodic crises in the economy which resulted in a higher than normal number of business failures.

The peak in 1858 followed on the overtrading between Britain and the United States which reached its peak in 1857. This resulted in bankruptcies in America which had a subsequent effect on the state of trading companies and banks in Britain who had made advances to the bankrupt concerns.[12] Evans criticised the management of such merchant houses saying that they utterly disregarded every sound commercial principle in their granting of credit.[13] In Scotland the crisis manifested itself in the failure of the Western Bank in 1857 which was eventually caused by the inability of four leading Glasgow firms to meet their debts to the Bank as a result of their involvement in the American commercial crisis.[14] Kerr however claimed that the crisis would not have been so great had it not been for the 'setting at defiance the soundest principles of good management, in the face of the often repeated remonstrances of friends and rivals.'[15] Nevertheless the bank failed with liabilities to the public of just under nine million pounds[16] which added to the upsurge in the number of bankruptcies. The *Annual Report* of the Accountant in Bankruptcy stated: 'The year ending 31 October 1858 was marked by a great Commercial Crisis: and the effect of this is obvious from the number of sequestrations applicable to that year.'[17]

In 1862 the slightly smaller peak was considered to have arisen as a result of the passing of the Joint Stock Companies Act in that year. This greatly expanded the work available to accountants[18] and increased the number of companies being incorporated under the Act. When Brown referred to the 1862 Act as the 'accountant's

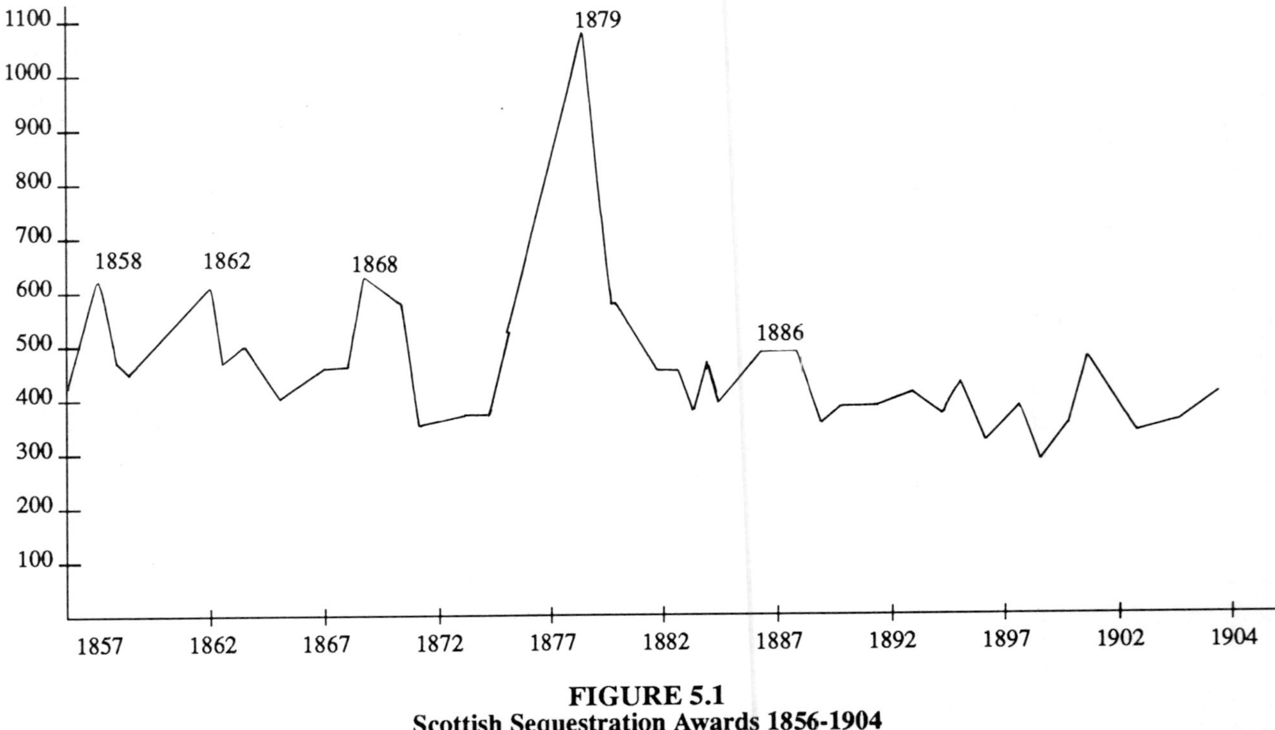

FIGURE 5.1
Scottish Sequestration Awards 1856-1904
Source: Annual Report of the Accountant in Bankruptcy 1857-1904

friend'[19] he was perhaps referring to the fact that the optional requirements in Table A to produce accounts and have them audited meant that there was an increasing tendency to see the accountant as the obvious person to attend to all aspects of business life and death. However, the more specific cause of this upsurge in Scotland was the blockading of ports of the Confederated States of America and the subsequent inability to ship raw cotton from there to Britain.[20] The early Scottish cotton industry had been built up around the linen traders of Glasgow and the surrounding area[21] and this starvation of raw material led to several of these failing in 1862.

The crisis of 1868 arose from the failure of Overend, Gurney and Co. resulting from its management having adopted unsound business practices. Overend, Gurney and Co. were originally bill-brokers but extended their business to include money-lending and dealing in credit. 'Increasingly, however, they drifted into a dangerous policy; in search for higher interest, money was lent on securities which offered none, and especially on questionable shares.'[22] Although this failure did not have too serious an impact on the banking system in Scotland, it did affect Scottish businesses that had dealings with Overend, Gurney and Co. and resulted in an increase in the number of sequestrations.

Without any doubt the most severe financial crisis to arise in Scotland during the period studied was that caused by the failure of the City of Glasgow Bank in 1878. The conclusions arising from their trial were that the directors had been guilty of falsifying and fabricating the balance sheets of the Bank and of uttering and publishing them knowing them to be false.[23]

The resultant expansion in the number of sequestrations formed a strong basis for many of the emerging accounting firms in Scotland. Thomson McLintock was heavily involved in handling failures resulting from the crash[24] and Robert Reid of Reid and Mair specialised in insolvency after originally training in the legal department of the City of Glasgow Bank and then embarking on an apprenticeship in accountancy. Ironically the Bank's crash also brought a great deal of work to his accounting firm.[25] Not all Glasgow accounting firms were as fortunate at this, in particular, John Mann Senior was precluded from dealing with this area of work since he himself was a shareholder in the Bank and narrowly escaped bankruptcy.[26]

Sequestrations were awarded in both the Sheriff Court and the Court of Session, although the latter was much less frequently used, being responsible for approximately one-quarter to one-fifth of the awards in any year.

(*b*) *Geographical Distribution of Sequestrations*

Sequestration awards were recorded according to the sheriffdom in which they arose and segregated into those awarded in the Sheriff Court and those awarded in the Court of Session. Over the period studied there were fluctuations in the number of cases arising in different locations, but a reasonably clear pattern emerged in an analysis of each year between 1856 and 1904.

Aberdeen generally accounted for about five per cent of the total number of sequestrations awarded in any one year and Dundee for approximately seven per cent. The percentage in Edinburgh fluctuated between ten per cent and twenty-two per cent, generally being around twenty per cent of the total and Glasgow was considerably higher at between thirty-five per cent and sixty per cent, generally around forty-five per cent of the total. There is nothing surprising in such a distribution since one would expect a higher number of sequestrations in the industrial area around Glasgow. Another point of interest is the fact that around fifty per cent of the cases arising in Edinburgh in any year were dealt with in the Court of Session, as compared to twenty per cent of cases from the other three centres. This may have been due to the proximity of the Court of Session or perhaps it indicated more complex cases. Around thirty per cent of sequestrations arose in areas of Scotland other than the four cities mentioned.

It is interesting to note the gradual decline in the number of sequestrations awarded by the end of 1902; although there were periodic peaks there is no doubt that the general trend was downwards.

(*c*) *Division of Awards Between Chartered Accountants, non-Chartered Accountants and Other Groups*

Table 5.2 provides an analysis of the groups who were appointed as trustees on sequestrated estates from 1856-1902. Perhaps the

TABLE 5.2

Percentage Analysis of Trustees on Sequestrated Estates by Occupation 1857-1902

Year	CA	Non-CA Acc.	Total Acc.	Legal Prof.	Banking	Misc. (Non-Prof.)	Total %	Total No.
1857	40	21	61	11	5	23	100	432
1858	39	18	57	11	6	26		636
1859	40	19	59	11	5	25		461
1860	35	24	59	12	6	23		443
1861	29	34	63	12	5	20		525
1862	25	40	65	11	5	19		572
1867	32	31	63	11	5	21		444
1872	26	34	60	8	4	28		368
1877	40	35	75	8	3	14		543
1882	37	33	70	11	6	13		452
1887	46	24	70	14	5	11		444
1892	47	30	77	10	5	8		346
1897	50	32	82	10	1	7		332
1902	54	24	78	14	2	6	100	294

KEY

Acc. - Accountants
Prof. - Profession

Scource: Annual Report of the Accountant in Bankruptcy 1857-1902

most significant fact to emerge from this overview is the decline in the involvement of non-professionals in sequestration work and the corresponding increase in the participation of accountants. Bankers were never of any general significance in this area of work and by 1902, had almost ceased to be involved while the legal profession retained almost the same proportion of the total throughout the period. Looking at the percentage of work undertaken by accountants it is apparent that the increase in the involvement of accountants in this area was almost completely due to chartered accountants. The comparative changes between these groups over the period can be seen from the graph in Figure 5.2.

While this overview is in itself interesting, it would be wrong to imagine that the pattern was the same throughout Scotland and, indeed, when the figures were further analysed, significant geographical differences emerged. Further analysis extracted figures for Edinburgh, Glasgow, Aberdeen and Dundee; the first three because of the formation of societies of Chartered Accountants in these cities and Dundee because, from 1891 onwards, eligible Dundee accountants were admitted to membership of the Glasgow Chartered Accountants' Institute.

The results of this analysis on the division of sequestration work between those who were or who became members of one of the Chartered societies, accountants who did not become chartered, and other trustees can be seen in Tables 5.3-5.6.

Records show that in Edinburgh from the time of the introduction of the new legislation on bankruptcy, this work had been largely dominated by accountants. It is surprising to see so little involvement of the legal profession in a city where so much importance was placed on lawyers but the fourteen per cent involvement in 1856 had fallen to just over two per cent by 1902. Bankers were rarely involved in this work and by the end of the century there is no doubt that the chartered accountants, with ninety-seven per cent, had monopolised sequestration work in Edinburgh.

In Glasgow, the involvement of the legal profession was insignificant and that of bankers negligible, and from 1856 onwards accountants were mainly responsible for this kind of work. This can perhaps be explained by the fact that business firms in Glasgow were more likely to employ an accountant than were firms in Edinburgh. Certainly the records of the Glasgow Institute would

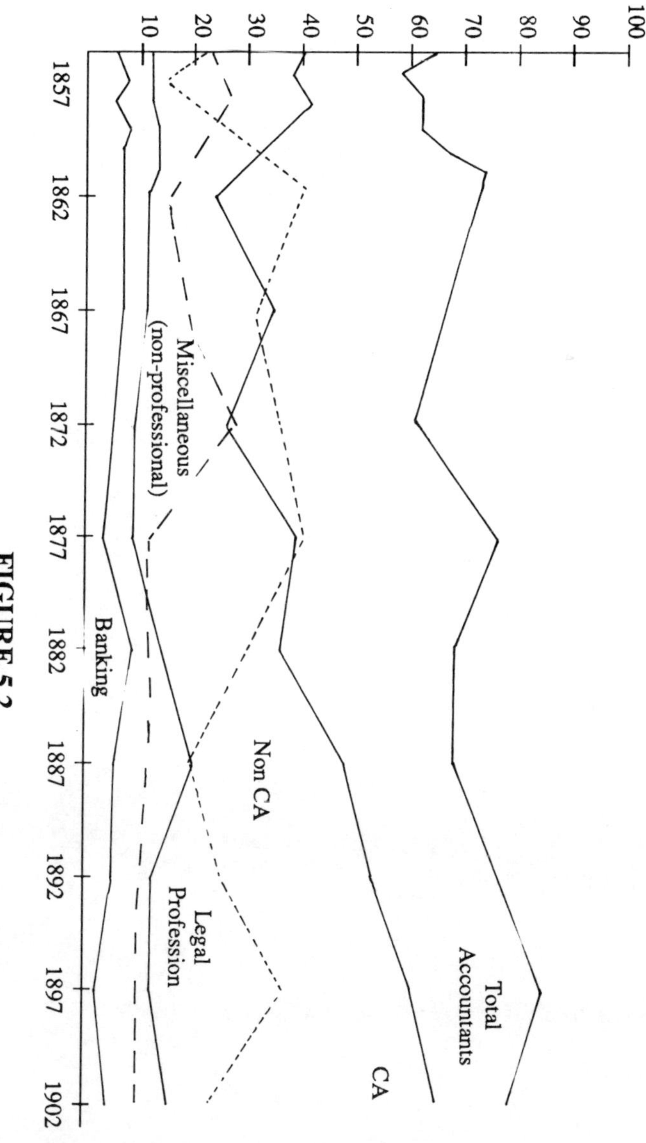

FIGURE 5.2
% Occupational Analysis of Trustees on Sequestrated Estates 1856-1902
Source: Annual Report of the Accountant in Bankruptcy 1857-1902

TABLE 5.3

% Occupation of Trustees in Edinburgh Sequestrations awarded in year ending 31 October 1857-1892 and 31 December 1897-1902

Year	Chartered Accountant	Accountant	Legal Profession	Banking	Others	Total
1857	45	28	14	-	13	100
1858	56	10	7	-	27	
1859	65	14	2	-	19	
1860	49	25	14	-	12	
1861	50	35	8	-	7	
1862	46	34	5	-	15	
1867	61	14	10	-	15	
1872	57	25	4	-	14	
1877	44	41	5	-	10	
1882	60	29	3	-	8	
1887	78	14	6	1	1	
1892	80	9	9	1	1	
1897	82	12	4	-	2	
1902	97	1	2	-	-	100

Source: Annual Report of the Accountant in Bankruptcy 1857-1902

TABLE 5.4

% Occupation of Trustees in Glasgow Sequestrations awarded in year ending 31 October 1857-1892 and 31 December 1897-1902

Year	Chartered Accountant	Accountant	Legal Profession	Banking	Others	Total
1857	63	29	1	1	6	100
1858	66	29	1	-	4	
1859	61	35	1	-	3	
1860	55	37	3	-	5	
1861	46	49	2	-	3	
1862	39	55	1	1	4	
1867	49	47	2	-	2	
1872	32	60	1	-	7	
1877	55	42	-	-	3	
1882	51	49	-	-	-	
1887	65	35	-	-	-	
1892	50	48	1	-	1	
1897	56	44	-	-	-	
1902	58	42	-	-	-	100

Source: Annual Report of the Accountant in Bankruptcy 1857-1902

TABLE 5.5

% Occupation of Trustees in Aberdeen Sequestrations awarded in year ending 31 October 1857-1892 and 31 December 1897-1902

Year	Chartered Accountant	Accountant	Legal Profession	Banking	Others	Total
1857	-	8	61	8	23	100
1858	-	-	76	14	10	
1859	7	-	71	-	22	
1860	7	-	50	-	43	
1861	10	-	50	-	40	
1862	-	6	61	-	33	
1867	-	-	56	-	44	
1872	25	-	50	-	25	
1877	-	-	44	-	56	
1882	7	-	36	14	43	
1887	45	-	45	10	-	
1892	50	-	30	-	20	
1897	10	-	80	-	10	
1902	7	-	79	-	14	100

Source: Annual Report of the Accountant in Bankruptcy 1857-1902

TABLE 5.6

% Occupation of Trustees in Dundee Sequestrations awarded in year ending 31 October 1857-1892 and 31 December 1897-1902

Year	Chartered Accountant	Accountant	Legal Profession	Banking	Others	Total
1857	61	-	17	-	22	100
1858	51	-	3	-	46	
1859	50	20	10	-	20	
1860	75	-	6	6	13	
1861	36	27	14	-	23	
1862	41	35	-	-	24	
1867	65	15	-	-	20	
1872	53	33	-	-	14	
1877	70	9	-	-	21	
1882	53	33	-	-	14	
1887	75	17	-	-	8	
1892	45	45	-	-	10	
1897	60	40	-	-	-	
1902	79	21	-	-	-	100

Source: Annual Report of the Accountant in Bankruptcy 1857-1902

support this in that the discussions over the introduction of the new bankruptcy legislation in 1856, suggested that there was very seldom any employment of Edinburgh accountants by firms prior to sequestration unlike the situation in Glasgow.[27] By 1902 all non-accountants were effectively excluded from this area of work in Glasgow although non-chartered accountants were still undertaking a significant proportion of it.

Figures for Aberdeen show very little involvement of the accounting profession and a continuing monopoly by the legal profession, but the number of cases in any one year was not large and they were mostly dealt with through the Sheriff Court. However, in Dundee, where numbers were generally not much larger than Aberdeen, accountants had completely eliminated other groups from this work in 1892 and by 1902 the work was being largely undertaken by chartered accountants. Table 5.7 illustrates the gradual increase of accountants as trustees outside the larger Scottish cities. The increased involvement of accountants in these locations was generally at the expense of the non-professional group, although the involvement of chartered accountants was still not significant by 1902.

(*d*) *Income from Sequestration Work*

Fee income from sequestration work was assessed either as a flat fee, ranging from five guineas upwards on small estates, or as a percentage of the gross receipts realised by the trustee on larger estates.

Table 5.8 shows the amount of trustees commission paid in each year and also shows this as a percentage of the gross receipts in the same year so that averages may be compared for the period 1856 to 1904. The percentage of legal expenses is also shown to indicate that although sequestration work might have been lucrative for accountants, it was even more so for lawyers.

While it is interesting to see the total pool of fee income available to trustees in sequestrations, the figure contains little information about the amount of fee income going to individual accountants. In theory we would compare this table with Table 5.2 and hypothesise, for example, that since in 1877, seventy-five per cent of sequestrations (407 cases) were dealt with by accountants

TABLE 5.7

% Occupation of Trustees in Sequestrations awarded in locations other than Edinburgh, Glasgow, Aberdeen and Dundee 1857 to 1902

Year	Chartered Accountant	Accountant	Legal Profession	Banking	Others	Total
1857	-	7	21	15	57	100
1858	-	11	19	17	53	
1859	-	3	26	15	56	
1860	-	12	20	17	51	
1861	-	16	25	14	45	
1862	-	24	22	14	40	
1867	-	22	21	13	44	
1872	-	16	17	10	57	
1877	2	21	25	12	40	
1882	5	18	30	17	30	
1887	3	19	34	14	30	
1892	3	21	28	20	28	
1897	-	35	28	6	31	
1902	8	27	35	10	20	100

Source: Annual Report of the Accountant in Bankruptcy 1857-1902

TABLE 5.8

Total Trustees Commission per annum and Trustees Commission and Legal Expenses as a % of Gross Receipts from Sequestrated Estates, 1857-1904

Year	£	Trustees Commission as % of Gross Receipts	Legal Expenses as % of Gross Receipts	Year	£	Trustees Commission as % of Gross Receipts	Legal Expenses as % of Gross Receipts
1857	5,028	3.03	2.10	1881	23,419	4.625	6.25
1858	3,963	2.97	3.05	1882	22,267	4.50	6.0
1859	4,501	4.99	9.17	1883	23,858	3.50	3.75
1860	5,564	5,375	8.75	1884	16,174	5.625	7.75
1861	12,187	4.50	6.50	1885	21,992	4.25	4.25
1862	10.354	4.625	6.0	1886	11,892	5.0	6.375
1863	16,614	4.50	5.25	1887	21,356	4.1	4.625
1864	11,487	4.625	8.0	1888	25,467	4.75	6.0
1865	10,450	5.25	8.25	1889	35,744	3.75	3.125
1866	16,234	5.0	7.0	1890	18,573	4.875	5.50
1867	11,307	4.625	7.25	1891	44,884	4.25	3.0
1868	14,763	5.25	7.875	1892	20,766	5.0	6.75
1869	13,426	3.125	3.625	1893	16,469	4.25	5.125
1870	17,081	4.50	7.125	1894	16,835	4.125	5.125
1871	15,096	4.75	7.375	1895	13,337	4.75	7.125
1872	17,899	4.50	7.50	1896	18,347	3.375	4.25
1873	14,812	5.0	7.625	1897	15,206	3.125	4.125
1874	12,806	5.25	7.875	1898	14,166	3.875	5.125
1875	13,459	4.75	6.50	1899	19,127	4.625	6.25
1876	29,766	3.0	3.75	1900	13,451	5.25	7.0
1877	30,029	4.375	5.25	1901	14,841	5.25	8.25
1878	26,422	4.25	5.0	1902	20,239	4.50	5.0
1879	21,480	5.125	5.75	1903	24,681	4.50	4.625
1880	20,740	4.25	5.625	1904	12,242	5.125	7.0

Source: Annual Report of the Accountant in Bankruptcy 1857-1904

TABLE 5.9

Number of Sequestration Fees equal to or greater than £350 per location, 1857-1904

	Edinburgh		Glasgow		Aberdeen		Dundee		Total	
YEAR	**CA**	**Others**	**CA**	**Others**	**CA**	**Others**	**CA**	**Others**	**CA**	**Others**
1857	-	-	2	-	-	2	-	1	2	3
1858	-	-	7	1	-	-	-	1	7	2
1859	-	-	-	-	-	-	-	-	-	-
1860	-	-	1	-	-	-	-	-	1	-
1861	-	-	-	-	-	-	1	1	1	1
1862	-	-	2	-	-	-	-	-	2	-
1863	2	-	3	-	-	-	-	-	5	-
1864	-	-	-	-	-	-	1	-	1	-
1865	-	-	1	-	-	-	1	-	2	-
1866	-	2	1	1	-	-	-	-	1	3
1867	1	-	1	-	-	-	-	-	2	-
1868	1	-	5	-	-	-	-	1	6	1
1869	-	-	1	-	-	-	-	-	1	-
1870	1	1	2	-	-	2	-	1	3	4
1871	-	-	3	-	-	1	-	1	3	2
1872	2	-	4	-	-	2	-	1	6	3
1873	-	1	5	-	-	-	-	-	5	1
1874	-	-	1	-	-	-	1	-	2	-
1875	3	-	-	1	-	-	-	-	3	1
1876	-	-	3	1	-	1	-	1	3	3
1877	1	1	7	-	-	-	-	1	8	2
1878	6	-	8	-	-	-	-	-	14	-
1879	3	1	8	1	-	-	-	-	11	2
1880	1	-	1	1	-	-	-	-	2	1
1881	-	1	4	-	-	-	-	-	4	1
1882	2	-	5	-	-	-	-	2	7	2
1883	2	-	3	1	-	-	-	-	5	1
1884	1	-	3	-	-	-	-	-	4	-
1885	2	-	3	1	-	-	1	-	6	1
1886	-	-	2	-	-	-	-	-	2	-
1887	6	-	8	-	-	-	-	-	14	-
1888	4	-	5	-	-	1	-	-	9	1
1889	2	-	7	-	-	-	-	-	9	-
1890	1	-	4	-	-	-	-	-	5	-
1891	-	1	7	1	-	-	-	-	7	2
1892	5	-	1	-	-	-	-	-	6	-
1893	2	-	2	1	-	-	-	-	4	1
1894	2	1	4	-	-	-	-	-	6	1
1895	1	1	1	-	-	-	-	-	2	1
1896	1	-	7	-	-	-	1	1	9	1
1897	3	1	1	-	-	-	-	-	4	1
1898	1	-	4	-	-	-	-	-	5	-
1899	2	-	2	-	-	-	-	-	4	-
1900	-	-	1	-	-	-	-	-	1	-
1901	3	-	4	-	-	-	-	-	7	-
1902	3	-	3	2	-	-	-	-	6	1
1903	6	-	7	-	-	-	7	-	14	1
1904	2	-	3	-	-	-	-	-	5	-
TOTAL	**72**	**11**	**157**	**11**	**-**	**9**	**7**	**12**	**236**	**43**
%	**26**	**4**	**56**	**4**	**-**	**3**	**3**	**4**	**85**	**15**

Source: Scottish Records Office. Records of Sequestration CS 322

who shared as fee income £22,522 (75% x £30,029), each case produced approximately £55 of income for the trustee. However, for two main reasons, this would be unrealistic. First, the time taken to settle a sequestration varied from two to four years,[28] the payment of fees being in some cases on a continuing basis and in other cases on completion and second, fee income varied tremendously depending on the size of the estate being sequestrated.

In an attempt to establish some indication of income from trusteeship an analysis was carried out on all fees of £350 or more and the pattern which emerged for the period 1856 to 1904 can be seen in Table 5.9. The analysis concentrated on the cities where Chartered societies were formed, with the addition of Dundee, where accountants were later admitted to membership of the Glasgow Institute. The designation CA included those who were or who became members of one of the Chartered societies. 'Others' included non-chartered accountants, members of the legal and banking professions and other miscellaneous non-professionals.

This analysis proves beyond doubt that the majority of large fee sequestrations were being dealt with by chartered accountants. In particular, Glasgow chartered accountants took ninety-three per cent of the large fees in their area compared with eighty-seven per cent for Edinburgh members. Interestingly, the picture is completely different in Aberdeen and Dundee with no involvement at all of Aberdeen chartered accountants in sequestrations of this magnitude and in Dundee only thirty-seven per cent of larger fees going to chartered accountants.

An examination of the involvement of the various non-chartered accountant groups in this analysis shows interesting geographical differences. In Edinburgh, five out of the eleven large fees concerned went to accountants, four to the legal profession and the remaining two to a plumber and an undesignated trustee. In Glasgow, nine out of eleven went to accountants and the remaining two to a glass merchant. Aberdeen had six out of nine going to the legal profession and one each to a banker, timber merchant and general merchant respectively, while in Dundee five out of twelve were awarded to accountants and the remaining seven to merchants. In addition to the 279 fees analysed in Table 5.10 a further thirty-seven large fees were noted in locations where no Chartered Accountants' society was established, and of these only two were awarded to accountants. The remainder were largely dealt with by the legal profession with fourteen, and bankers with eight. Of the remaining thirteen, ten were dealt with by merchants, two by spinners and one by a rate-collector.

More detailed examination of the records for sequestrations dealt with by chartered accountants shows that some of the accountants specialised in sequestrations which yielded large fees, possibly because a particular expertise was required to administer complicated and large bankrupt estates.

For example, in Glasgow, Walter Mackenzie only dealt with twelve sequestrations during the period from 1858 to 1888, with fee income ranging from £361 to £5,488, while James McClelland, also of Glasgow, had only five trusteeships between 1858 and 1863 with fees ranging from £1,008 to £2,391. The largest single fee paid to any trustee in the period studied was one of £13,229 paid to William Mackinnon in 1891. At the other extreme were various members of the Glasgow Institute such as David McCubbin, William Mudie jnr, Robert Craig and James McLay who undertook up to fourteen sequestrations per year, not one of which involved a single fee in excess of £350.

The pattern to emerge in Edinburgh was similar, with members such as James Howden, Fred. Carter and James Molleson concentrating mainly on a few large estates, while others, such as Charles Munro, Charles Romanes and especially James Balgarnie, handled anything up to twenty-nine small cases in any one year.

As far as can be ascertained from the records, at least 177 members of the Glasgow Institute, 112 members of the Edinburgh Society and nine members of the Aberdeen Society were involved in sequestration work during the period covered.

3. Summary

The foregoing analysis has shown how the members of the Chartered societies in Scotland gradually increased their involvement in sequestration work and has also proved that the higher fees went to chartered accountants rather than to any other group of trustees. Although it can be argued from this analysis and from the arguments put forward at the time of the formation of the Chartered societies that bankruptcy work formed an important element of fee income at the time of their formation, it is also clear that over the period studied this work was in decline. During the first six years following the introduction of the Bankruptcy (Scotland) Act 1856 the number of sequestrations averaged 512 per year, while by 1902 this had dropped to 294.[29] To some extent this decline was balanced by an increase in the number of sequestrations yielding large fees, but an additional factor which cancelled out this advantage was the increase in the number of accountants being admitted to membership of the three societies.

As a consequence, accounting firms were forced to look elsewhere for fee income, not only to maintain the income of the earlier members but also to provide earnings for this continuing supply of new entrants to the profession. The main new source to be tapped was that of audit work and during the last quarter of the nineteenth century there was a great deal of pressure from the professional accounting bodies, both in Scotland and England, for the annual audit of limited liability companies to be made compulsory and for this work to be undertaken by chartered accountants.

VI

Development of Other Areas of Practice to 1900

1. Introduction

Company legislation passed during the latter half of the nineteenth century developed in two ways. General provisions were developed for the control of joint stock companies and there was a subsequent development of legislation specific to certain classes of companies, such as banks and insurance companies, and changes in the legislation for local government. All of this was to have an impact on the work available for accountants and lead to competition between the members of the new professional bodies and other accountants.

2. Changes in General Legislation

The passing of the Bubble Act in 1719 had virtually removed the possibility of limited liability for shareholders and incorporation for companies in industry but its repeal in 1825 relaxed the legal constraints upon incorporation.[1] Jones identified the 1840s as a critical decade for the development of the English accountancy profession because of government legislation and the growth in the size and complexity of businesses which created a demand for expanding numbers of accountants.[2]

The Joint Stock Companies Act 1844 was preceded in 1843 by a Select Committee under the Chairmanship of Gladstone 'appointed to inquire into the state of the Laws respecting Joint Stock Companies (except for Banking), with a view to the greater security of the Public.'[3] Considering the implications that the subsequent Act was to have on accounts and accountants it is perhaps surprising that no accountants were called as witnesses.[4] However, the accountancy profession had not yet been formed so it might have been unreasonable to expect any single accountant to present anything other than a personal viewpoint to the committee.

Witnesses certainly held differing opinions as to whether or not there should be periodic publication of accounts. One opinion was that companies 'would feel proud of having an opportunity of showing their solvency; and that company which would refuse to do so, I should say unhesitatingly was a company to be suspected.' But the more commonly held view was 'that assets and liabilities ought certainly to be laid before the whole body of proprietors at least once in every year, and twice if possible,' though doubt was expressed as to how any way could be found to compel businessmen to keep clear and distinct books of account to be balanced every year.[5]

These comments indicate that accounting at that time had little, if any, degree of uniformity, possibly as a result of a shortage of trained bookkeepers. By that time, several books had been published on double entry bookkeeping and the preparation of different types of accounts, but there was little, if any, formal training available. This makes it somewhat surprising that the subsequent Act made no attempt to indicate the format of the accounts that it required to be kept by companies.

The 1844 Act was described enthusiastically by Stacey 'from an accountant's view-point, its provisions in regulating accounting safeguards were nothing short of visionary.'[6] But its only stipulations were that the accounts be properly kept and a full and fair balance sheet prepared and sent to the company's proprietors, that the balance sheet and accounts be audited within fourteen days and the balance sheet and auditors report filed with the Registrar of Joint Stock Companies. However the schedules to the Act did not contain an outline balance sheet so there was no move towards a uniform or improved reporting system although the requirement to keep proper accounts may have increased employment opportunities for those practising accountancy.

The Companies Clauses Consolidation Act of 1845, applied

in Scotland by the Joint Stock Companies Act 1845,[7] further improved the climate for accountants, since it allowed the auditors of the company to employ accountants, at the company's expense, to report on the accounts or confirm them. In addition, the Act required the directors to appoint a bookkeeper to enter the accounts. Auditors were required to hold at least one share in the company so that, while it was necessary for the auditor to have some interest in the company in order to report on it, it was not expected that he be skilled in accountancy. Of course, it is impossible to ascertain how many auditors did employ accountants to report on the accounts, but the fact that bookkeepers were being employed to enter the accounts points to a more professional approach to the maintenance and preparation of the accounts. One disadvantage was the fact that any person could describe himself as a bookkeeper and it is reasonable to assume that much of this work was undertaken by relatively unskilled men so that the company would be seen to be complying with the letter of the law.

In 1856 the Joint Stock Companies Act, which repealed the previous legislation, provided a model set of Articles in Table B. However only a draft balance sheet was included and the compulsory accounting provisions of the 1844 Act were repealed. If a company chose to adopt Table B, then it had to comply with rather more detailed requirements for keeping the accounts, such as using double entry and keeping specific books of account but the compulsion to employ shareholder-auditors was removed as a departure from the principle that auditors were shareholders checking on management. Both of these Table B changes must have enlarged the opportunities for accountants, first as bookkeepers or accountants in preparing the accounts of companies and secondly in permitting the position of auditor to be filled by professional accountants.

New consolidating legislation appeared in 1862 in a further Joint Stock Companies Act. Although this was after the formation of the societies of accountants in Edinburgh and Glasgow, their Minute Books reveal no interest being expressed in this legislation, but both Stacey[8] and Brown[9] stated that the Act had a tremendous impact on accountants. Although it was perhaps visionary in a theoretical sense, it again suffered from its failure to detail the form and content of the balance sheet to be produced; to require the provision of a profit and loss account or to detail any qualifications required for appointment as an auditor of a joint-stock company.

This golden opportunity for accountants to make an impact on large companies was apparently not always taken advantage of, since the witnesses to the Select Committee on the Limited Liability Acts in 1867 were extremely critical of the way in which accounts were kept and audits carried out. Chadwick, an accountant, described accounts as being 'sometimes stated in forms which are quite incomprehensible'[10] and suggested that the model balance sheet be made compulsory. Thus it would appear that the Act of 1862 had not achieved one of its desired effects, that of improving the standard of information supplied by companies. This failure was attributed by Jeal to the fact 'that the profession at that time was hardly advanced enough in numbers of men of the degree of professional integrity required for such work'[11] and this was probably a very fair comment, since numbers of professional accountants, even in Scotland, were still small in relation to the new developments in practice.

It would appear that towards the end of the nineteenth century accountants gradually became more involved with auditing. In 1881, an address by the President of the Manchester Society of Chartered Accountants referred to auditing as being a duty 'of a pleasanter nature, and to which many accountants have devoted much attention'[12] although the main areas referred to in his speech were still bankruptcy work and executorship and trust accounts. Sir John Mann described the accountant's work in the 1840s to 1880s as being mainly involved with bookkeeping, balancing and the preparation of accounts, with audit only being carried out as a follow up when an accounting firm was called in to investigate a defalcation case. But by the end of the century, a steady flow of auditing and company work had taken over from the more spasmodic bankruptcy and other work, although the standard of auditing was described as being rather primitive and mainly concerned with establishing arithmetical accuracy.[13]

Writing in 1886 on the role of chartered accountants as auditors of companies, Ernest Cooper referred to auditing as one of the three principal branches of an accountant's duties, but complained that 'auditing is still in great part and probably in a large majority of instances, in the hands of unskilled or at least unduly qualified persons' stating that such audits could not in most cases be efficiently conducted.[14] He also noted that the systems of accounts used by companies were so varied as to necessitate the auditor having training in more than one system. Companies were not always efficiently run, and Jones stated that 'Fraud was a disease endemic in the Victorian economy, and public accountants were the physicians employed to drive it out,'[15] so the accountant's tasks included investigation as well as audit but there was no legislation to limit this work to the qualified professional public accountant.

The desirability of having qualified public accountants acting as auditors of joint stock companies was still being claimed in 1891,[16] but by 1896 it was stated that it was almost solely chartered accountants who were being appointed auditors of the many public companies being floated.[17] Nevertheless, in 1897 it was asserted that a large number of provincial audits were still in the hands of amateurs[18] and Pixley confirmed this when he stated, also in 1897, that the advantages of employing professional accountants as auditors were becoming more and more recognised but were not yet fully appreciated.[19]

In 1895 the Davey Committee[20] recommended that audit should once again be made compulsory for all companies registered under the Companies Act and this was enacted in the Companies Act 1900,[21] though there was no requirement for the auditor to be a professional accountant. This reimposition of compulsory audit led to an increase in the volume of audit work and also to a wave of protectionism in the accountancy profession.

> Since the qualified accountant thought himself better equipped to cope with the audit of companies than his professionally untutored brethren, and furthermore since the accountant who was a member of a professional accounting body is subject to ethical standards and disciplinary codes, members of accounting associations who passed vigorous examinations felt more entitled to the audits of companies and sought to protect their pastures against unqualified intruders.[22]

Edey stated that there was at the time some support for making audit by professional accountants obligatory,[23] but this requirement was not introduced until the Companies Act of 1947.[24] This did not prevent the anonymous author of an article in the *Accountant* from stating in 1901 that the 1900 Act proved that 'the tendency of the legislature is thus clearly shown to be favourable to professional accountants.'[25]

By 1906 an Edinburgh chartered accountant, George Lisle, described auditing as one of the two main branches of the business of an accountant[26] and Jones also noted that by the 1890s auditing provided a sizeable proportion of the fee income of Ernst and Whinney.[27]

Thus, it was not until the end of the nineteenth century that general company legislation did much to increase the need for professional accountants. However, legislation dealing with specific areas such as banking, insurance and railways did increase this need.

3. Auditing

(*a*) *Banks*

At the time of the formation of the accounting profession in Scotland the Act which regulated bank accounting was the Joint Stock Banking Act 1844 which had been applied to Scotland by the Joint Stock Banking (Scotland) Act 1846. The provisions in this Act relating to the publication and audit of accounts were similar to those in the Joint Stock Companies Act 1844, providing specifically:

> For the Publication of the Assets and Liabilities of the Company once at least in every Calendar month: . . . For the yearly Audit of the Accounts of the Company by Two or more Auditors chosen at a General Meeting of the Shareholders, and not being Directors at the Time: . . . For the yearly Communication of the Auditors Report, and of a Balance Sheet, and Profit and Loss Account, to every Shareholder.[28]

Only the most basic information was disclosed and this secrecy was approved of by the bankers of the period. In 1857, John Hubbard the ex-Deputy Governor of the Bank of England stated in evidence to a Select Committee on Banking: 'a great deal too much information is given to the public, because the public has not yet arrived at a due understanding of it.'[29] This view was not held by all bankers and a Report from the Select Committee on Savings Banks showed a distinct appreciation of the need to improve bank audit. Suggestions for improvement included the appointment of Government auditors or inspectors entirely independent of managers, which would give security to depositors; the employment of 'a professional public accountant, independent of all other paid officers, whose duty shall be to audit the accounts of the bank every month, or quarter, in small banks, and report the result in writing every month, or quarter, as the case may be' and the weekly audit of savings banks by professional accountants, paid by the trustees and managers or governors. The fee accompanying this last suggestion was £20 per year plus an allowance of about five guineas to a clerk so it can hardly be imagined that at such a level of remuneration professional accountants would find the work particularly attractive.[30]

In spite of these clear concerns as to the state of disclosure and audit requirements for banks, the Joint Stock Companies Act 1862 extended the abandonment of compulsory auditing to all companies, banks and insurance companies having been previously excluded from the provisions of the 1856 Act. 'The abandonment seems to have been the result of the strong contemporary feeling that matters of accounting should be dealt with by private contract between shareholders and directors.'[31] Although audit was not compulsory, banks could apply any accounting and audit requirements that were felt necessary, but there seems to have been a general feeling at this time that any audit being performed was complying with the letter rather than the spirit of any such audit requirements. In 1860, Scratchley wrote, with reference to bank audit:

> Audit, without inspection, is not a security to be relied on. The experience of numerous Joint Stock Companies has shown that Auditors are too apt to act in a perfunctory way, forgetting the real spirit of their duties. From a desire to prevent a shock that would ruin 'the credit of the Company', they have been known to abstain from reporting on improprieties or irregularities in the management, and to have said

> nothing respecting deficiencies in the funds - sometimes from a species of foolish sympathy - sometimes from a bona fide sort of idea that the concern could recover itself. Had the Auditors properly discharged their duties, or been possessed of sufficient powers of inspection, the Royal British Bank, and other grievous frauds would not have been perpetrated.[32]

Scratchley's suggested solution to this problem was the appointment of Government Inspectors to examine both the management of the bank and its financial condition. In addition, he advocated the appointment by the Government Commissioners of a local professional accountant who would be attached to each bank which was too small to keep a full staff of officials. As an alternative, he suggested the appointment of an Audit Committee, such as was already in operation in 1860 in certain banks in the United States.[33]

In Scotland, where admittedly there were far fewer banks, conditions were somewhat better than those in England. Tyson[34] reported that by 1865 all of the Scottish banks were publishing annual reports with abstract balance sheets and profit statements although prior to that 'almost absolute secrecy shrouded their affairs. Except the amount of their capitals, and the rates of dividends they paid, but little was known regarding them which could serve as a guide to intending purchasers of bank stock.'[35]

Once more, however, there was no independent audit of the information provided: 'it was strongly felt that outside investigators were incompatible with the privacy necessary in dealing with the financial affairs of the banks' customers.'[36] Two points make this attitude particularly difficult to accept in Scotland. First, the formation of the Societies of Chartered Accountants in Edinburgh and Glasgow had led to an increase in the involvement of chartered accountants in railway audit and it seems strange that they did not also attempt to secure a role for themselves in the audit of banks. Second, some of these early chartered accountants were directors of different banks and might have been expected to encourage independent audit.

It can only be concluded that, in spite of the failure of the Western Bank in 1857 and the subsequent temporary weakness of the

City of Glasgow, Edinburgh and Glasgow and Union Banks, both the banks and professional accountants were unconvinced of the need for the independent audit of banks at that time. Even the failure of the great English merchant bank of Overend, Gurney & Co. in 1866 with liabilities of over £18 million was insufficient stimulus.[37]

Scotland not only produced the first modern accounting society in the world but it also produced the first banking institute: the Institute of Bankers in Scotland, which was formed on 6 July 1875. There is no obvious reason for the formation of this Institute, but the Edinburgh bankers in particular had many examples of professional bodies in their community and perhaps saw the need to raise the status of bank employees and to formalise the training of bankers. Up to this time, Kerr commented:

> the education of bankers in the theory and practice of their profession - nay, even the ascertainment of their most ordinary educational acquirements - was of the most haphazard description. Not the smallest attempt was made either to encourage, or to provide means for, the study of the theory of banking.[38]

Indeed the comment of an eminent banker on the teaching of bookkeeping in schools reinforces the viewpoint that the training of bank employees was an extremely basic affair:

> as to school knowledge, we like that he should write well, that he should have had as thoughtful an education as possible, and that he should not have learned bookkeeping. We have our own system of accounts, and the spurious commercial phraseology used in school-books, would only hinder him from acquiring it. Give us a lad of cultivated intelligence, and a good general knowledge of arithmetic, and we will undertake to teach him all that is special to our own business in three days.[39]

The Institute swiftly introduced examinations to ensure a minimum standard for entrants and from 1878 it was almost impossible to gain admission other than by examinations.[40]

Unfortunately, these steps to improve the quality of the work being done in banks did nothing to prevent the failure of the City of Glasgow Bank in 1878 which brought financial disaster to hundreds of people in the West of Scotland.

The City of Glasgow Bank failed through a combination of misfortune and unethical direction and management. The directors of the bank allowed themselves to become over-extended in their lending to a very few companies, basically four large borrowers in which they had a financial interest so in effect they were lending money to themselves. When the debtor companies began to have difficulty in repaying the loans, the directors of the bank falsified the annual balance sheet and continued to pay out handsome dividends in order to attract investors. At the time of the collapse the bank had 1891 stockholders and, during the liquidation, calls amounting to £2750 were made for each £100 of stock held. From this the creditors received a dividend of 6*s* 8*d* in the £. Such was the degree of public interest in the trial of the directors and manager of the bank that a special report reprinted from the *Glasgow Herald*, was published and sold at a price of sixpence.

In the three years immediately prior to the City of Glasgow Bank failure there had been several select committees covering various aspects of banking, and the evidence given to them proved that there were great differences of opinion among bankers as to what information should be disclosed in the accounts and as to whether or not they should be audited. However nothing had come to the statute books by 1878 and early in 1879, in response to the City of Glasgow Bank failure, a Bill was introduced into Parliament, for the 'better auditing of the Books and Accounts of the Chartered and other Joint Stock Banks in Scotland.' This required auditors to certify that the accounts gave a true and correct view of the bank's affairs and also made the auditors liable to any shareholder who acted on the auditors' report when the auditors made or sanctioned any statement which they knew to be untrue or misleading or which they might, by due diligence have ascertained to be untrue or misleading.[41] This Bill which would have had serious repercussions for bank auditors was talked out but the Government immediately introduced a Bill which resulted in the Banking Companies Act 1879.

This was a wide-ranging Act and the most significant section for accountants was that on audit, which required every bank registered as a limited company to have its accounts examined at least once a year by an auditor or auditors elected annually at the general meeting of the company. Directors and officers of the bank were not allowed to be auditors, the auditors were to have access to all the books and accounts of the bank and were required to report on whether or not the balance sheet was a full and fair balance sheet properly drawn up so as to exhibit a true and correct view.[42] Apparently some banks, seeing that the legislation was being passed quickly through Parliament, altered their practice of using only internal auditors and appointed external examiners for the first time.[43]

While there was no requirement that the appointed auditors be professional accountants, records of many of the Scottish banks show that their directors considered professional accountants to be the most appropriate people to fill this position. The Royal Bank of Scotland immediately began to have its accounts audited by professional accountants.[44] The North of Scotland Bank was also in the van of change and presented its first auditors' report to the AGM of 1879, the auditors being John Young FCA of Turquand, Youngs & Co., London, and James Meston, CA, Aberdeen.[45] The Clydesdale Bank submitted its 1879 balance sheet to the audit of two chartered accountants, J.M. MacAndrew and Alex. Moore, for the first time.[46] The Union Bank acted before a resolution was passed at its May 1879 AGM requiring the appointment of auditors, its directors having already appointed Jas. Haldane, CA, Edinburgh and Wm. Mackinnon, CA, Glasgow as auditors. Their report, in addition to the regular form of audit report, also stated their satisfaction with the system of continuous audit maintained by the Bank.[47] The British Linen Bank went even further in that the Governor and Deputy Governor of the Bank sent a proposal to their Head Office 'recommending that a chartered accountant in Glasgow and another in Edinburgh be appointed as Auditors. This the Court of Directors immediately agreed to do, though the Bank as a Corporation was exempted from the provisions of the Companies Act.'[48] Indeed within three years of the failure of the City of Glasgow Bank, each of the ten remaining Scottish banks had appointed two independent professional accountants as auditors. 'The auditors now occupied a vital role in reassuring the public that the practices perpetrated by the management of the City of Glasgow Bank would not be repeated.'[49]

Compliance with the new legislation was seemingly less

complete in England than in Scotland, since Ernest Cooper, FCA, stated in October 1886 that he had examined 159 banks and found that 128 had appointed auditors.[50] Nevertheless, this was a tremendous increase on previous figures. By 1894 James Howden, President of the Edinburgh Society of Accountants, was reporting that the greater number of bank auditors in England were either fellows or associates of the ICAEW and that in Scotland, with one exception where a Writer to the Signet was employed as a joint auditor, all bank auditors were chartered accountants.[51] Howden's confidence in the quality of bank auditors in England was not universal, since a leading article in the *Accountant* in 1897 stated that the audits of many banks were in the hands 'of gentlemen who have no claim, and very little qualification, to discharge these duties . . .[and] hold their appointments on account of their local and personal influence.'[52] Apparently there were still some lay auditors in 1907 when H. Woodburn Kirby wrote, in support of registration for the profession, that it should no longer be possible for such auditors to certify 'the accounts of banks, insurance companies, and other important undertakings, involving themselves and the public in unknown risks.'[53]

No doubt the switch to the appointment of professional auditors was easier in Scotland where there were fewer banks and where there were already a number of chartered accountants involved in the direction of some of the banks, but it is interesting to note that the pressure for independent professional audit of banks did not come from within the profession and was not considered necessary until imposed by legislation. The Scottish Chartered Accounting societies probably gained some prestige from the fact that all of the Scottish banks entrusted them with their audits, but their number was very limited and provided limited business for their members.

(*b*) *Local Government*

Around 1830, many Scottish cities including Aberdeen, Dundee, Paisley and Dunfermline became bankrupt and it became obvious that there was a need for a new system of local government and local government accounting. Municipal corporations were reformed in 1835, but the Act which first increased the work for professional accountants was the Municipal Corporations Act of 1882[54] which dealt with burgh audits. The Local Government Act 1888[55] which established county councils in England was extended to Scotland by the Local Government (Scotland) Act 1889 and legislated for the appointment of parish council auditors by the Local Government Board and those of county councils and burghs by the Secretary for Scotland.[56] Jones commented that some accounting firms developed considerable expertise in this area of work, where auditors would cut their teeth on parish council audits in the hope of being promoted to successively larger councils.[57]

None of the Acts contained any requirements as to the professional qualification of the auditors appointed, though the ICAEW had made a submission to Parliament in 1887 suggesting that the accounts of all local government offices should be audited only by properly qualified accountants.[58] This was refused. However, the system of allowing unqualified auditors was found to be inadequate and unsatisfactory to many municipal corporations although they did value the right to appoint their own auditors.[59] Some local authorities did appoint professional accountants and the first instance of a borough obtaining powers from Parliament to appoint professional auditors was the West Bromwich Corporation (Consolidation of Loans) Act 1889, which required that the borough auditor should be a chartered accountant or a member of the Incorporated Society of Accountants and Auditors.[60] The Act does not specify a member of the ICAEW only 'a chartered accountant', but it was assumed by most writers that, since this was an English Act, the implication was that the chartered accountant would be a member of the ICAEW. However the importance of this Act for the chartered bodies cannot be underestimated since it 'created a precedent upon which subsequent acts were modelled.'[61]

Although Scotland had far fewer local authorities to audit, this branch of work grew steadily towards the end of the nineteenth century and the professional audit of such accounts became compulsory.[62] Brown claimed that in almost every case the auditor appointed was a duly qualified accountant[63] so that the situation in Scotland was better than that said to exist in the country as a whole by Carr-Saunders and Wilson, who reported that 'in local government the professional audit of accounts has not for the most part been adopted.'[64]

Local authority audit was not exclusively the province of

chartered accountants. The audits of the thirty-three Scottish counties were divided up by the Secretary for Scotland between ten chartered accountants and chartered accountants had a near monopoly over the audit of parish councils.[65] When the local Government (Scotland) Bill of 1894,[66] which constituted parish councils, was introduced into the House of Commons it contained a provision that the auditors of county council accounts should also audit the parishes within the counties for which they were auditors, a provision which would have meant an average of 130 parish audits for each of the ten chartered accountants. Ultimately, this clause was altered by the Grand Committee and left the appointment of parish auditors to the Local Government Boards which: 'distributed the appointments very widely among professional gentlemen - principally accountants - in all parts of the country, and in a manner that gave very general satisfaction.'[67]

Matters in this area were not always satisfactory. Under the Burgh Police (Scotland) Act 1892[68] the auditor was appointed by the Sheriff of the County, but this led to accusations in some sheriffdoms of family patronage or political bias so the power to appoint auditors was transferred to the Secretary for Scotland under the Town Council (Scotland) Act 1900.[69] There was also criticism that the rates of payment to burgh auditors were inadequate for the services rendered.[70]

So, once again, a new area of work appeared and what was without doubt the most prestigious part of it, the audit of county councils, went exclusively to the chartered accountants. Since only ten of them were involved in such work the impact on the profession as a whole could not have been great, but no doubt to the individual firms concerned the fee income was significant. What was probably much more important was the fact that members of the Chartered Bodies had shown themselves to be preferred over others for the most important areas of this type of work.

(*c*) *Insurance Companies*

The Select Committee on Joint Stock Companies looked at, among other things, the accounting and auditing requirements for insurance companies and extracted various opinions from different witnesses. As far as reporting to shareholders was concerned, it was felt that an annual balance sheet would be sufficient. In reply to questions as to the quality of audit generally carried out, a group of actuaries replied that some audits were carried out much more severely than others and that there was a belief that auditors did not generally go into the details of the assurance accounts. It was also stated that most insurance companies employed an accountant but that a public accountant was not called in to assist in the preparation of the accounts.[71]

When the Joint Stock Companies Act was passed in 1844 it applied to Assurance and Insurance Companies and it was unusual for the Acts incorporating such companies after that date to contain any specific requirements with regard to accounting or auditing. Several companies had been formed prior to that Act. For example, the Scottish Union Insurance Company was formed in 1833 and was granted incorporated status in 1847,[72] and the Scottish Equitable Life Assurance Society was formed in 1838 and was also incorporated in 1847.[73] Such companies, coming under general company legislation, were relieved of any compulsory accounting or auditing requirements with the passing of the 1856 Companies Act, though some of them included requirements voluntarily. The Scottish National Insurance Company, which had been formed as a partnership under the name of the National Fire and Life Insurance Company of Scotland included in its incorporating Act of 1859 a requirement that 'The Directors shall cause the Books and Accounts of the Company to be kept in such Form as shall seem to them most suitable for preserving an accurate and distinct View of the Company's Affairs,'[74] but no more detail was given.

This lack of regulation of insurance and assurance companies was not popular in all quarters and, in a very detailed investigation of Associations for Provident Investment in 1859, Scratchley suggested that any future legislation should require the appointment of a professional accountant as auditor.[75]

In 1870 the Life Assurance Companies Act was implemented and required all such companies to prepare an annual revenue account and balance sheet as outlined in the first and second schedules to the Act. Copies of the statements were to be supplied on request to shareholders and policy holders but there was no requirement that the statements should be audited. However, the Act did attempt to compensate for this deficiency by requiring life assurance companies to deposit £20,000 with the Accountant General of the Court of

Chancery as security; this amount would be returned to them as soon as the life assurance fund had accumulated premiums amounting to £40,000.[76] This was apparently considered to be sufficient security to ensure that the company was being properly managed and that no fraud would take place. Thereafter, these companies continued to be dealt with under special legislation.[77]

Many companies imposed additional accounting and auditing requirements in their incorporating Acts, often including in statute what they were already doing in practice. The Act which in 1878 amalgamated the Scottish Union Insurance Company and the Scottish National Insurance Company allowed the directors to determine the form of the accounts, but also required the examination of the accounts at least once a year by one or more auditors who could have no personal interest in the company other than as a policy holder.[78] In fact the Scottish Union Insurance Company, which was founded in 1824, had from the beginning employed an accountant, John Greig of Edinburgh[79] and the Scottish National, established in 1841, had had its books 'From the beginning . . . minutely audited and the Balance Sheet certified by an independent accountant.' From its establishment until at least 1924 this particular company was audited by a succession of Edinburgh Chartered Accountants.[80]

This was not unusual, since the records of the Scottish Provident Institution, founded in Edinburgh in 1837, show that it appointed three auditors from the start, one of them being the Edinburgh accountant James Watson[81] and the Scottish Amicable Life Assurance Society was audited for many years by partners of McClelland, Ker and Company of Glasgow.

Accountants were involved far more in other aspects of insurance companies than they were in their audit, many of them being involved in their formation[82] and management, or as agents.[83] The strong ties between the Scottish accountancy profession and insurance companies can be further evidenced by the fact that many Edinburgh chartered accountants were also members of the Faculty of Actuaries and that on the formation of the Insurance and Actuarial Society of Glasgow in 1881, the first President was John Graham, then President of the Institute of Accountants and Actuaries of Glasgow, and one of the initial vice-presidents was also a Glasgow chartered accountant.[84] However, the situation in England at this time appears to have been less satisfactory since Pixley complained in

1881 about the fact that the Life Assurance Companies Act of 1870 had not required the compulsory audit of accounts. He further remarked that nearly all such companies did have auditors but that 'their names show that their qualification for these important appointments is less considered than the fact of their being men of position and influence.'[85]

The difference between the two countries appears to have continued since the *Accountant* criticised the involvement of amateur accountants with insurance companies in 1891 and again in 1897,[86] while by 1894 James Howden, then President of the Society of Accountants in Edinburgh, stated that there were twenty insurance companies with their head offices in Scotland who employed twenty auditors, all of whom were Scottish chartered accountants.[87]

So another area of work had developed during the second half of the nineteenth century and had gradually become the exclusive domain of the Scottish chartered accountant. The ability to capture the whole of this particular field of audit had no doubt been helped by the fact that there was such a close association between the accountancy and actuarial professions and also because a significant number of chartered accountants had, over the years, been involved as agents, secretaries, managers and directors of various insurance companies. However, it also demonstrated the reputation of members of the profession as a well-trained and trustworthy group of accountants.

4. Railway Companies

(*a*) *Legislation affecting accounting and audit requirements*

Any examination of the economic development of nineteenth-century Scotland confirms the view that the advent and development of railways were of tremendous importance. Indeed, it is perhaps no exaggeration to refer to this as 'The single most dramatic development across the face of virtually all Lowland Scotland, and later and to a lesser extent in the Highlands.'[88]

The first recorded railroad in Scotland was opened by the Duke of Portland in 1812, built, at a cost of £50,000, from

Kilmarnock to Troon to facilitate the movement of coal from his collieries to the coast for shipping. Once in operation it was also used to convey timber, grain, slates, lime and passengers all in horse-drawn wagons. Significantly, the first railway in the modern sense was also built for the easier conveyance of coal from the Monkland Collieries. This was the Monkland and Kirkintilloch Railway which consisted of ten miles of single-track line with passing places and, originally, horse-drawn wagons although these were quite soon replaced by steam locomotives.[89] The line linked the eastern end of the Monklands Canal to the Forth and Clyde Canal, opening up a quicker route for coal and other freight to Edinburgh and ports on the East Coast.[90] Many of the early railway lines were considered to be complementary to the existing canal structure, but before long they were being built in direct competition to the canals, initially for the conveyance of freight, and then for passengers. The first of these competitive lines was the Glasgow and Garnkirk Railway which was opened in 1831 and which utilised locomotives, enabling the company to reduce the cost of carrying coal to Glasgow from 3*s* 6*d* to 1*s* 3*d* per ton. By 1836 the line was carrying 140,000 tons of minerals and 145,000 passengers.[91] Not only did the railways facilitate the movement of minerals, they also enabled the development of the rich mineral deposits of the West of Scotland.

The continuing growth of the railway system had many repercussions for different sections of the community. For example, each new line and any alteration or extension to an existing line required a separate Act of Parliament, thus providing fees for the legal profession. Lines and sleepers were originally cast in iron, but, although the Scottish iron industry in the West of Scotland experienced significant expansion at this time, most of the iron produced in this area was marketed abroad[92] while the iron rails used in Scotland were mainly imported from England. However, most of the early locomotives used on Scottish lines were built in Scotland and the West of Scotland remained an important centre of locomotive manufacture well into the twentieth century.[93]

Each railway company was incorporated under a separate Act of Parliament which detailed any requirements for the maintenance of accounting records and audit of the accounts. These conditions were generally outlined in an extremely vague fashion; for example, the Act to enable a railway to be constructed from Spittal to Kelso in

1811 only required that 'proper Books of Account, and other Matters relating to the said Undertaking, shall be kept.'[94] As railway building increased, some of the Acts became more detailed in their requirements, particularly in respect of audit. The Act enabling the construction of the North British Railway from Edinburgh to Berwick-upon-Tweed in 1844 required the election of two auditors, each of whom was to have no office or interest in the company other than a requirement that each hold at least the same number of shares as a director. At the time of incorporation this would have required the purchase of twenty shares at £25 each, i.e. £500 investment. So although one auditor was to retire each year but be eligible for re-election it is not surprising to find the same auditors in office for a long period of time. The Act required the audit of the periodical accounts and balance sheet and the appointment of a bookkeeper to enter the accounts in the books.[95]

In 1844 the government passed the Railway Regulation Act in an endeavour to set minimum requirements for various aspects of railways, including accounting. The Act provided for the maintenance of full and true accounts of all receipts and disbursement of cash; the preparation of half-yearly accounts comprising a receipts and expenditures account plus a statement of the balance of the account, and the auditing and certifying of such accounts by two or more directors of the railway companies.[96] Section I of the Act implied that railways were very profitable concerns since it stipulated that profits for a railway company must not exceed ten per cent per £ of paid up capital stock and in the event of them so doing then fares were to be reduced to a level which would produce profits of ten per cent or less.

The mid-nineteenth century view of the auditor was obviously rather different from that held today: 'he was not required to be either independent of management or to be a qualified accountant. In practice, in most cases, he was a shareholder appointed by his fellow members.'[97] This viewpoint was enforced by the Companies Clauses Consolidation Act 1845 which required an auditor to have at least one share in the company but not to hold office;[98] ensuring that, in theory at least, the auditor was independent of management and would have the interests of his fellow shareholders uppermost in his mind. Once more, only a balance sheet was required to be prepared and audited, but two clauses were of importance to accountants. First, section cxix required the directors to appoint a bookkeeper to enter the accounts in the company's books, recognising the fact that if a balance sheet was to be prepared then it was necessary to keep proper books of account. Second, section cviii allowed the auditor to employ accountants and other persons at the company's expense in order to enable him to carry out his audit properly, an acknowledgement that shareholder-auditors might not themselves have the necessary expertise. The Railway Clauses Consolidation Act, 1845 again contained provision for the preparation of accounts of receipts and expenditures.

However, an article in the *Railway Magazine* of 24 July 1841 suggested that auditors paid lip service to their task by merely examining receipts placed before them by the secretary and that they failed to make suggestions for improvement to the companies by which they were engaged.[99] *Herapath*'s *Journal* of 27 September 1851, criticised Quilter and Ball for their inconsistency in the work they performed for railway companies, pointing out that in the accounts of the Berwick Railway the repair of carriages and wagons was charged to general charges, while in the accounts of the South Eastern and Eastern Counties Railway the same item was charged to locomotive expenses.[100] It is small wonder that Pollins commented:

> The officially published annual railway returns invariably contained a pathetic statement to the effect that the statistics printed were those given by the companies, and the compilers of the returns had no responsibility for their accuracy or for their completeness; and there were always delinquent companies which did not bother to deliver any information at all.[101]

In 1849 the increasing number of railway companies and mounting dissatisfaction with the accounts provided by them led the government to appoint a Select Committee of the House of Lords to examine the question of the audit of railway accounts. The reports produced by this committee and the minutes of evidence taken provide a valuable insight into the accounting and auditing of railway companies in the mid-1800s. Charles Russell, chairman of the Great Western Railway Company, stated that, in his opinion, the information contained in the accounts of railway companies provided an insufficient basis for decision-making while claiming that the information rendered was ample. When questioned as to whether or not difficulties arose because of different railway companies having different sorts of accounts, he replied:

> That is true to a certain extent, but I am afraid that the attainment of entire uniformity of accounts would be a matter of considerable difficulty. I know that theoretically it is considered that a general uniformity of account is desirable; but the circumstances of Railways, to a considerable extent, differ; Railways are still progressive. If you had established uniformity of account in the commencement, I am satisfied that there would or ought to have been a considerable divergence from that uniformity before this, and the same if you establish it in the present state of Railway progress. I think that circumstances will change, and will occasion considerable divergence hereafter. Uniformity will go far to arrest improvement in the system, of which the accounts may be quite susceptible.

When questioned on the subject of the choice of auditors, Russell was firmly of the opinion that the system of shareholder-auditor was entirely adequate: 'I believe there is an amount of supervision exercised now over Railway accounts generally that renders it entirely impossible that any accounts can be insufficiently or improperly kept.' He dismissed the claim that such an auditor might be solely concerned with the amount of dividends to be received and with the subsequent value of his shares, stating that the auditor was more interested in the permanent prosperity of the company particularly if he was a large shareholder.

Russell was also asked whether or not he thought it a good idea to allow the government to nominate an auditor or accountant to work in conjunction with the auditors of the company and who would comment on the accounts. He believed that:

> in many instances such an auditor would be deeply

> injurious. If such an audit had existed during the last year, and had been rigidly enforced, many Railway Companies would have been brought into very great difficulties, even if they were not absolutely reduced to bankruptcy. I am satisfied it was because they were subject to the audit of their own shareholders, who could look to questions of expediency or necessity as well as questions of rigid law, that they have been enabled to weather the storm . . . Men of high character and position now become the Directors of Railways, and the public may suffer from such persons declining to continue in that position, if they are to be subject to the cavils of mere official Accountants, empowered to interfere with their system of management by raising technical objections to their accounts.[102]

What Russell seems to have been saying was that railway companies should be allowed to prepare their accounts as the Directors saw fit and without being encumbered with rules and regulations and the interference of external auditors. It is little wonder that the government had felt the need to investigate this whole area.

Lengthy evidence was also given by William Quilter, of Quilter and Ball, who had at that time been an accountant in the City of London for about twenty years and who was firmly of the opinion that a system of uniform accounts for railway companies would be to the advantage of the public. Quilter made specific recommendations as to the form of accounts which should be produced, suggesting a Parliamentary account showing how much capital the company was authorised to raise and how much it had raised; a capital account, showing capital raised and expended; and an income and expenditure account for the computation of profit and the declaration of dividends.

Unlike Russell, Quilter stated that railway accounts could only be reliable if the auditor was independent of the company, i.e. not a shareholder: 'I think that a man can act more independently when he has no pecuniary interest in the subject than when he has.' Perhaps it is not surprising that Quilter also expressed his opinion 'That a professional accountant, from the nature of his practice and the habit of investigation which his mind acquires from it, may, as a general rule, be considered as the fittest sort of person to perform that duty.'[103]

Other witnesses were equally scathing about the quality of audit work generally performed on railway companies at that time. Mr Swift described the audit of the accounts of the North Western Railway Company as 'moonshine as against dishonest Directors' and Mr King, who had acted as Secretary to two railway companies, was even stronger in his condemnation referring to the audit as the 'greatest farce possible' and of no value or importance. When the committee came to discuss its findings on achieving the improvement and independence of audit, it was clearly stated that the auditor must be independent of the shareholders. In evidence there had been general agreement by the witnesses that this was necessary in order to gain public confidence in the audited accounts. Indeed some witnesses such as Mr Morrison went so far as to say that the auditor should be appointed by an outside body such as the Railway Board; and Mr Andoe preferred a government auditor because he would be wholly unbiased.[104]

In the face of such evidence, the Committee was of the opinion:

> that the Railway Commission should be empowered, from time to time, by law to name one Auditor to act in conjunction with the two Auditors named by the several Companies, or to act singly in case of neglect on the part of the Companies to appoint such Auditors, or of a refusal or neglect of such local Auditors to act . . . it is obvious that the whole success of the measure will depend upon the character and the abilities of the Public Auditors selected. They . . . should therefore be selected from their character for integrity, and from their knowledge and experience, and from such qualifications entitled to public confidence.

The Committee recommended the adoption of Quilter's triple account system and also that of a system of keeping separate accounts for different branches of the same company. One of the main drawbacks of many of the existing railway accounts was the failure to distinguish between income and capital and on this the Committee said: 'it is impossible to overrate the importance of the strictest adherence to an invariable separation between the Capital and the Income of Railway Companies.'[105] In total, the Report reflected a very thorough examination of the problems of railway company accounts in the late 1840s and suggested sensible and straightforward ways of improving both the information contained in the accounts and the credibility of that information. The report's recommendations were, however, not implemented until twenty years later in the Regulation of Railways Act 1868.

On 26 February 1850 a public meeting was held in London to establish a Railway Shareholders' Audit Association. One of the speeches delivered at that meeting by Thomas Buckton, described as 'Railway and General Auditor and Accountant; (lately Secretary to the London, Brighton and South Coast Railway; previously General Superintendent and Accountant of the London and Brighton Railway Company); one of the Vice-Presidents of the Institut d'Afrique at Paris; author of *China Trade, Western Australia*, etc.,', was highly critical of the state of railway audit and accounting. Buckton commented that in his experience very few shareholders ever took the time to look at the accounts and if they did they were rarely competent to know anything about them. He claimed that he had not known any auditor who had reported on railway accounts in the spirit of the Act and advocated the necessity of a fuller and more independent audit.[106]

The Joint Stock Companies Act 1856 did introduce one of the findings of the Select Committee in removing the requirement for an auditor, if appointed, to be a shareholder in the company; but again, the auditor was only required to report on the Balance Sheet and to examine the accounts and vouchers relating to it. Most important for auditors, the audit requirements were contained in Table B of the Act - Regulations for Management of the Company - and were therefore not compulsory since directors had the choice of adopting Table B or compiling regulations specific to their company. The Joint Stock Companies Act 1862 continued this policy by placing the audit requirements in Table A which companies could opt out of by preparing their own Articles of Association. Pixley, in a paper delivered to the Liverpool Society of Chartered Accountants in 1904, explained the lack of compulsory audit at this time by commenting that: 'One can only assume that auditing at that time was generally recognised as the farce it really was.'[107]

This continued abandonment of the principle of compulsory audit for companies in general meant that legislation was provided for specific groups of companies as the necessity for it was deemed to arise. Under the Railway Companies (Scotland) Act 1867, prior to the declaration of a dividend, the auditors were required to certify that the half-yearly accounts contained 'a full and true Statement of the financial Condition of the Company.' Additionally, the auditors had the right to give extra information to the shareholders of the company at any time regarding the financial condition and prospects of the company which they might deem to constitute material information for the shareholders.[108]

Although railway companies were now required to employ some sort of auditor, there were still strong views being expressed against the suggestion that an audit was necessary. A.B. Hyde, giving evidence to the Select Committee on the Limited Liability Acts, stated that 'the system of audit is a bad system for large companies, and I think that it will be found that, at some future day, it will lead to fraud.' He expressed the opinion that an audit should not be compulsory since it led to false security and was not at all efficient. As a substitute he recommended a return to the earlier system: 'if it was left to the directors and officers, then the public would have the opportunity of knowing who the directors and officers were, and of trusting them if they liked it.'[109] Hyde apparently saw little of value in the performance of professional audits, which is perhaps surprising given that his evidence was being offered to a Select Committee which had been appointed as a result of the 1866 financial panic following the failure of Overend, Gurney & Co.. Cottrell commented that:

> Little of the factual evidence of the substantial incidence of abuse and near-fraud during the 1860's financial boom made any impact upon members of the Select Committee, who similarly took no heed of the large number of calls for the tightening up of the law in order to protect the investor.[110]

The Regulation of Railways Act 1868 removed the necessity

for the auditor to be a shareholder and gave the Board of Trade the power to appoint an additional auditor if so requested by the members of the company. This was unlikely to have much effect on auditing but the Act did contain other provisions which were bound to have an impact on the work of the auditor in that it required the preparation of audited accounts and balance sheet at least half-yearly.[111] The First Schedule of the Act detailed the form of the accounts referred to in Section 3 and listed fifteen different statements that had to be provided. Half of the statements dealt with matters pertaining to the capital account, the remainder dealing with receipts and payments, appropriation, abstracts of expenditure, track authorised and constructed, train mileage and a general balance sheet. This Act must have imposed a greatly increased burden on railway company accountants and auditors and have led railway companies to consider the appointment of professional auditors with the skills necessary to audit these detailed statements.

In 1868, the accountancy profession was still in its infancy and it was often difficult to distinguish, particularly in England where no professional body had been formed, between a competent auditor and one claiming to be a professional auditor. Certainly Pixley, writing in 1881, stated that:

> One of the most important qualifications an Auditor should possess is a thorough knowledge of, and experience in, Commercial Book-keeping, but . . . (very often unfortunately for themselves) a meeting of Shareholders does not always in its selection of an Auditor take this into consideration.

Commenting further on the appointment of an auditor: 'One of the most absurd qualifications, and yet the one most frequently put forward by a candidate, is the fact of his being a Shareholder and for this reason alone most incompetent persons are frequently selected to fulfil the office.'[112] Pixley was only expressing his personal view of the amateur approach which he saw with regard to auditing but Joseph Slocombe, a Birmingham accountant, said of amateur auditors in 1882 'Their number is thinning down year by year, and some of you may probably live to see the day when the amateur auditor will be almost extinct as the dodo. The non-professional auditor is generally a man of business - frequently retired - whose friends think he has an aptitude for figures and investigation.'[113]

Although the 1868 Act specified detailed accounts and required the auditor to report on the company's financial position, Dicksee suggested that the burden was not as onerous as might first have been thought and, writing in 1892, he stated that railway companies had accountants and audit staff to do the detailed work. He also disagreed with Slocombe's statement on the demise of the amateur auditor: 'All professional Auditors would like to share Mr Slocombe's pious hope for the ultimate extinction of the amateur Auditor; but some will doubt whether that consummation is very appreciably nearer than it was when the words . . . were spoken.'[114]

It was not until the passing of the Companies Act of 1900 that all companies were required to appoint an auditor. Lee argued that the reintroduction of compulsory audit was probably in response to the high economic failure rate over the period from 1862 to 1904, adding that the reintroduction was aimed at the prevention and detection of fraud and error in the accounts.[115] Although the Act did not require the auditor to be a suitably qualified accountant, it would appear that in some areas of work that was the case, since Brown noted in 1905 'it may safely be said that the audit of the accounts of all the leading railways in the kingdom is now in the hands of professional accountants.'[116]

(*b*) *Railway company auditing in Scotland*

The number of railway companies in existence in the United Kingdom and abroad can be assessed by referring to the alphabetical listings in successive editions of *Bradshaw's Railway Manuals and Directories*. (Table 6.1)

In Scotland there was a steady growth in the number of companies during the 1850s followed by a steady reduction generally caused by companies amalgamating, rather than by companies failing. Railway company formation reached a peak in Scotland ten years earlier than in the rest of the United Kingdom, where the peak occurred in 1870.

The information contained in subsequent editions of *Bradshaw's* was not produced in uniform format, which is hardly surprising considering the lack of uniform disclosure in railway

TABLE 6.1

Railway Companies Listed

Year	England, Wales and Ireland	Scotland	Total
1848	106	28	134
1849	104	28	132
1850	97	28	125
1851	117	29	146
1852	127	28	155
1853	128	26	154
1854	225	40	265
1855	177	30	207
1856	187	35	222
1857	201	42	243
1858	209	47	256
1859	212	49	261
1860	230	52	282
1865	364	47	411
1870	400	30	430
1875	392	35	427
1880	324	28	352
1885	291	27	318
1890	277	25	302
1895	249	28	277
1900	229	27	256

Source: *Bradshaw's Railway Almanac, Directory, Shareholders' Guide and Manual; Bradshaw's General Railway Directory, Shareholders' Guide, Manual, and Almanack; Bradshaw's General Shareholders' Guide, Manual, and Railway Directory; Bradshaw's Shareholders' Guide, Railway Manual and Directory*

accounts. In some editions, and for some companies, more detail was given than in others but, generally, the emphasis was on disclosure of capital changes, expansion and dividend payments. Some large items of expenditure were separately listed, but only those for rolling stock purchases were consistently disclosed. The directors of each company were noted, as were the secretary, engineer and solicitors, and, in many cases, the auditors.

The incidence of railway company audit for the period from 1848 to 1900 varied considerably (Table 6.2) and these figures might seem to suggest that railway audit became less common towards the end of the nineteenth century. However, several new companies appeared in each of the years in question, while existing companies were either failing or amalgamating. Of the twenty-eight railway companies listed in the 1848 edition of *Bradshaw's*, only three, the Caledonian, Great North of Scotland and North British, were still listed in 1900. The fifteen companies listed in 1900 and not disclosing auditors can be readily explained. One of them was leased to another company which would then have been responsible for its accounting and auditing and none of the remaining fourteen had begun to operate by 1900. Many companies during the period examined were taken over before they began to operate and so never produced accounts or had auditors. It must be remembered that railway companies, during the second half of the nineteenth century, formed a constantly changing population and the explanations for the absence of auditors in earlier years are the same as those for 1900. There was a significant increase in the number of listed auditors from 1854 onwards and since no legislation affecting railway companies was passed to take effect in that year the most likely cause was the formation of the Edinburgh and Glasgow chartered bodies in 1853. This could have been an influence in one of two ways: either members of the chartered bodies who had previously acted as auditors of certain railway companies were anxious to display the involvement of the new Societies and therefore encouraged disclosure of their involvement, perhaps as a means of indirectly advertising their expertise in this area; or, the directors of railway companies were so impressed by the formation of the accounting societies that they began to employ chartered accountants to do this audit work as a means of increasing the credibility of the figures in the accounts. It is difficult to weigh the influence of these, but both were probably

TABLE 6.2

Auditors of Scottish Railway Companies

Year	Companies Listed	Companies Listing Auditors	% Companies Listing Auditors
1848	28	4	14.3
1849	28	2	7.1
1850	28	2	7.1
1851	29	4	13.8
1852	28	3	10.7
1853	26	3	11.5
1854	40	22	55.0
1855	30	23	76.7
1856	35	23	65.7
1857	42	30	71.4
1858	47	34	72.3
1859	49	37	75.5
1860	52	41	78.8
1865	47	37	78.7
1870	30	24	80.0
1875	35	23	65.7
1880	28	20	71.4
1885	27	18	66.7
1890	25	18	72.0
1895	28	16	57.1
1900	27	12	44.4

Source: *Bradshaw's Railway Almanac, Directory, Shareholders' Guide and Manual, 1848, etc.*

contributing factors.

Not all of the railway auditors were accountants but by 1900 chartered accountants were either completely or partly responsible for the audit of all of the railway companies in operation in Scotland (Table 6.3).

The only Aberdeen company consistently showing auditors was the Great North of Scotland with John Smith, advocate, Aberdeen and R.R. Notman continuing in partnership until 1854, when Notman was described as an accountant in London and when his joint auditor was shown as R. Fletcher, accountant, Aberdeen. In 1867 Fletcher is shown as joint auditor with J.A. Sinclair, accountant, Aberdeen, and Fletcher continued to hold this post until at least 1875, in spite of the fact that he had moved to London to practise some years earlier; the move being to assist in the reorganisation of the London, Chatham and Dover Railway.[117] In 1880 Sinclair was joined by William Milne, an Aberdeen chartered accountant, a partnership which continued until Sinclair's death in 1891.[118] From then until 1900 Milne, who had spent the earlier part of his professional life in Edinburgh accountancy circles, was joint auditor with J. Robertson-Durham, an Edinburgh chartered accountant. With the exception of Notman, who left Aberdeen to work in London, all the auditors of the Great North of Scotland were or became chartered accountants. The Great North of Scotland - Eastern Extension became the Scottish North Eastern in 1856 and from then until 1865 was audited by George Marquis, accountant, Aberdeen and James Morison, accountant, Perth.

Although this group of companies had been launched by the same people they did not continue to have the same auditors. The Aberdeen Railway company which was formed in 1845 disappeared from *Bradshaw's* between 1849 and 1853 and on its reappearance in 1854 listed as auditors, Notman and George Marquis. This partnership continued until 1857 when Marquis was joined by James Morison, accountant, Perth, there being no further mention of the company, which presumably amalgamated with another one. Marquis became a member of the Aberdeen Society but Morison, although responsible for founding a thriving accounting firm in Perth, died in 1878 before membership of the three Scottish societies was opened to accountants practising outwith the three cities.[119]

The Alford Valley Railway Company appears in the 1848

TABLE 6.3

Occupation of Auditors of Scottish Railway Companies

Year	Companies listing Auditors	CA only No.	CA only %	Auditors Part CA No	Auditors Part CA %	Others No.	Others %
1848	4	-		4	100.0	-	
1849	2	-		2	100.0	-	
1850	2	-		2	100.0	-	
1851	4	-		4	100.0	-	
1852	3	-		3	100.0	-	
1853	3	-		2	66.7	1	33.3
1854	22	5	22.7	7	31.8	10	45.5
1855	23	4	17.4	9	39.1	10	43.5
1856	23	6	26.1	7	30.4	10	43.5
1857	30	9	30.0	13	43.3	8	26.7
1858	34	12	35.2	11	32.4	11	32.4
1859	37	12	32.4	12	32.4	13	35.2
1860	41	13	31.7	13	31.7	15	36.6
1865	37	12	32.4	7	18.9	18	48.7
1870	24	12	50.0	1	4.2	11	45.8
1875	23	12	52.2	1	4.3	10	43.5
1880	20	9	45.0	1	5.0	8	40.0
1885	18	14	77.8	-	-	4	22.2
1890	18	14	77.8	1	5.5	3	16.7
1895	16	11	68.8	5	31.2	-	-
1900	12	10	83.3	2	16.7	-	-

Source: Bradshaw's Railway Almanac, Directory, Shareholders' Guide and Manual, 1848, etc.

Bradshaw's as a line on which work had not yet commenced and was not listed between 1852 and 1858. In 1851, its auditors were Smith and Notman but in 1858 they were shown as Fletcher and Sinclair who continued in this office until the late 1860s, when the company disappeared from the directory. The Deeside had a similar sort of audit history with Smith and Notman being listed in 1848 and no note of the company from then until 1854, when they were still listed as auditors. In 1855 Notman joined forces with Sinclair, who in 1857 became joint auditor with Marquis, this partnership continuing until 1875, when the company ceased to exist. Again, the fact that all of those Aberdeen railway companies appointed as auditors men who were accountants and who almost without exception became members of the Aberdeen Society of Accountants indicated either that Aberdeen entrepreneurs appreciated the need to appoint auditors who understood accounts, or that the small group of Aberdeen accountants quickly developed a near-monopoly of this work.

Further evidence of this near-monopoly can be seen in later railway companies in the vicinity of Aberdeen. The Banff Macduff and Turiff Railway was audited by Fletcher and H. A. Smith, an Aberdeen actuary, from its first listing in 1857 until it disappeared in the late 1860s as was the Fortmartine and Buchan Company from 1860 until its closure in the late 1860s. The Montrose and Bervie line is listed in 1870 and 1875 as having Marquis and James Meston for auditors and in 1880 as having Meston and Harvey Hall. In 1875 Fletcher and Meston were shown as being auditors of the Aboyne and Braemar Railway Company. Only eleven auditors appear to have been involved in railway company work in the Aberdeen area and ten of them were accountants. Eight of these ten were or became chartered accountants and it is arguable that the other two would have, had one not moved to London and the other been debarred through being in practice in Perth.

Two auditors were appointed for each company and, for the companies disclosing auditors, these appointments were increasingly awarded to chartered accountants so that, by 1900, seventy-five per cent of Scottish railway auditing was completely in the hands of professionals and the remaining twenty-five per cent partly so. This movement towards professionalization seemed to accelerate from 1880 onwards. Certainly James McClelland did not consider railway work to be of any significance to accountants earlier than that, since he made no reference to it in a lecture, given in 1869, detailing the areas of work that were important to accountants.[120] This, in spite of the fact that he had been employed as one of the auditors of the Monkland Railway from 1854 to 1865.

Given that many of the leading accountants in Edinburgh, Glasgow and Aberdeen were involved in the audit of railways and other commercial concerns, it is surprising to discover that there is no mention of this work in any of the petitions submitted by the three Scottish chartered accountants' societies in applying for a Charter. The involvement of professionals was apparently also considered relatively slight by Pixley, since he noted in 1881 that it was unfortunate that the majority of auditors were not professionals.[121]

By the end of the nineteenth century matters had changed, and in 1894 Howden, President of the Edinburgh Society of Accountants, referred to the introduction of the railway system as being one of the factors which had contributed to rescue the profession from obscurity. In Howden's opinion, the demand for satisfactory audit arose from the damage which resulted from the speculative mania that raged through the railway's financial system. This was aggravated by the fact that such large schemes, requiring huge amounts of capital, were in many cases supervised completely by directors who were neither independent nor skilled in accounting matters. As a result:

> a supreme moment in the history of the profession appears to have arrived. The public wanted, and would not be satisfied with less than, an independent professional superintendence of the expenditure which was going forward, so that their interests might be protected. Clearly, therefore, it was the profession of accountants whose services were desired, and whether the name of 'auditor' was known before, it was now and onwards to receive greater significance than it had yet attained.[122]

The auditors of companies not employing a chartered accountant to assist in the audit were either lawyers, bankers, other accountants, or were given no designation. Assuming that a professional person would have identified himself as belonging to a professional group, we can assume that non-designated auditors were not lawyers, bankers or accountants.

One possible explanation for the appointment of non-professional railway auditors was the location of a particular railway line. In companies located other than in the vicinity of Edinburgh, Glasgow or Aberdeen, it was normal for the auditors to be appointed from men in the local community. Since many of those lines were financed by local investors, it is understandable that the directors preferred as auditors men who were known to these investors. Thus, the auditors were accountants who could not be members of the chartered societies because they did not live or work in Edinburgh, Glasgow or Aberdeen. Examples of this category would be W. Myles and J. Sturrock of Dundee who audited the Dundee & Perth and the Dundee & Arbroath Companies; J. Morison from Perth who was widely involved in railway company audit; W. Grant from Elgin who audited the Morayshire railway and J. Young, a London accountant who was involved with the audit of the Caledonian Railway from 1857 to 1895. Young was a partner in Turquand Youngs, London but he originated in Moray and went to London to work with Robert Fletcher of the Aberdeen Society of Accountants who spent most of his professional life in London.[123]

There were only two instances where both auditors were members of the legal profession, the Findhorn and Wigtownshire Companies. Generally, a lawyer was paired with either an accountant or a banker, presumably so that one could provide the financial expertise and the other could ensure that the railway company was operating within the law. Such appointments must cast doubts on the quality of the audit work being done at that time but perhaps these short, local lines had no real need of the services of one or two chartered accountants. As these smaller lines either closed or were amalgamated with larger companies, the involvement of this non-chartered accountant group completely disappeared, there being no mention of it after 1890. In those cases where the company was audited by a chartered accountant along with another, the most common combination was that of a chartered and a non-chartered accountant. There were also a few examples of chartered accountants being teamed with lawyers, bankers and actuaries or with another auditor who was named, but his occupation was not revealed and this group steadily diminished during the period apart from the odd increase in 1895.

The amount of work involved in the audit of the larger railway companies must have been considerable since the Regulation of Railways Act of 1868 required the preparation and audit of accounts at six-monthly intervals. The heavy burden of responsibility which lay upon railway auditors is indicated by the fact that, by 1894, railway companies had total authorised capital of £1050 million.[124] *Bradshaw's* published excerpts from the most recent six-monthly accounts, which occasionally disclosed auditors' fees and expenses separately, but which more commonly included them under the heading 'fees for direction and audit.' When the audit fees were disclosed separately, there is no indication as to whether they were for six months or for a year, so it is difficult to interpret the figures. None of the figures quoted is very large. The Scottish Central paid fees of £137 in 1857 and the Stirling and Dunfermline paid £241 10*s* in 1855 and an auditors' allowance of £346 in 1858; the latter company was the only one to have four auditors as compared with the statutory two. The auditors of the Crieff Junction only received £15 in 1857, and those of the Castle Douglas and Dumfries Company, a fee plus expenses amounting to £11 in 1859. The two Glasgow chartered accountants who shared the audit of the Glasgow, Dumbarton and Helensburgh Company received a fee of £20 for both 1859 and 1860, this amount also being the fee for the audit of the Kirkcudbright Company in 1865.

Some of the larger Scottish railway companies also employed accountants, the need for bookkeepers and clerks being increased by the detailed accounting requirements of the Regulation of Railways Act 1868. The Scottish Central listed an accountant in 1848, before the line had opened. In 1850 D. Rankine was noted as being the treasurer, accountant and cashier of the Caledonian Railway and George Hodge the accountant and cashier of the Caledonian and Dunbartonshire Junction. Henry Watson was the accountant of the Edinburgh Perth and Dundee railway in 1850 but, in 1854, after the formation of the Edinburgh Society of Accountants of which he was a founder member, he was listed as one of the auditors with a new accountant for the company. Similarly, Walter Mackenzie was the accountant of the Caledonian and Dubartonshire Junction in 1854 and one of its auditors by 1856. The Glasgow and South Western was the only Scottish railway company to list an Audit Inspector who presumably filled the role of internal auditor. After the formation of the chartered accountants' societies no chartered accountants could have been employed as full-time railway accountants, since the rules of the societies required that members be in public practice.

So, by the end of the nineteenth century, another area of work had become almost exclusively the domain of the chartered accountants. However, the actual amount of railway audit work was very limited and had declined during the century. Certainly there was no increase in the work to compare with the increase in the number of chartered accountants during the same period.

5. Emigration of Accountants

The development of legislation over the second half of the nineteenth century undoubtedly led to a gradual but steady increase in the opportunities for accountants. However, in many cases certain classes of companies actually went further than required by legislation in, for example, requiring annual audit prior to the passing of the Companies Act 1900. Given the various scandals that had appeared at this time in areas such as banking and in railway companies it is hardly surprising to see groups of companies working to regain the trust of investors and their respectability through improving their accounting information by the employment of auditors. The fact that, in many cases, Scottish chartered accountants had by the end of the century built up a monopoly in certain areas can be attributed to various factors. First, over the years they must have convinced such companies that a qualified accountant would do a better job than an unqualified one and second, it would appear that companies gradually came to the conclusion that an audit certificate signed by a chartered accountant carried with it a guarantee of quality.

This followed the same pattern as the near-monopoly in bankruptcy but the development of this new work was insufficient to compensate for the decline in the volume of bankruptcy work and the increase in the number of Scottish chartered accountants by the end of the nineteenth century. This was a problem that was obviously of concern to the profession at that time, since Brown commented on it in 1904. He saw a partial solution to the problem in the further development of work in joint-stock companies and in complicated taxation disputes. However it would appear that he also foresaw continuing and expanding opportunities for the Scottish chartered accountant abroad when he stated that:

> in many parts of the civilised world the accountant is still unknown. In other parts where he has only just presented himself before the public, these words of wise and far-seeing men may perhaps strengthen his courage and endue him with a proper pride; and for further encouragement, let us only add in conclusion that, if we read the signs of the times aright, a far greater measure of development all over the world awaits the profession during the next fifty years than that which we have witnessed during the half century which has just elapsed.[125]

Brown further noted that, at November 1904, twenty-six per cent of the membership of the three Scottish accounting societies were practising outside Scotland, with almost eleven per cent of the total membership practising overseas. This does not appear to have been at all unusual; in 1896 it was claimed that twenty-five per cent of the members of the Edinburgh Society practised in England and that of the thirty-two members of the Aberdeen Society, 'there are in ordinary practice in Aberdeen, as accountants, only 7, the remaining 25 being either out of Scotland or engaged in business, not as accountants, but as solicitors, stockbrokers, and in other occupations.'[126]

This outflow of accountants is explained quite simply by the fact that the needs of Scotland were adequately met, with one chartered accountant per 6500 of population, whereas England and Wales, with one for every 10,500, had scope to absorb more.[127] However, it was a concern which had been in existence for some years as can be seen by a letter from 'An Embryo Accountant' in 1883 who was in despair as to his opportunities in the United Kingdom and was asking for advice with regard to opportunities in the Colonies.[128]

Table 6.4 shows that the Edinburgh Society was the largest exporter of accountants, followed by Aberdeen and then by Glasgow. The percentages are, if anything, on the conservative side since

TABLE 6.4

Comparison of residence at death of members of three socieites 1854-1904

	Edinburgh		Glasgow		Aberdeen	
Edinburgh and District	276	49.7	20	3.5	-	-
Glasgow and District	9	1.6	306	53.7	2	2.9
Aberdeen and District	1	0.2	1	0.2	37	52.8
Dundee and District	6	1.1	19	3.3	2	2.9
Other Scottish Locations	25	4.5	28	4.9	1	1.4
Total Scotland	317	57.1	374	65.6	42	60.0
London	37	6.7	24	4.2	3	4.3
Others England	56	10.1	44	7.7	3	4.3
Ireland	3	0.5	1	0.2	1	1.4
Abroad	70	12.6	61	10.7	6	8.6
Not Known	72	13.0	66	11.6	15	21.4
	555	100.0	570	100.0	70	100.0

Sources: Scottish Records Office, the *Accountants Magazine*, R. Brown, *History of Accounting and Accountants*, (Edinburgh 1904), J.C. Stewart, *Pioneers of a Profession*, (Edinburgh 1977).

obituaries of chartered accountants dying in Scotland often state that the member had practised in England or abroad and had returned to Scotland on retirement.

These trends continued and there was a steady increase in the number practising abroad from thirty-three in 1896 to ninety-seven in 1904 compared with an apparent reluctance to practise in towns in Scotland other than those in which the Societies were established and the additional reluctance of Glasgow members to practice in Edinburgh and vice versa. Of the three societies, Glasgow was the one which consistently exported the lowest proportion of its members a fact which might be explained by there being more opportunities for employment of accountants in the industrial west of Scotland at that time than in other areas. It was claimed in 1909 that approximately thirty-three per cent of all Scottish chartered accountants practised outside Scotland.[129]

Without doubt, the most popular country for resettlement was England with large numbers working in London. These Scottish chartered accountants were not entirely welcome in England, indeed the *Accountant* was accused of being absurdly hostile to them.[130] But the Association of Scottish Chartered Accountants in London appears to have been confident of the demand for their services and the opportunities still open to them when it stated: 'There is room enough in England for all. The number of qualified accountants there is still a long way short of the number in Scotland in proportion to the population.'[131]

In earlier years the most popular destination for emigrating Scottish accountants was the United States of America, but this was closely followed by South Africa, a few men having stayed there or returned after service in the Boer War. India was next in line, followed by Canada. Other countries where accountants are known to have settled include Australia, Ceylon, Philippines, Japan, China, Ethiopia, Gibraltar, Switzerland, Egypt, South America, Polynesia, Russia, Belgium, New Zealand, Siam, West Indies and France.

United States of America

All three societies exported accountants to America and John Niven of the Edinburgh Society had the honour, in 1924, of being elected

President of the American Institute of Accountants.[132] Another Edinburgh member, Edward Fraser, was deeply involved in the profession as is evidenced by an award made to him for twenty-three years of service to the Missouri State Board of Accounting.[133] The most famous Glasgow accountant to go to America was James Marwick who had first tried his luck in Australia, but then went to New York and formed the partnership of Marwick, Mitchell and Co.[134] which was to be one of the founding firms of KPMG Peat Marwick McLintock.

South Africa

In 1894, a group of accountants in the Transvaal formed The Institute of Accountants and Auditors in the South African Republic and by November 1894 it was attracting attention from the Society of Accountants and Auditors in England.[135] The reason for this interest was stated to be the securing of 'the complete trustworthiness of the accountants on whom the investing public in the last resort depends.'[136] The real reason may well have been the desire of the Society to increase its membership since James Martin, Secretary of the Society of Accountants and Auditors embarked on a trip to South Africa at the end of 1894. A report on his trip showed that he had been responsible for the formation of a South African committee with the intention of legalising the profession and introducing registration for accountants in South Africa.[137]

Progress in the area of registration was interrupted by the outbreak of the Boer War, but it also ran into difficulties because the articles of the Society limited the scope of its activities to the United Kingdom, British Dominions, dependencies and colonies. In 1903, after the end of the Boer War, the Society approved the affiliation of the Institute of Accountants and Auditors in the Transvaal (formerly the South African Republic) as the Transvaal Branch of the Society.[138]

However, this move did not meet with unanimous approval from the members of the Transvaal Society. In particular:

> this did not suit the [Scottish] chartered accountants, who, while supporting the local institute so long as it

> was an independent body, had no wish to become merged in an English Society which continued to admit members without examination. They preferred to maintain their separate identity as chartered accountants, with all the guarantee of professional efficiency which that title conveys.[139]

At that time, there were reputed to be thirty-six chartered accountants in South Africa with the likelihood of a considerable increase in numbers and in January 1903, a number of them formed the Institute of Chartered Accountants in South Africa.[140] Initially, the members were of the opinion that it would be sensible and beneficial for men who were apprenticed to members of the Institute to become members of one of the three Scottish institutes, but this suggestion was not acceptable to the home bodies.[141]

Attempts to provide for the registration of accountants in the United Kingdom has continued to be fruitless but the change in government and move towards the reorganisation of many areas in South Africa after the war led the members of the Transvaal Branch of the Society of Accountants and Auditors to believe that progress on that front would be successful.[142] Accordingly, a joint committee of the Society and the Institute met and agreed upon terms and the necessary legislation was passed in August 1904, allowing registration to residents in the Transvaal, to members of the Transvaal Branch of the Society of Accountants and Auditors, or members of any of the five Chartered societies or the Society of Accountants and Auditors in the United Kingdom. Brown conceded that although this was not an ideal solution, it did at least ensure 'that only those who registered shall be permitted to describe themselves to the public by the title which implies proper qualification for undertaking such work.'[143]

Of the population studied, thirteen Glasgow chartered accountants and fourteen Edinburgh chartered accountants are known to have gone to work in South Africa. Little is known of the Glasgow chartered accountants, apart from James Leisk who stayed in South Africa after war service and became chairman and managing director of the National Bank of South Africa,[144] but a few of the Edinburgh members are known to have made some contribution to accountancy in South Africa, most notably James Findlay who became Professor of Accounting at the South African School of Mines and Technology, Johannesburg. Robert Hemphill who went to South Africa during the Boer War stayed on to work in the Repatriation Department and then went into public practice in Johannesburg, and at one time was President of the Transvaal Society of Accountants.[145] James Douglas went to practice in Cape Town immediately he was admitted to membership of the Edinburgh Society in 1904 becoming one of the founders of the Cape Society of Accountants and Auditors and its first Secretary; he also served two periods as President from 1924-6 and 1944-6.[146] Peter Warden went to practise in South Africa in 1897 because of his health and later became Town Clerk of Salisbury.[147] T. Cullen Young qualified in 1902 but decided to be a missionary and went to Livingstonia in 1904 where among his duties were the teaching of commercial subjects and maintenance of the mission accounts.[148]

Canada

Although eleven Edinburgh chartered accountants and ten Glasgow chartered accountants are known to have gone to Canada to practice, little is known about their progress there. Canada had several accounting societies, the earliest known being the Association of Accountants in Montreal which was formed in 1880.[149] Subsequently associations were formed in Ontario, Nova Scotia, Manitoba and British Columbia.

Scottish chartered accountants are known to have had connections with four of these associations. Joseph Bell of the Edinburgh Society spent some years as a member of the Manitoba Society, but settled in London after the First World War.[150] James Hutchinson went to Montreal two years after being admitted to membership of the Edinburgh Society and was President of the Montreal Society in 1919.[151] William Stein of Edinburgh was the first President of the Institute of Chartered Accountants of British Columbia and Thomas Sime of the Glasgow Society was elected President of the Ontario Institute of Chartered Accountants in 1917.[152] Members of the Scottish societies continued to go to Canada to practise and by the end of 1936 there were reckoned to be forty-four Scottish chartered accountants in Montreal alone.[153]

The presence of Scottish chartered accountants in so many corners of the old Empire arose because of various factors. Records show that many of those who practised in South Africa first went there as a result of the Boer War. Some who went to other countries went into occupations other than public practice and perhaps had family or business contacts. Mainly though, young Scottish chartered accountants left Scotland because they could see that the profession in Scotland was becoming crowded and that the best prospects for their future lay in the uncrowded and comparatively undeveloped colonies.[154]

The profession had the reputation of being more adaptable than most and therefore opening opportunities for success in any country to which members went.[155] There was an acute shortage of qualified men in the colonies and there can be little doubt that Scottish chartered accountants were 'in demand in all parts of the world.'[156]

VII

The Establishment of Entry Standards

1. Introduction

If the newly-formed accounting profession was to be successful and to grow in size and in stature, it was necessary to attempt to exclude non-members from specific areas of work and to convince those using the services provided by accountants that a member of the Edinburgh or Glasgow societies was the most competent person to fulfil their needs, 'the main thing was to create a preference for the qualified man as against the unqualified, and to maintain professional standards.'[1]

Much of the basic framework of the new professions of the mid-nineteenth century was adapted from the examples of the so-called 'liberal professions' of the eighteenth century - the Church, medicine and law. Until well into the nineteenth century these professions had no written examinations and yet had very clearly conceived ideas as to the proper qualifications necessary for admission to professional standing. They assumed that anyone choosing to enter a liberal profession would have had a liberal education and that, before the population explosion of the nineteenth century, there would not be too many men of such liberal education and so professions would remain small in terms of numbers of members.

However, the Victorian age brought tremendous growth in industry and the development of technology. 'Victorian business was

TABLE 7.1

Admission to membership of three Scottish Chartered Societies

Year of Admission	Edinburgh	Glasgow	Aberdeen	Total
1854	65			65
1855	18	58		76
1856	1	3		4
1857	1	6		7
1858	1	-		1
1859	1	-		1
1860	6	-		6
1861	2	2		4
1862	2	3		5
1863	3	1		4
1864	6	-		6
1865	3	-		3
1866	1	1		2
1867	2	6	12	20
1868	4	2	-	6
1869	6	7	1	14
1870	3	10	-	13
1871	8	2	1	11
1872	6	4	-	10
1873	8	4	1	13
1874	3	-	2	5
1875	6	3	-	9
1876	4	4	3	11
1877	8	16	1	25
1878	9	8	1	18
1879	4	5	-	9
1880	8	4	4	16
1881	12	6	1	19
1882	13	6	-	19
1883	13	6	-	19
1884	14	3	1	18
1885	13	6	1	20
1886	20	11	1	32
1887	13	9	-	22
1888	10	7	1	18
1889	17	8	1	26
1890	10	10	1	21
1891	15	29	3	47
1892	11	18	3	32
1893	16	19	4	39
1894	11	20	1	32
1895	16	13	2	31
1896	14	19	1	34
1897	16	24	3	43
1898	18	29	2	49
1899	17	20	4	41
1900	16	23	2	41
1901	17	23	5	45
1902	16	25	3	44
1903	19	43	4	66
1904	29	44	-	73
	555	570	70	1195

Source: Society Minute Books and Records

a large employer of all the professions, both traditional and new; and it created several.'[2] With the emergence of the new professions there developed an almost structured approach to their formal organisation. On formation and in its early stages, a professional association was usually an unofficial body with no legal authority. Respectability was considered to be achieved on receipt of a Royal Charter which conferred official recognition by the State that the occupation concerned was worthy of professional status. Having achieved this recognition, the new professions saw their role as being to 'Reform: train: examine: inspect: these were the Victorian precepts which created a self-reproducing cadre of experts.'[3]

This approach to the creation of properly-qualified professions was not new: 'Training through apprenticeship and testing at the time of admittance to full membership were characteristic of the guild system.'[4] This approach was adopted by most of the new professions. Certainly, as far as accountancy was concerned; 'The leading principle of professional education was apprenticeship: learning by doing.'[5] and this principle has survived in Chartered Accountancy up to the present.

2. Society of Accountants in Edinburgh

(*a*) *Admission to Membership*

At the second meeting held on 22 January 1853 to discuss the formation of a Society of Accountants in Edinburgh, those present divided into groups: 'and arranged to wait upon the gentlemen who are to be requested to join the Institute who have not yet been seen.'[6] From that date until 31 January 1853, when the Institute formally came into being, membership was by invitation. It would seem reasonable to assume that those approached to be members were accountants in the city who were considered to be of sufficient standing to become members of a prestigious profession.

The need to be known to existing members continued after the Institute was formally established and paragraph 6 of the Constitution and Laws stated that: 'New Members are admitted into the Institute at any General Meeting, annual or special. They must be proposed by one Member, and seconded by another, and their election shall be carried by the votes of three-fourths of the Members present, ascertained by ballot.' This ruling appears to have been strictly adhered to since, when William Myrtle wrote to the Institute claiming a right to be admitted to membership, he was told that the list had closed on 31 January 1853 and that he would have to apply for admission according to the Laws of the Institute. Myrtle was admitted on 29 December 1854 at the special request of the Lord Advocate.[7] Somewhat surprisingly these regulations for the admission of new members were not entirely acceptable to the members of the Scottish legal profession, who, while approving of the new society since it consisted of 'nearly all the respectable Accountants in Edinburgh,' disapproved of what they saw as being insufficient provision of control over the admission of members. This and other comments led them to conclude that 'Altogether, the "Rules and Regulations" bear unsuitable evidence of having been hastily and crudely concocted.'[8] However, despite these criticisms, the Edinburgh accountants had achieved their principal objective, the formation of a recognised society.

(*b*) *Classes of Membership*

Initially there were two classes of membership in the Edinburgh Institute: 'Ordinary Members are Gentlemen who are engaged in practice in Edinburgh as professional Accountants - The Honorary Members consist of Gentlemen who have formerly practised as Accountants in Edinburgh, but who are now engaged in the management of Life Assurance or other public Companies in Edinburgh or elsewhere, or who hold Official Appointments in connection with the Courts.'[9] The annual subscription was set at two guineas per Ordinary Member and one guinea per Honorary Member.[10] This was critically commented on by the legal profession who were concerned that, although Honorary Members contributed to the funds, they were not involved in the management of the society and stated that this must be remedied. It is perhaps possible to assess the importance of the opinion of the legal profession to the society in Edinburgh at that time by the fact that the class of Honorary Member was dispensed with in 1854 at the time of the Petition for a Royal Charter, which was worded on the assumption that all the petitioners were practising accountants: 'That, in these circumstances, the

TABLE 7.2

Accountants listed as being in practice in Edinburgh

Year	Accountants	Edinburgh CAs	Members ICAEW	Total
1840-41	111	-	-	111
1850-51	132	-	-	132
* 1855-56	63	77	-	140
1860-61	56	73	-	129
1870-71	81	79	-	160
1880-81	93	117	-	210
1890-91	59	209	3	271
1900-01	57	232	1	290

Source: Edinburgh and Leith Post Office Directories

* Members of Society of Accountants in Edinburgh first identified as so being.

Petitioners were induced to form themselves into a Society called the Institute of Accountants in Edinburgh, with a view to unite into one body those at present practising the profession.'[11] The Institute could hardly terminate the membership of people whose support they had actively canvassed some months earlier and avoided this by giving the Honorary Members the opportunity to become Ordinary Members by paying up arrears of the difference between the two annual subscription rates. The minutes for 18 December 1854 show that thirteen members were known to have been Honorary Members, of whom seven chose to become Ordinary members and six declined and ceased membership of the society. Some of the seven had an interest in accountancy in addition to their stated occupation; four of them were involved in insurance, two as actuaries and two as officials of insurance companies, one was manager of the Edinburgh Savings Bank and the remaining two held appointments with the Courts.

In the period prior to the receipt of its Royal Charter of Incorporation no mention had been made by the Institute of any pre-entry test of competence. However, the Charter empowered the society to examine entrants and others:

> And we will and ordain that the Corporation shall have power from time to time, and in such manner as may be fixed by the bye-laws, rules, and regulations, to constitute and appoint a Committee of Examinators for the purpose of regulating and conducting such examinations of entrants and others as the Corporation may from time to time direct, and in such manner as they may appoint, in furtherance of the objects of the Society; and that the course of education to be pursued, and the amount of general and professional acquirements to be exacted from entrants, shall be such as the Corporation shall from time to time fix.

The Royal Charter of Incorporation which contained this enabling clause was dated 11 December 1854 and it was only a few months later that the Society of Accountants in Edinburgh recognised that: 'There is only one royal road to entrance to a profession, and that is by passing the professional examinations and acquiring professional training and experience;[12] and began to insist on the examination of entrants to the profession, both during their period of indenture as apprentices and on entry to membership. The Royal Charter also stated the need for members of the profession to have had a liberal education, but without enlarging on ways of judging this.

(*c*) *Apprenticeship*

On 7 February 1855 new Bye-laws, Rules and Regulations were adopted at a Stated General Meeting of the Society.[13] These were much more detailed than before, especially with regard to apprentices and admission. Bye-laws 37(2) and 37(3) provided transitional regulations for eligibility for examination and admission for a five-year period. The two groups covered by these Bye-laws were, first, those who had served an apprenticeship with a member of one of the legal bodies (Writers to the Signet, Society of Solicitors before the Supreme Courts of Scotland or Incorporated Society of Solicitors at Law) and who, after the completion of such apprenticeship, had been employed for at least three years in the chambers of a member or members of the Society and, second, those who had not served any apprenticeship but who were at least twenty-three years of age and had been employed for at least six years in the chambers of a member or members of the Society.

The most important part of Bye-law 37, however, was Section (1) which defined eligible candidates as those having served as apprentices under indenture to a member of the Society, duly recorded and discharged. Bye-law 38 stated that, after the five year transitional period, this would be the only way to qualify for examination and admission. The necessity to complete an articled apprenticeship with a member would certainly have constituted a barrier to entry to a large section of the population of Victorian Scotland. In order to embark on such a course the aspiring accountant would have to know a chartered accountant who would be prepared to accept him as an apprentice and also have access to sufficient funds to pay his indenture fee and to support him during the period of his apprenticeship. Since the indenture fee was set in 1855 at one hundred guineas to be paid on entering articles, the new profession was scarcely open to young men other than those from a professional or socially-privileged background.

The period of service under indentures was set at five years and the minimum age at sixteen, although the period of service could be reduced to as short a period as three years if the apprentice had previously been in legal chambers. The reduction in the period of articles was to be computed on the basis of two years legal training to one year accountancy training. In 1874 the Rules and Regulations removed the three year minimum requirement for articles in the case of service in a legal office, allowing deduction of one half of the time so spent, however the minimum requirement was reintroduced in 1877. By 1889 the minimum age for apprenticeship was raised to seventeen and remained so until at least 1904. The ability to reduce the period of indenture with a member of the Society by service in a legal office was still in force in 1904, and it was not until 1899 that holding a degree from any university in Great Britain or Ireland entitled the holder to a reduced apprenticeship of four years, although such a provision had been discussed in 1876.[14]

The effectiveness of these requirements in limiting applications for membership can be seen in the admission figures for the Society. At 1854, admissions stood at sixty-five and a further eighteen accountants were admitted in 1855. Current indentures in 1855, 1857 and 1858 were thirty-one, thirty-three and forty-seven respectively,[15] figures which might lead to an expectation of around twenty new members per year. However, records of admission to membership do not support this and in no year up to 1880 were more than nine new members admitted. Indeed, the average annual number of admissions to the Edinburgh Society between 1856 and 1880 was four.[16]

On completing his indenture and on passing the examinations, each candidate was required to pay an entry fee. In 1874 this was set at fifty guineas for all candidates, but for candidates who entered into indentures subsequently to 31 July 1888 the fee was raised to one hundred guineas.

An examination of the Register of Indentures recorded in Edinburgh reveals that, prior to the Bye-law and Rules of 7 February 1855 the apprentice fee could vary. Indenture Number One for James Latta shows a fee of £80 but this had been entered into on 21 December 1837, registered on 18 January 1855 and discharged on 29 January 1855 to prove Latta's qualification for membership.[17] The most common apprentice fee was one hundred guineas for indentures entered into prior to the formation of the Society, so the Bye-laws appear to have formalised a system already in operation.

There were some departures from this *norm*. Charles S. Murray's fee was one hundred and fifty guineas for a four year apprenticeship in 1850 and Dugald Kerr's ninety-nine pounds nineteen shillings. Duncan Mackenzie's fee was one hundred and twenty guineas and Archibald Horne jnr paid no fee at all, since he was indentured to his father. In some cases, part of the indenture fee was returned to the apprentice in the form of a small salary. Patrick Morison agreed to pay his apprentice James Small a salary in quarterly instalments of ten, fifteen and twenty pounds per annum for years one, two and three of his apprenticeship. Archibald Borthwick and Samuel Raleigh appear to have had the same approach, since they paid Alexander Dunlop jnr and James Molleson a salary of fifteen, twenty-five and thirty pounds for the first three years of their apprenticeship.[18]

What is clear from the records of the Edinburgh Society is the high level of indentures recorded compared with the extremely low level of admissions. Even in the early days of the Society, when long standing indentures were being formally recorded the Register shows that five of the first sixteen apprentices failed to become members. This pattern continued, since the list of indentures outstanding at 31 December 1873 shows a total of 130 apprentices, the indentures of eighty-three of whom had expired without the apprentices presenting themselves for examination, representing a drop out rate of sixty-four per cent.[19]

It is conceivable that some of the young men who embarked on an apprenticeship did not find the work to their liking and abandoned the profession before completing their period of indentures. Pixley, in 1897, did not consider that chartered accountancy was a career suited to all intellects, claiming that those who had studied mathematics were more likely to succeed than those who had studied classics.[20] He also raised the question of chances of success in the profession after qualifying, suggesting that passing the examinations and being admitted to membership was no guarantee of success. This view is reinforced by an article in the *Pall Mall Gazette* in 1890, stating that it was not advisable or prudent to become a chartered accountant without having capital of between two and three thousand pounds or influential friends in business circles. Of the two, the latter was considered to be more important but the best combination was to have both.[21] This situation obviously continued for many years since on 27 February 1902 disquiet was expressed as to the availability of jobs for apprentices passing their examinations or the ability of those passing the examinations to get jobs. The shortage of jobs in Scotland for qualified men can perhaps be judged from the fact that in 1903 approximately 125 Scottish chartered accountants were known to be practising in London and other parts of England,[22] and that, out of a total membership of 832, twenty-five per cent practised outside Scotland.[23]

Another reason for failing to complete articles may have been the offer of more attractive paid employment elsewhere. From the comment that the object of the system was to produce fully qualified chartered accountants: 'and not the creation of a half-formed class who look upon the examination Certificates merely as a means of getting better situations as Clerks'[24] it is apparent that the partly qualified accountant was a marketable product. Some young men such as Fred and John Moir who went on to found the African Lakes Company, regarded their time in an Edinburgh chartered accountant's office as part of their business training.[25]

Difficulty in passing the examinations is unlikely to have been a reason in the early stages of rather informal examination systems, but perhaps some who passed the examinations did not go into practice as public accountants and did not apply for admission. Finally, due to the prevalence in the nineteenth century of many diseases such as tuberculosis, it is possible that many teenage apprentices did not survive to complete their period of indenture.[26]

(*d*) *Examinations*

The 1855 Bye-laws required that all candidates for admission to the Society should be examined, but left the form and extent of the examination to the examinators. The subjects considered necessary for the practice of accounting at that time were listed as:

> algebra, including the use of logarithms - annuities - life assurances - life rents - reversions - book-keeping - framing of states under sequestrations, trusts, factories, executries - the Law of Scotland, especially that relating to Bankruptcy, private trust and arbitrating rights and preferences of creditors in rankings.

Very few of these subjects would be familiar to the present-day candidate, but they reflected the type of work undertaken by chartered accountants in the mid-nineteenth century. It is particularly noticeable that there is no mention of auditing.

The first minuted meeting of the Committee of Examinators took place on 22 March 1855.[27] At this meeting, eight young men produced evidence that they were eligible for examination having completed the required period of apprenticeship. They were examined on an informal basis - the minute makes no mention of the type of examination, but no formal written examination system was in operation at this time - by the President, the Secretary and four members of the Society. The Minute noted that all eight passed and received a Certificate of Qualification as provided by Article 40.

At this period, growth in the membership of the Society was slow and the Minutes often show candidates being examined singly. On 25 January 1856 the President, the Secretary and three Members examined James Haldane and reported that: 'the Committee after a careful examination found him qualified and granted the Certificate to that effect, as provided by Article 40 of the Society's laws.'[28] Again, no detail whatsoever was provided as to the subject matter or duration of this examination process. A little more information is found in 3 February 1858 when the Minutes state that: 'the Committee carefully examined him on Scotch Law: the general principles of Annuities and Assurance, and Book-keeping: and have great pleasure in reporting that he made a most creditable appearance and is well qualified to be admitted a member of the Society.'[29]

On 3 February 1863 the Minutes recorded a recommendation: 'that the Examinations should be conducted in writing' and in July 1864 the records, for the first time, laid down 'General Regulations, and Syllabus of Examinations for Candidates for Admission as Members of the Society'.[30] The General Regulations provided that examinations could be conducted viva voce or in writing, or both, and that each candidate should undergo two examinations, the first in October and the second in the following January.

The Syllabus of Examinations gave details of the amount of knowledge required in each subject area, as follows:

> *Arithmetic*: On the operations of addition, Subtraction, Multiplication, Division - both Simple and Compound Practice, Proportion, Compound Proportion, Interest, Simple and Compound Discount, Vulgar and Decimal Fractions, Square Root and Cube Root.
> *Algebra*: On the Simple Rules of Addition, Subtraction and Division - simple Equations - Quadratic Equations.
> *Annuities and Life Assurance*: Explanation will be required of the general principles on which Annuity

and Life Assurance transactions proceed; how Annuity Tables are framed, how Policies are valued; and the particulars of all different classes of Annuities and Assurances.

Logarithms: Explanation will be required how Logarithmic Tables are formed, and how they are used.

Book-Keeping: On the method of keeping Mercantile Books - Single and Double Entry; Bankers' Books, Insurance Company Books, Professional Books - such as WS or SSC.

Framing States: As to method of framing States in Sequestrations, Private Trusts, Factories - Judicial and others, Executries.

And in connexion with the preparation of these states as to the Management, generally - In Sequestrations - Particularly as to preparing Claims for ranking and Voting.

In Private Trusts - Particularly as to preparation of Claims and mode of Ranking.

In Judicial Factories - As to the requirements of the Act of Sederunt, 13 February 1730.

In Factories - As to the requirement of the 'Pupils Protection Act, 12 & 13 Vict Cap 51' and relative Acts of Sederunt (11 December 1849, etc.).

In Judicial Factories - Under 19 & 20 Vict Cap 79, and relative Act of Sederunt (25 November 1857).

In Executries.

Law of Scotland:

(1) The dates, import, and effect of the Statutes on which the original Bankrupt Law of Scotland was founded, and the principles thereby established applicable to alienations by Insolvents in favour of parties related to the Granters, and to transactions involving preferences to particular Creditors.

(2) The dates, import, and effect of the modern Sequestration Statutes, and the leading rules

of Law applicable to the administration of Bankrupt Estates.

(3) Specially the rules of Ranking of Creditors, secured and unsecured, at common law, and under the Statutes; and the mode of treating Claims against Companies and individual Partners, and upon Accommodation Bills.

(4) The dates, import, and effects of the Statutes and Acts of Sederunt relating to the estates and affairs of Minors and incapacitated persons, and to property subject to Judicial Factory, and the legal principles applicable to the powers and duties of the Officers appointed by the Court to manage such Estates.

(5) The principles of law and practice applicable to Judicial Reference and Private Arbitration, and the powers and duties of Arbiters acting under the same.

(6) The Law relating to Partnership, Personal Succession and Life Assurance.

This represented a formidable list of topics to be studied by aspiring chartered accountants from 1864 onwards, and it indicates the sort of work for which their training was designed to equip them. The provisions for arithmetic, algebra and logarithms were in order to enable them to cope with work on annuities and life assurance. In Edinburgh there were strong links between the Society of Accountants and the Faculty of Actuaries; indeed, five of the first fourteen Presidents of the former were also members of the latter.[31] The detailed requirements for the study of Scots Law suggest that a large proportion of the work of these early chartered accountants was in the management and winding up of Bankrupt Estates and Trusts and Judicial Factoring. Bookkeeping receives very scant attention and shows that there was little interest in becoming involved in mercantile work in preference to servicing the professions of Banking, Insurance and Law.

A contemporary comment on the necessity to study these subjects can be found in a copy of a lecture on 'The Origin and

Present Organisation of the Profession of Chartered Accountants in Scotland' by James McClelland, a President of the Institute of Accountants and Actuaries of Glasgow - partly published in the *Accountant* of December 1874,[32] but written and delivered more than five years previously. The first category of work mentioned by McClelland pertained to legal work:

> Besides the employment which accountants have always found under insolvency and bankruptcy, many of them, from time-to-time, have been engaged under the courts in remits relative to intricate accounts; in appointments as judicial factors for landed proprietors and deceased partners, and in numerous family trusts, needing men trained to keep accounts and analyse the wishes and directions of testators under family trusts.

In describing an apprentice's progress through his period of indentures, he notes that:

> he sees the necessity of becoming more intimately acquainted with the higher branches of arithmetic and algebra, with a more definite knowledge of the art of book-keeping, and learning for himself to note entries for books kept by double entry. His mind is led again to the knowledge of commercial, bankrupt, and civil law . . . he will find it necessary to study and make himself master of the various exchanges with foreign countries, to enable him to turn them into sterling values . . . in remits from the court - in adjustment of partnership accounts - in judicial factories for deceased, insane, or incapable parties - and in family trusts under wills of deceased parties . . . and another important area of Life Insurance, and of the preparation necessary in the higher branches of arithmetic and algebra, to make the student an expert in the necessary calculations and problems.

Given the preponderance of work relating to legal matters, it is not surprising to find a suggestion in 1865 that apprentices should attend the Scots Law, Conveyancing and Civil Law Classes at the University of Edinburgh,[33] although this did not become compulsory until the next major review of the examination system. The Council Minutes for 7 May 1869 show that examinators were not remunerated for their service, but there was a suggestion that perhaps they should be and 'the Secretary was instructed to make enquiries as to the practice which obtained in Societies of Writers to the Signet and Solicitors.'[34] The matter seems not to have been considered to be of crucial importance, since the Secretary's reply was not noted until 26 January 1870; 'he found the universal rule was that the Examinators acted without remuneration' - and the chartered accountants decided to follow suit.

The meeting of the Examinators of 3 January 1872 noted that Charles Pearson was still carrying out duties in this sphere although he was then seventy years of age and still in practice. However, the wind of change was beginning to be felt in the examination system. Brown noted that the examinations were 'from time-to-time rendered more exacting with the general advance of education and the introduction of competitive examinations into business life.'[35] Discussions began to take place as to how the system should be altered in order to ensure, firstly, that all applicants were of a sufficiently high educational standard to be admitted as apprentices and, secondly, to test their progress after they had served part of their apprenticeship. The revised Bye-laws, Rules and Regulations of the Society, which came into effect in 1874, stated the new conditions for apprentices: Paragraph 33: 'Every Applicant before entering into an indenture with a Member of the Society, shall undergo an examination in regard to his general education.' This examination was not to be carried out by a Member of the Society, but, for the first time, by someone employed specifically for this purpose.[36]

> It was agreed on the recommendation of Mr Jamieson at a meeting on 12 February 1873 to appoint Mr A.M. Bell, of Fettes College, to conduct the preliminary Examinations of Gentlemen coming forward to be apprentices to Members of the Society; and also to undertake the Examination of Apprentices in the third year of their Apprenticeship with such assistance from his Colleagues as he may consider necessary, having

> in view the Subjects of Examination both voluntary and Compulsory, as laid down in the Society's Report.

The third year professional examination was described in Bye-law 37 of the revised Bye-laws, Rules and Regulations as follows:

> Every Apprentice shall, during the third year of his apprenticeship, undergo an examination, to test the progress made by him, and in the event of any Apprentice failing to pass such examination to the satisfaction of the Committee of Examinators at the time fixed for such examination, it shall be competent for him to present himself for re-examination at any time during the remainder of his apprenticeship, and within six months of the expiry thereof. Such examination must be passed by each Apprentice before he can present himself for final examination for entrance into the Society.

In July 1873, Mr Bell presented a syllabus for the third year examinations which was amended and adopted. At this same meeting it was agreed that specialist examiners should be appointed for the Actuarial and Law examinations and subsequently Mr Spencer Thomson of the Standard Insurance Company and Mr A.S. Kinnear, Advocate, were appointed to carry out the examination of candidates in the Actuarial Branch and Law respectively. The final minute on the new system provided that the preliminary examinations, the Imperative examinations marked A and the examinations marked B Voluntary might all be conducted by extramural examiners.[37] It further stated that the examination in Actuarial Science should be conducted by a Gentleman possessing Actuarial acquirements who may or may not be selected from within the Society. As might be expected, all examinations in Professional subjects were to be conducted exclusively by Members of the Society.

As well as having to cope with the new examination system, apprentices were required to complete their eligibility as candidates for admission as Members of the Society by attending the Scots Law, Conveyancing, Commercial Law and Political Economy classes in the

University of Edinburgh.[38] In 1877 this was altered to compulsory attendance at Scots Law and Conveyancing classes and recommended attendance at those for Political Economy and Commercial Law.[39] The new system presented candidates for apprenticeship and admission to membership with a stiffer path to follow and this fact was perhaps recognised by the Society.

> Some juicy carrots, however, were offered with the view of encouraging apprentices in the prosecution of their studies. These took the form of a bursary of £20 per annum tenable for two years for the apprentice who at the third year examination should attain the highest proficiency in all branches, 'Imperative' and 'Voluntary' and a Fellowship of £30 per annum tenable for three years for the 'Candidate who shall attain the highest proficiency at the Final Examination, on the subjects prescribed in both classes, termed 'Imperative' and 'Voluntary'. The above Bursary and Fellowship being always subject to such regulations as the President and Council may from time-to-time deem proper.[40]

Each set of Accounts for the period 1874 to 1889 included an entry for Bursaries and Fellowships.

Paragraph 40 of the 1877 Rules detailed the subjects for examination for candidates for admission who had passed the intermediate examination and whose indentures had been discharged. The subjects to be examined were:

> First, 'The Law of Scotland.' To be conducted by a professional examiner to be selected by the Committee of Examinators.
> Second, 'Actuarial Science.' To be conducted by a gentleman with actuarial knowledge to be selected by the Committee of Examinators.
> Third, 'The general business of an Accountant.' To be conducted by Members of the Society exclusively, under arrangements to be made by the Committee of Examinators.

Despite the recommendation in 1863 that examinations should be conducted in writing there were for many years examples of candidates being examined in a very informal manner. F.D. Hunter reports the experience of his master, W.H. Cook, who was admitted to membership in 1878:

> I was admitted to the Society without sitting any examinations. One day when my indenture was at an end I dressed myself in a frock coat and silk hat and presented myself before the members of the Council. They all shook me by the hand and said they were sure I would be a credit to the profession, and that is how I became a chartered accountant.[41]

At a meeting of the President and Council on 10 March 1879 there was a suggestion that, since some of the examinations of the Society and the Faculty of Actuaries were in many respects similar, they should enter into a joint examination system. However, it was decided not to pursue this line of enquiry and the existing system continued unaltered for the following ten years.

The first official reference by the Scottish Education Department to a school-leaving certificate appeared in Circular 74, dated 15 January 1886: 'In connection with the inspection of schools, the suggestion was made that their lordships should issue a certificate, based on the results of the highest classes in these schools, which would serve as a measure of attainment fairly to be expected in the case of pupils completing a course of secondary education.' Professor Chrystal, Professor of Mathematics at the University of Edinburgh, was given the task of determining whether or not a national examination was possible and in carrying out this task he 'took into account the opinion that pupils from the highest classes of a well-conducted secondary school should be academically equipped to enter university. It followed from this that the minimum standard of proficiency should be equivalent to that of the University Entrance Examination for the three years' Arts course.'

The objects of a system of school-leaving certificates were to attempt to eliminate the wide differences existing between the range and achievement of schools nominally of the same class and, also, to explore the potential use of the examination as a substitute for the varied entrance examinations set by the professional bodies.[42] In fact, in his submission to the Scottish Education Department, Pirie, one of the four examiners who made the preliminary investigations, argued 'that co-operation and goodwill from employers and professional bodies were essential to the success of the certificate,' and categorically stated that the scheme should be dropped if these were not obtained. To this end, the Scottish Education Department sent letters requesting recognition of the proposed leaving certificates to, among others, the Institute of Accountants and Actuaries - the professional body of the Glasgow Chartered Accountants - on 6 January 1888 and that body noted its recognition of the certificate as granting exemption from its entry examinations on 26 September 1888. The first leaving-certificate examination was held on Monday, 18 June 1888, the subjects covered being English, including questions on History and Geography, Mathematics, German, French, Greek and Latin; in other words, a broad classical education such as would be required for those attempting university entrance examinations.

In 1889 the Rules and Regulations of the Edinburgh Society were altered to take account of the introduction of the school leaving certificate. Paragraph 32 included the provision that; 'Any Applicant who may have taken a degree of BA or MA at any University in Great Britain or Ireland, or who may have obtained the Government School Leaving Certificate, consisting of three subjects, including Mathematics, shall be exempt from the Preliminary Examination.'

Paragraph 36 still required apprentices to attend Scots Law and Conveyancing classes in the University of Edinburgh for one complete session and, in addition - 'such lectures on special subjects as the Society may in General Meeting approve.' The form of the final examinations was more specifically defined in Paragraph 38. The examination on the 'Law of Scotland' - 'shall consist of written papers, as well as a viva voce Examination' and that on 'The general business of an Accountant' - 'shall consist of written papers, as well as a viva voce examination before a Board of not less than three of the Committee of Examinators.' So the accountancy profession followed the general trend of the educational system in Britain in the nineteenth century with: 'a move to almost complete dependence upon written examinations as the main criterion of success at each stage in the system.'[43]

3. Institute of Accountants and Actuaries in Glasgow

The original Rules and Regulations of the Glasgow Institute which were drawn up in September 1853, made initial provision for the admission of applicants for membership to be dealt with by the Council of the Institute without the need to have applications sanctioned by a meeting of the Members.[44] This admission procedure was only to be extended until 31 December 1853 when interim provisions came into force for the period to 31 December 1856, making it necessary for Council's recommendations as to the suitability of applicants to be ratified by a quarterly meeting of the Institute. These early admission procedures were in keeping with Reader's view of professions such as accountancy having 'conceived of themselves as admitting educated gentlemen to small, self-governing groups of their social equals, to whom they would be personally known and by whom their fitness would be judged.'[45]

Commencing on 1 January 1857, applicants for admission were required to have completed at least four years of articled apprenticeship 'with a Member of the Institute or of some other Institute or Society of Accountants or Actuaries.'[46] The only other such bodies in existence at that time were the Edinburgh Society of Accountants, formed earlier that year, and the Institute of Actuaries which had been formed in 1848.[47] The Faculty of Actuaries in Scotland, which was formed by a secession of the Scottish Members from the Institute of Actuaries, was not constituted until January 1856.[48]

During this initial stage up to the end of December 1856 the entry money for the Institute was set at ten guineas, but for those who delayed in applying to join, this was to increase on 1 January 1857 to fifty guineas. In including a provision for this increase it was hoped that by that time 'the Institute would have attained a degree of eminence and usefulness, and could hold out advantages to the members.'[49]

A loophole permitted admission to membership of special cases, designated as those who had not served an articled apprenticeship but who were recommended by two-thirds of the Council of the Institute and approved at two successive quarterly meetings of the Institute. On applying for admission each applicant had to state that he was not engaged in the business of a manufacturer,

TABLE 7.3

Accountants listed as being in practice in Glasgow

Year	Accountants	Glasgow CAs	Members ICAEW	Total
1840-41	48	-	-	48
1850-51	135	-	-	135
* 1855-56	93	52	-	145
1860-61	115	54	-	169
1870-71	165	73	-	238
1880-81	282	107	-	389
1890-91	302	106	15	423
1900-01	193	232	13	438

Source: Glasgow Post Office Directories

* Members of Institute of Accountants and Actuaries of Glasgow first identified as so being.

merchant or law agent; occupations which were apparently considered to be incompatible with the business of an accountant, unlike those of house-factor, insurance agent and stockbroker, which were among those carried on by Glasgow accountants.

It was not long before the Glasgow Institute discovered that, although in theory the requirement that applicants be recommended for membership by Council might be sufficient, there were practical difficulties when someone applied who had been hitherto unknown to them. On 16 December 1853 Robert Scobie applied to be admitted under Rule 5, but on it being discovered that he 'was found to be personally unknown to any of the gentlemen present the consideration of his application was postponed till the next meeting of Council - Enquiries regarding Mr Scobie's qualifications to be made in the meantime.'[50] Scobie had been practising as an accountant for six years and was also the Glasgow agent for the Commercial Credit Mutual Assurance Society of London and was admitted at the next meeting of Council on 5 January 1854 after satisfactory enquiries had been completed. At the same meeting it was resolved to introduce a new Bye-law stating that in future each applicant should be instructed by the Secretary of the Institute to produce a recommendation from three members of the Institute, who were not members of Council, before the application would be considered by the Council.

By the end of 1854, before the Glasgow Institute had been granted its Royal Charter, Council re-examined its admission policy and discussed 'the propriety of introducing an examination of applicants previous to admission, as was the plan of all similar bodies.' The reference to similar bodies can only have meant the Society of Accountants in Edinburgh and both bodies were ultimately empowered by their respective Charters to constitute and appoint Committees of Examinators.

In January 1855 the Council of the Glasgow Institute had already determined that examination should be undergone by applicants for admission and that these examinations 'should imply a knowledge on the part of the applicant of the elementary principles of Bankrupt Law; of Book-keeping and Accounts; of the practical working of Bankruptcies; Trust Estates, Voluntary and Judicial Factories, and of the rudimentary principles of Arithmetic and Algebra.' This recommendation was passed by the Members at the first Annual General Meeting of the Glasgow Institute on 30 January 1855 and implemented through the introduction of Rule 41. Rather than appoint outside examinators it was agreed to designate all members of the Council as such. The first admission examinations were held in July 1855 for three candidates, one of whom, Ruthven Todd, was referred to be re-examined four days later, at which time he was passed for admission. It is presumed that his re-examination was due to some apparent lack of knowledge and not the fact that he was a native of Edinburgh!

No copies or details of examination papers or tests survive

but it would appear that for quite a few years they were mainly oral and administered in an informal manner. Certainly Sir John Mann, who was admitted to membership of the Glasgow Institute in 1885, recalled his examinations as being a quaint, homely affair conducted on a one-to-one basis with the Secretary of the Institute.[51] James McLelland, in a lecture delivered to apprentices in 1869 outlined the preparation for examinations as being mainly training by experience in a professional office. In addition, however, it was necessary for apprentices 'to go back to school, and attend the prelections of the professors of commercial and civil law' for at least two sessions.[52] Any Glasgow apprentice who wished to broaden his education at that time had ample opportunity to do so in his spare time. John Mann, for example, attended evening classes at the Mechanics Institute and the Andersonian in George Street to widen his general education which had been curtailed when he left school at the age of twelve.[53]

In order to qualify for admission, candidates not only had to satisfy the Institute's examiners but had to intend either to set up as an accountant on their own account or to go into an accounting partnership. As numbers of accountants slowly grew these opportunities became more elusive with the result that there arose a surplus of qualified accountants who were ineligible for membership of the Institute. Admission records show that during the period from 1856 to 1876 the highest number of new members in any one year was nine; in six of these years there were no admissions and the average number of admissions per year over that twenty-year period was less than three.[54]

As early as January 1857 the Council of the Glasgow Institute had discussed the possibility of admitting qualified men to the Institute although they had no intention or prospect of practising on their own account, but the matter did not proceed any further at that time.

Apprentices and clerks in Glasgow accountants' offices were required to attend Scotch Law classes at the University in order to equip themselves for the entrance examinations of the Institute. However, in 1871 a petition was presented to the Institute pointing out the inadequacy of these classes due to the wide scope which they covered and requesting the Institute to establish a course of lectures on Mercantile and Bankruptcy Law. This suggestion was acted upon and classes were provided out of office hours with an attendance fee of one guinea per student; this was the first known instance of classes being provided specifically for accounting apprentices.

In November 1876, almost twenty years after the first discussion on this topic had taken place, the problem of qualified men being unable to become members of the Institute through not fulfilling the practising requirements was again raised. The suggestion was that a class of Associate Member be introduced and the members of Council present at the meeting felt:

> that some recognition on the part of the Institute of young men training for the profession would tend to stimulate their interest in the study of those subjects best calculated to prepare them for taking an honourable position therein; and it was thought that the admission of such as Associates by preliminary examination & payment of a small entrance fee, would at least be a step in the direction indicated.

The members of the Glasgow Institute agreed at their Annual General Meeting in January 1878 to introduce the category of Associate Member and the Admission Books show that for the period from 1878 to 1899 it was possible for a candidate to complete his apprenticeship and pass the appropriate examination to become an Associate member. Full membership could be achieved at a later date on passing the Final Examinations, paying an entry fee and on either becoming a partner in an existing accounting firm or setting up on one's own account as an accountant or actuary.

Considering that the normal age for entering an apprenticeship at that time was sixteen and that to qualify for Associateship, a candidate had to be twenty-one years of age, thus having completed perhaps five years in an accountant's office, the subjects to be passed in the matriculation examination seem rather a strange mix of general and professional subjects. The subjects deemed necessary by the Council in 1877 for Associateship were: Arithmetic and the Elements of Algebra and Mathematics; Geography, with particular reference to Commerce; English Composition and Writing to Dictation and Spelling; Framing of Accounts and States with reference to Branching and General Arrangement; Style and Penmanship and Principles of Bookkeeping.

The inclusion of Geography and Pure Mathematics can be explained by James McClelland's comments in 1869. The former would be necessary since in insolvencies or bankruptcies most parties would have transactions with foreign countries for Glasgow merchants traded actively all over the world. The latter might be explained by his claim that:

> A branch of the profession, which has hitherto had but a limited scope in Glasgow, compared with its development and practice in Edinburgh, we should like to see cultivated among the members of our Institute. The branch to which we allude is the important one of Life Insurance, and of the preparation necessary in the higher branches of arithmetic and algebra, to make the student an expert in the necessary calculations and problems required in this very large business.

Some important areas of present-day practice are noticeable by their absence, particularly auditing, which John Mann noted as being unusual in 1878.[55] Taxation was also unexamined and, although John Mann notes that this work was quite common after Peel reimposed income tax in 1842, this can perhaps be explained by the small amount of such work in comparison with other areas and by the fact that taxation work was also carried out by the legal profession in Scotland. Most significant, however, despite the fact that bankruptcy work was commonly undertaken and was of great importance in the formation of the Institute, there was no examination in this subject at Associate Level.

The introduction of Associateship status led to an immediate increase in membership, although the category was only intended to be a temporary one and Associates were required to qualify as Members within six months after commencing business as accountants or actuaries either on their own account or in partnership with others.

At the Annual General Meeting of the Glasgow Institute on 27 January 1885, Council was asked to consider: 'The question of the expediency of widening the constitution of the Institute so as to provide for the admission of thoroughly qualified men who may not have received their training in the offices of members, also of admitting members of other Institutes on certain terms without payment of Entrance Money.' The matter was deferred for discussion until the quarterly meeting of 28 July 1885 when various possible categories of applicant were considered. These included men who had been in practice as public accountants for at least four year prior to application; young men trained in offices other than those of members of the three Chartered Bodies in Scotland and members of other Institutes of Chartered Accountants - this presumably being a reference to the Institute of Chartered Accountants in England and Wales.

This attempt to widen membership was probably made for two reasons. First, although the Glasgow Institute had been in existence since 1853, the *Glasgow Post Office Directories* consistently listed approximately three non-chartered accountants for every one chartered accountant. Second, the Institute of Chartered Accountants in England and Wales which was formed in 1880 had admitted to membership some Glasgow accountants who did not qualify for membership of the Glasgow Institute. The most prominent of this group was Thomson McLintock, who founded an accounting firm in Glasgow in 1877 and who was admitted to the English Institute as an associate member in 1880.[56] Not surprisingly, and to the intense annoyance of members of the Glasgow Institute, the members of the English Institute designated themselves 'Chartered Accountant' as provided for in their Charter. An obvious way of removing this irritation would have been to recognise that anyone considered suitable for membership of the English Institute was also acceptable to the Glasgow Institute. However after discussion and further consideration at a Council meeting in October 1885, it was agreed that no rule change was necessary at that time.

The admission policy of the Glasgow Institute was once again called to question at the Annual General Meeting of the Institute on 31 January 1888 when John Mann, jnr, proposed an alteration of the rules so as 'to open the doors of admission to the Institute to all capable men willing to undergo the prescribed Examinations whether they should have served with a member of a Chartered Institute or not.' Mann's reason for resurrecting this proposal was clearly stated: 'The younger members, he said, met with a large amount of competition from outsiders, who, if connected with the Institute, would come under its rules and be guided by its etiquettes.

It is difficult to establish, at this distance in time, precisely what factors were of concern to Mann, but the 'large amount of competition' must have referred to the fact that there were more accountants outside the Glasgow Institute then there were members and perhaps also to the fact that this sector consistently dealt with between forty and fifty per cent of the bankruptcy work in the Glasgow area. At that time there were no areas of professional practice confined only to members of recognised accountancy bodies and, in Glasgow at least, it would appear that it had proved impossible for chartered accountants to achieve a monopoly in at least one major specialist area. Once again, the Council of the Glasgow Institute declined to alter the admission rules[57] but reversed this decision in October 1888 and agreed 'that some effort should be made so to widen the basis of the Institute as to open the door to all capable and qualified men.'[58] This was, of course, only an acknowledgement that the matter ought to receive further serious consideration and discussions were to carry on for quite some time.

It was not until six months later, in April 1889, that a draft proposal was submitted to the Quarterly meeting of the Institute, suggesting that it would be:

> competent for the Council, in special circumstances, to recommend for admission as a Member, without requiring him to become an Associate any gentleman who has been practising as an Accountant for at least ten years, either in Glasgow or elsewhere, who shall be recommended by five Members of the Institute, whose position in the profession would render him suitable, and regarding whose qualifications the Council have satisfied themselves.

In addition, any application would have to be passed by three-quarters of the members present at a Quarterly General Meeting. Once again, no decision was taken and the matter was shelved for future consideration.

On 24 February 1890, the Council once more discussed the subject of admission requirements and combined this with an acknowledgement that there were suitably qualified accountants in practice, notably in Dundee and Greenock, who would be welcomed as members of the Chartered Societies. The most positive suggestion came from the Aberdeen Society whose members envisaged the amalgamation of the existing Chartered Bodies into one body, with a new Charter, which would be empowered, for a limited period, to admit to membership suitably qualified and eligible applicants. Such an amalgamation was not, however, to take place for a further sixty-one years. The Glasgow Institute eventually agreed to alter its admission rules in July 1890, and to implement the open door policy only until 1 January 1893.

The *Glasgow Post Office Directory* for 1890-1 listed approximately 106 members of the Glasgow Institute, fifteen members of the English Institute and 300 accountants who were not members of any Institute. Since the members of the Glasgow Institute were not unanimous in their support of the new admission policy, this pool of potential members might have appeared to threaten a takeover of the established members by new admissions. This concern was expressed in a letter signed by fifty-seven Members of the Institute which was sent to the Council urging caution over the admission of applicants and suggesting that the Council should consider requiring such applicants to take the Associateship examination as proof of their professional ability. This, it was claimed, would prevent the embarassing situation of an applicant being recommended for membership by the Council but being voted down by the members. Council took heed of this opinion and agreed that examination should be the norm, but that the Council should retain the discretion to dispense with it in special cases.[59] The *Accountant* explained the necessity for this dispensation as being that 'The exercise of this power has occasionally been found desirable in Glasgow, owing to the large amount of commercial work carried out by the profession in that city; whereas in Edinburgh accountants are more particularly occupied with court work, and such exceptional cases have not been generally experienced.'[60]

This special dispensation was only granted in a few cases such as the admission of Walter Galbraith in 1891 who was exempt from examination because of his age, being sixty-four at the time of his admission. At the same time, Louson Walker from Greenock was admitted without examination presumably on the grounds of his position as an accountant in Greenock, since was elected to the

Council of the Glasgow Institute in 1892. In 1891 a group of Dundee accountants applied for admission and all five were admitted without examination.

4. Society of Accountants in Aberdeen

Much of the wording of the application for a Royal Charter by members of the Society of Accountants in Aberdeen was an exact replica of that contained in the Royal Charter incorporating the Society of Accountants in Edinburgh, but the Aberdeen application omitted any reference to Actuarial work and to work directly involved with suits before the Court of Session.

The original Rules and Regulations of the Aberdeen Society were also closely modelled on the Rules and Regulations of the Edinburgh Society which were in force in 1867. Paragraph 12 empowered the Society to appoint examiners: 'The Society shall also at said stated Annual General Meeting elect three Members, who, with the President and Council, shall form the Committee of Examinators (of whom three shall be a quorum) for regulating and conducting the examination of entrants.' Since the first Council of the Society consisted of four members this meant that the possible maximum size of the Committee of Examinators was eight - out of a total original membership of twelve. Apprentices could apply for examination immediately the discharge of their indenture was completed and registered with the Society.

During a transitional period lasting for ten years after the formation of the Society, the conditions for admission to the Society were widened to include applicants who had not served five years apprenticeship under indenture to a member of the Society. If such applicants had been employed for three years in the business chambers of a member of the Society subsequent to completing a regular term of apprenticeship with a member of the Society of Writers to the Signet, a member of the Society of Solicitors before the Supreme Courts of Scotland, or with a member of any Incorporated Society of Solicitors-at-Law, or with a member of the Society of Advocates in Aberdeen, then they were eligible for examination and admission. The Rules and Regulations also provided retrospectively for persons who were twenty-three years of age or over, and who had

TABLE 7.4

Accountants listed as being in practice in Aberdeen

Year	Accountants	Aberdeen CAs	Members ICAEW	Total
1840-41	8	-	-	8
1850-51	13	-	-	13
1860-61	25	-	-	25
* 1867-68	13	12	-	25
1870-71	15	13	-	28
1880-81	23	15	1	39
1890-91	40	21	-	61
1900-01	43	22	-	65

Source: Aberdeen Post Office Directories

* Members of Society of Accountants in Aberdeen first identified as so being.

not undergone a traditional apprenticeship under indentures, but who had been employed for at least six years in the business chambers of a member of the Society or of the societies of Chartered Accountants in Edinburgh or Glasgow, to present themselves for examination and admission. These conditions were identical to those laid down in the Rules and Regulations of the Edinburgh Society, but in Edinburgh the transitional period had only lasted for five years from the date of incorporation.

Although the application for the Royal Charter of

Incorporation did not mention actuarial work, Paragraph 40 of the Rules and Regulations was identical to Paragraph 39 of the Rules and Regulations of the Edinburgh Society and identified subjects for examination as being 'algebra, including the use of logarithms - annuities - life assurances - liferents - reversions - book-keeping - framing of States under sequestrations, trust, factories, executries - the Law of Scotland, especially that relating to Bankruptcy, private trust and arbitration, and rights and preferences of creditors in rankings.' Thus, although at its formation, members of the Aberdeen Society were not involved in Actuarial work they presumably felt that it would be sensible to extend the possible boundaries of their work to cover the same areas as those covered by the Edinburgh Society.

The Royal Charter for the Aberdeen Society was dated 18 March 1867 and registered on 10 April 1867. The Rules and Regulations were approved by the Society at a meeting on 10 May 1867 and on that same date the first apprentice, John Knox Greig was indentured to Marquis and Lunan. No indenture fee was noted, perhaps because Greig's father was deceased, and his cautioner was an Aberdeen advocate. An apprentice was required to pay a fee of one guinea to the Society for the recording of his indenture in the Minute Books and the indenture fee was fixed by Rule 33 at twenty-five guineas. The period of indenture was five years, the same as that for the Edinburgh Society, but the minimum age for apprenticeship was fourteen years. The period of apprenticeship could be reduced on a one year for two years basis to a minimum of three years and the permitted service included any with a member of the Edinburgh or Glasgow Societies, the Writers to the Signet, the Society of Solicitors before the Supreme Courts of Scotland, of any Incorporated Society of Solicitors at Law, the Society of Advocates in Aberdeen or any other body of solicitors in Scotland.

The original members of the Aberdeen Society had strong links with the legal profession, at least five of the twelve having received their training in legal offices.[61] Since three of them had been trained in accountant's offices in Edinburgh and a further two in an insurance company and with an advocate in Edinburgh, it is hardly surprising that they modelled their Charter and Rules and Regulation closely on that of the Edinburgh Society rather than the Glasgow Institute.

Membership was restricted to those who intended to practise

as accountants and the Aberdeen Society seems to have administered this quite strictly, regularly refusing admission to applicants, though there were examples of the rules being altered to allow an accountant to become a member.

In February 1868, Robert Cran, bookkeeper to a firm of advocates, was refused membership on the grounds that he had no intention of practising as an accountant. Then in December 1876, Alexander McConnachie had his application refused on the grounds that his experience of four years in an advocate's office did not fulfil the requirements of the Society. A.M. Walker, Sheriff Clerk Depute was refused admission in April 1878, despite the fact that J. Leslie, Sheriff Clerk had been an original member of the Society. The requirement to have completed the accepted apprenticeship system in Aberdeen was also adhered to and James McLaren who had been apprenticed in Edinburgh was refused admission to the Aberdeen Society in 1880. However, in 1893 John McBain was admitted to membership on the grounds that he had been practising as an accountant in Aberdeen in partnership with his brother, George, a member of the Society, for five years. This move gave rise to a telegram of protest from Joshua Gladstone, a member of the Society practising in London - 'I object most strongly to admit McBain or anyone without examinations - It will tell most effectually against English Institute amalgamating with Scotch Society.'[62] His protest was in vain and had no effect on the decision taken at the Special General Meeting.

During his apprenticeship an apprentice was required to attend a course of at least two sessions of Scots Law lectures at the University. The first examination of apprentices was carried out in 1876 on two apprentices whose period of indenture had expired. Both were successful and were admitted as members at a Special General Meeting on 29 February 1876, having paid the required entry money of twenty guineas.

By 1877 only nine new members had been admitted to the Aberdeen Society. Since it had started with such a small number of members and the shortest method of apprenticeship was with a member, the Society had a very limited base on which to build. The requirement that intending members went into practice on their own account or in partnership, meant that a group of men developed who had completed their indentures and passed their examinations but were still unable to qualify for membership. The Aberdeen Society solved this problem in the same way and at approximately the same time as did the Glasgow Institute, by introducing a category of Associateship. On 15 November 1877, a Special General Meeting of the Society agreed to admit applicants as Associates until such time as they began business on their own account, when they would be raised to full membership without further examination. The entry fee was to be paid half on Associateship and half on full membership, but at no time did the Minute Books show more than one Associate.

By 1880, the entry money had been increased to forty guineas and in 1893 to fifty guineas, but no reason was given for the increases and in 1885 the Society refused to reduce the term of an apprenticeship for graduates. Indeed, the Aberdeen Society seems to have been completely unimpressed by graduate entrants, since in 1886 the minute of the Annual General Meeting refers to three apprentices who had satisfied the examiners of their fitness prior to entering on the apprenticeship when two of the three held MAs.

At the Annual General Meeting in 1889 recommendations were put forward for the more formal examination of prospective members. The proposed scheme consisted of three levels, pre-admission to apprenticeship, during apprenticeship and on application for admission to membership. At the first level the subjects covered were general educational subjects - English composition, Writing, Writing to dictation, Arithmetic, British History, Geography and Elements of Latin, German or French - presumably to test whether or not the applicant had had the benefit of a liberal education as would befit a member of a profession such as accountancy. During apprenticeship the examinations would be on practical matters: Arithmetic, profit and loss, stocks, partnerships, simple compound interest, foreign exchange, commercial bookkeeping by single and double entry, geometry and algebra. At the final level the examinations were to be more specific: Algebra - logarithms, Compound Interest, Theory and Practice of Bookkeeping, Accounts and States in Trusts, Factories and Sequestrations, Procedure and Requisites in the Audit of Accounts and Books, Law of Bankruptcy, Trusts, Partnership, Joint Stock Companies, Bills of Exchange, Intestate Succession. It was a comprehensive spread of subjects and it is particularly interesting to note the inclusion of auditing.

The new regulations were passed at a Special General

Meeting on 2 March 1889 and at the same time graduate apprenticeships were reduced to four years plus exemption from the first two levels of examination.

On 25 November 1890 the Society was asked by the Edinburgh Society to consider the desirability of admitting to membership certain classes of practising accountants who had not fulfilled the conditions of apprenticeship or passed the entrance examinations. At a further Special General Meeting on 8 December 1890 the members resolved to admit practising accountants who had been in business on their own or in partnership for at least five years and those holding respectable positions as businessmen and considered qualified, although not by examination, in Aberdeen or any of the other towns in Scotland. The minute specifically mentioned Chamberlains of Cities or towns and opened the way to membership for Peter Cran, Chamberlain of Aberdeen who was admitted to membership as from 1 January 1891, having been refused entry on 5 February 1868 at which time he was employed as an advocate's cashier and also on 4 July 1873 when he was described as clerk to a firm of advocates. Cran then became a member of the Scottish Institute of Accountants and rose to become Vice-President by 1889.[63] He was almost fifty years of age when he was eventually admitted to membership of the Aberdeen Society and probably applied for admission to gain status (or perhaps equality with those other members of the Scottish Institute of Accountants who were taking advantage of the rule changes and applying for admission to the chartered bodies at this time), since he had no intention of practising as an accountant. At his death at the age of sixty-three he was still City Chamberlain of Aberdeen, a position which might have been thought to carry just as much if not more status than membership of the Society of Accountants in Aberdeen.

5. Joint Examination Scheme

At the beginning of 1890 when the three Societies of Chartered Accountants were co-operating in their opposition to the application for a Charter by the Scottish Institute of Accountants, Alexander Ledingham of Aberdeen suggested that a solution which would strengthen their opposition might be the establishing of a general

Accounting Society for Scotland.[64] This would be formed by the granting of a new Charter to a Society consisting of the members of the three existing Societies and the formation by this new Society of an examining board. The suggestion of amalgamation came to nothing at that time and by the end of 1890 all three Societies had introduced new rules allowing them to admit applicants previously considered unqualified, thus dispelling the threat from the Scottish Institute of Accountants. However, the idea of having standard examinations throughout Scotland did receive further attention and discussion.

In December 1891, the Edinburgh Society contacted the other two Societies about the desirability of having a joint examination board for Scotland.[65] The response of both the other Societies to this suggestion was enthusiastic[66] and several meetings were held to iron out differences of opinion between the three, particularly those raised by the Glasgow Institute. Members of the Glasgow Institute were unwilling to abandon Rule 8 which allowed them to admit in exceptional circumstances, without apprenticeship or examination, accountants whom they considered duly qualified. Eventually this was agreed to, with the condition that before admission the names of such applicants be submitted to and approved by the General Board of Examiners. By the beginning of 1893 the agreements for the Joint Examining Board had been completed and the syllabus was published in the *Accountant* of 25 March 1893.[67] The first diet of the new examinations was held in June 1893, when only the Preliminary Examination was held and all three levels, Preliminary, Intermediate and Final were examined in December 1893.

The *Accountant* published an anonymous series of four articles on the new examination scheme in January and February 1893. The first article pointed out that the previous arrangement by which each Society had admitted its own members had been a weakness in the Scottish system and that the new system would be a great improvement in that, 'there will, in future, be but one class of chartered accountants in Scotland - a class with definite qualifications, and of untainted reputation. It is beyond question that the real gainers in the long run will be the community where affairs will be supervised by a body of upright, vigilant, and intelligent gentlemen - the Scottish Chartered Accountants.'[68]

The article appearing on 4 February 1893 compared the old

Preliminary and Intermediate examinations of the Edinburgh and Glasgow Societies with one another and with those of the English Institute. The Preliminary examination was held to be extremely elementary when compared to that of the English Institute though apparently mainly on the grounds that over forty per cent of candidates in England failed this level. However, most of the article was concerned with the Intermediate examinations and noted the main difference between the two countries as being the fact that in England this level was concerned solely with professional subjects, while in Scotland, more than half of this level was concerned with scholastic subjects such as arithmetic, algebra, English, etc. The Glasgow Intermediate level had only one four hour paper in bookkeeping, but two days covering six non-professional subjects, this level being referred to as the Associates Examination. The high level of mathematics in the Scottish examinations was held to be necessary preparation for the final examination in actuarial science. In England this was considered to be a separate profession and one which an accountant could pursue, if he so desired, after completing his accountancy education.[69]

The Final examinations were examined more critically, the subjects for examination being: The law of Scotland; the elements of actuarial science; the elements of political economy and the general business of an accountant.[70] In Glasgow, the paper on political economy was replaced by one on bookkeeping and accounts because of the large amount of commercial work carried out by Glasgow accountants as compared to the Edinburgh accountants who were more particularly occupied with court work. Auditing was dealt with in the paper on general professional knowledge, although the author commented on the lack of knowledge required in this paper of different classes of accounts and the best method of auditing them. He also noted the difference between Edinburgh and Glasgow in the emphasis on mercantile law in Edinburgh and company law in Glasgow, Glasgow also included a question specifically related to shipbuilding.

In conclusion, the author judged the Edinburgh and Glasgow papers to be of an even standard and excused the lack of concentration on pure accountancy by saying that the accountant could easily make up for this after qualifying.[71]

The new scheme dispensed with the differences between the

three societies apart from the provision that apprentices who had entered indentures prior to the adoption by the three societies of the new regulations could, in place of the paper on political economy, take a second more advanced paper in actuarial science. In addition paper four on the general business of an accountant, although largely concerned with bankruptcy and other court work, did specifically include the 'procedure and requisites in the Audit of Accounts and Books; including those of Public Companies, Private Firms and Trust Estates.'[72]

One further article appeared after the first full diet of the new examinations had taken place in December 1893 and in this the author was critical of the balance of knowledge required of a Scottish chartered accountant as compared to an English one with particular criticism of two aspects of the papers. First, that the standard of accounting knowledge required in Scotland at a Final level was no more difficult than that required at an Intermediate level in England. His second criticism was the high concentration on mathematical, legal and economics questions concluding that, 'a more stringent test upon accountancy pure and simple should be exacted from any one who desires to become a chartered accountant.'[73] This contention was repeated in 1896 after an article in the *Accountant* on examination standards drew the response from Richard Brown, Secretary of the Society of Accountants in Edinburgh, that the average pass rate in Scotland was seventy-eight per cent. The article claimed that since in England the pass rate was generally lower than this the examinations were obviously harder: 'The fact remains - for it is a fact, and must remain however long the discussion might be continued - that the Examinations of the Scottish Chartered Accountants' Societies are not so severe in the accountancy subjects as the English.'[74]

In 1898 an intimation of evening classes for apprentices to be conducted in Edinburgh on bookkeeping and accounts, political economy, bankruptcy and company law and advanced bookkeeping was accompanied by Richard Brown's comment: 'Of course, the classes have not been got up with the view merely of enabling students to pass these examinations with greater facility, but for the purpose of giving them opportunities of acquiring a thorough knowledge of subjects which are indispensable to the efficient discharge of the professional duties, which they will be - or hope to be

- called upon to perform.'[75] It is difficult to believe that the finalists paying 10*s* 6*d* for each class per quarter held the view that the classes were designed for anything other than to help them pass their Final examinations. However, Brown's own perception of the new examination scheme of which he was the first Secretary was that: 'The arrangements made under this agreement have worked admirably, and the step has brought about the practical affiliation, for all public purposes, of the Chartered Accountants of Scotland.' Perhaps Brown was rather optimistic in his claim but the practical effects of the new system were at least twofold. First, the saving of costs in preparing separate examinations for each society and second, the undoubted strengthening of the position of Chartered Accountancy in Scotland by this outward evidence of standardisation of testing of entrants similar to that adopted much earlier by the Institute of Chartered Accountants in England and Wales. Certainly Beresford Worthington was impressed by the status which the profession had achieved in Scotland by 1895, 'There can be no doubt whatever that in Scotland accountancy has developed a degree of importance, and that Scotch Accountants rank higher than in any other part of the world. The gentlemen at the head of the profession are thoroughly accomplished, and possess very extensive acquirements and experience.[76]

6. Summary

The Charter for each of the Scottish Chartered Accountancy bodies included a requirement for members to have had a liberal education and also empowered the societies to examine candidates for admission. In their early years the societies had no formal test as a pre-entry requirement and probably had no need of them when the number of apprentices was small and when many of them would be known to their master. Also during this period examinations were on an *ad hoc* basis since there were very few candidates. Furthermore, their progress would have been carefully monitored during their apprenticeship, for the small number of members in each of the societies would have meant that apprentices were not removed from the senior members and this would have reduced the need for formal examination systems.

However, as the societies became established, the numbers of apprentices in Glasgow and Edinburgh gradually outgrew these informal systems and it became necessary to adopt more formal methods of admitting young men to articles and apprentices to membership. These changes were also logical steps in the development of the profession and in indicating to the public that certain standards were required of prospective chartered accountants.

The most important change in Scotland came with the introduction of the joint examination scheme for the three societies and it is possible that the formation and growth of the Institute of Chartered Accountants in England and Wales had something to do with this move. It is not surprising to find criticism of the Scottish examination system in the columns of the *Accountant*, which was an English Institute publication, particularly at a time when English chartered accountants were complaining about the competition of Scottish members for business in London.

By the end of the nineteenth century the numbers being admitted annually to the Scottish Chartered Societies were certainly of such a magnitude as to require a formal examination system. In addition, the developments in these two areas can only have enhanced the status of Scottish chartered accountancy in the eyes of other professional groups and throughout the world.

VIII

Attempts to Maintain a Monopoly over Professional Work

1. Exclusion of competing Societies

(a) *Introduction*

In 1853, the *Edinburgh and Leith Post Office Directory* showed 132 accountants practising in that area, but when Alexander Robertson sent out his letter suggesting, once more, the formation of a society of accountants in Edinburgh, he contacted only fourteen practising accountants. At their third meeting on 31 January 1853 at Gibbs Royal Hotel, Edinburgh, the policy of the embryonic society with regard to protectionism was clearly outlined by Archibald Borthwick, who, after referring to the various important duties which accountants practising in Edinburgh were called upon to discharge, said he presumed there could be 'no difference of opinion as to the expediency of endeavouring by such an Association as that now proposed, to have those important duties intrusted only to those who were qualified by their education and business acquirements to fulfil them with credit.'

Interestingly, the Glasgow society was not limited to accountants, but included actuaries, as its title, Institute of Accountants and Actuaries in Glasgow, makes clear and it was the only one of the three Scottish chartered bodies to admit to membership persons who had dual professional capacity such as accountant/stockbrokers. Although such members gradually disappeared, a report on the composition of The Institute of Accountants and Actuaries in Glasgow in 1870 states that at that date it consisted of 'thirty-seven stockbrokers, twenty-seven accountants, and not one actuary.' By 1885 the picture had changed little - 'at the present date while there are only three actuaries, who are by the way merely honorary members, a high proportion of stockbrokers to pure accountants is still kept up.'[1]

As was the case in Edinburgh, and later in Aberdeen, membership of the Glasgow Institute was initially limited to practitioners within its own urban area. None of the societies specifically mention the geographical limitation placed on membership in their Rules and Regulations, but the wording of the various petitions for Royal Charters reveals this. For example, the application by the Aberdeen accountants for a Royal Charter describes the petitioners as being accountants in Aberdeen and refers to the business of an accountant as it is practised in Aberdeen.

Various instances can be found of one of the societies refusing to admit an applicant on the grounds that he did not practise within the area covered by its charter. At a meeting of the Council of the Institute of Accountants in Edinburgh on 9 January 1860 an application from William McBean was considered. McBean was described as having served six years in the business chambers of a member of the Society and now working as a Clerk in Dundee. He was refused admission on the grounds that his residence outside Edinburgh disqualified him. However, he subsequently moved to Edinburgh and was examined and admitted to membership in June 1860.

Apparently, too, in thesc carly days a member might resign from the Institute if he moved away from Edinburgh, since the Minute Books show Christopher Douglas' resignation on the grounds that he was living permanently in London.[2] In its early days the Institute of Accountants in Edinburgh had two classes of members, Ordinary Members: 'being gentlemen practising at present in Edinburgh as Accountants' and of Honorary Members; 'being gentlemen who were formerly in practice as Accountants, and who now act as Managers of Life Assurance Companies or hold appointments from the Courts.'[3]

There is no doubt that the members of the Institute of Accountants in Edinburgh, probably because of its foundations having been largely in the legal profession and because of the proximity of its members to the main courts of Scotland, considered that they ought to be allowed a monopoly of court work. On 19 April 1854, the Glasgow accountants complained that appointments of accountants as interim factor on sequestrated estates were being made from a list that did not contain the names of any Glasgow accountants. The matter was quickly rectified to the satisfaction of both groups of accountants, and bankruptcy statistics show that Glasgow CAs resumed the undertaking of this type of work, although never to the same extent as their Edinburgh counterparts.

Without any known exception, Robinson's comment on the admission policies of the Scottish Chartered societies held true until 1891: 'The members of the Scottish societies were limited to accountants practising in one of the three cities, and this limitation was at the outset very strictly interpreted by the Scottish Chartered bodies.'[4]

These policies were implemented through the application of various requirements for admission. The first was the necessity to complete articles with a member of one of the three Societies. Not only did this limit the numbers of apprentices but it effectively limited membership to professional accountants. Secondly, the Charters of the respective societies make it clear that admission was only to be available to qualified persons practising in the city for which the Charter had been obtained and did not even extend, for example, to an apprentice training in Glasgow and being considered for admission to the Edinburgh Society. Thirdly, on admission members had to prove their intention to enter into practice on their own account or in partnership as a public accountant. This rule was more strictly interpreted on admission than at later stages in a member's career and there are very few cases of members resigning on moving into other areas at a later stage in their career. These policies effectively excluded from membership men employed as accountants in industry or with railway companies or utilities, or employed by local authorities, mainly because they had not completed recognised articles.

As a consequence of these restrictive admission policies, a sizeable group of practitioners developed over the years who practised outside the specific geographical areas covered by the Chartered bodies or who were either not willing, at their level of experience, or able to afford to embark on articles of apprenticeship in order to gain entry 'it appears to be inevitable that if successful accountants could not be accommodated within the existing framework of the profession's institutional organization, new avenues had to be found.'[5]

(*b*) *Scottish Institute of Accountants*

It would be reasonable to describe the activities of the new societies in restricting membership as normal for a fairly new profession. Generally the members were anxious to establish status and tended towards premature exclusiveness which led to the formation of rival institutions.[6] The first such move in Scotland came in 1880 when a group of practitioners joined together and formed the Scottish Institute of Accountants, based in Glasgow.[7]

The minutes of the Annual General Meeting of the Society of Accountants in Aberdeen on 2 February 1881 illustrates the attitude of the Chartered bodies to this new society.

> The Secretary mentioned that he had noticed in the newspapers that an Institute of Accountants was about to be organised at Glasgow by the City Chamberlains of that and other towns in Scotland, and that he had been told they were about to apply to the Home Secretary for a Charter of Incorporation; and thus an effort would be made to overturn the position of the Edinburgh and Glasgow Chartered Societies, and make the name of Chartered Accountants to mean any kind of Accountant public or private. The meeting considered that the matter ought to be noticed and enquiry made by the Secretary as to what the Edinburgh and Glasgow Chartered Societies intended to do and if necessary to call a meeting of the Society so that this Society may act with them.

At the meeting in Edinburgh between the Edinburgh and Glasgow societies it was agreed that a memorial should be prepared and presented to the Lord Advocate, urging him to refuse to grant a charter to the Scottish Institute of Accountants. The rumours that the

Scottish Institute was about to apply for a Charter appear to have been unfounded since no further mention of the matter was made until March 1883, when the Council of the Edinburgh Society again received a report from their Secretary to the effect that he understood that the Scottish Institute was now about to apply for one. The Council of the Glasgow Institute also discussed it and agreed that they too were willing to oppose such a plan, although their legal adviser assured them that no application by the Scottish Institute for a Charter had yet been made.

On 2 February 1884 the Council of the Society of Accountants in Aberdeen were reported to be discussing the application and they agreed to join with their fellows in Edinburgh and Glasgow in opposing the application.

The Glasgow Council noted that the petition would be considered on 24 March 1884 and a deputation from the society went to London, along with a deputation from the Edinburgh Society, and put their case to the Lord Advocate.

In England, the attitude towards the proposal was rather different. An editorial in the *Accountant* foresaw no problems in the matter of a Charter of Incorporation: 'This consideration will probably be a pure matter of form, and we congratulate the accountants of Scotland, men well and honourably known in business circles, on taking this step, which must ultimately tend to raise the profession in the eyes of the outside public, and give recognised status to members of an important and painstaking community.'[8] However the application was either unsuccessful or withdrawn.

There is no further mention in any of the Chartered Bodies' minute books of the Scottish Institute of Accountants until the Council minutes of the Glasgow Institute for 6 October 1886 stated that a letter had been received from J.L. Selkirk, Secretary of the Scottish Institute of Accountants suggesting that the time was now ripe for an application for a National Charter for all existing bodies of accountants in Scotland. A copy of the letter had also been sent to the Aberdeen and Edinburgh Societies; Aberdeen was the first to respond and sent a copy of its response to the other two societies. Part of the reply from the Aberdeen Society leaves no doubt as to the opinion of the Scottish Institute that was held by the Chartered Bodies:

> however desirable a National Charter may be it is not

> likely that the Members of the Society here would agree to the application if the chief object of it be to incorporate your Society and give the Title of Chartered Accountant to its Members and thereby deceive the public by admitting a set of men who however high their qualifications in other respects are not Professional Accountants and have had no experience or practice in such a business.

Both the Glasgow Institute and the Edinburgh Society declined to co-operate in the move for a National Charter. This clearly indicated to the Scottish Institute of Accountants that the only path open to them was to resuscitate their own application for a Charter of Incorporation and an intimation of the application appeared in the *Edinburgh Gazette* of 12 July 1889.

All of the existing Chartered societies called meetings to discuss what tactics they ought to pursue in dealing with the application. At a Special General Meeting held on 13 July 1889 the Aberdeen Society agreed to take any necessary steps. The Glasgow Council discussed the matter on 26 July 1889 and instructed their agents to adopt the same procedure in opposing the granting of the Charter as had been followed on the earlier occasion in 1884. The Council of the Edinburgh Society called a meeting on 19 July 1889, and extracts from their submission to the Privy Council demonstrate the strength of their feelings about the application.

They:

> humbly submit that the incorporation craved is uncalled for, unnecessary and inexpedient, and would, if granted, be detrimental to the interests of the public, injurious to the well-being and estimation of the great body of the professional Accountants in Scotland, and unjust to your Petitioners and the other two bodies of chartered accountants in Scotland . . . your Petitioners are decidedly of opinion, contrary to the views of the Scottish Institute of Accountants that it is for the benefit of the profession and the public that the Accountants of Scotland should receive their education and training in the University towns, where

> the great bulk of the legal and general business of the country is conducted, and where the education and training are more varied and efficient than in small provincial towns.

Membership of the Scottish Institute of Accountants had been thirty-three at its formation, but at the time of the application for a Charter it stood at 155, several of the members being permanent, salaried officials of Municipal Corporations. The Institute had its headquarters in Glasgow and members in Edinburgh, Glasgow, Dundee, Aberdeen, Greenock, Inverness, Paisley, Elgin and other towns. An editorial in the *Accountant* of 5 January 1889 states clearly some of the arguments in the case, pointing out that the application for a Charter:

> alleges and suggests that by restriction imposed in regard to the reception of new members, the chartered bodies have practically limited the right of admission in their respective cities to their own clerks and apprentices, thereby making an unfair use of the privileges conferred on them; that thoroughly qualified accountants practising in other towns possessing the requisite qualifications are not eligible for membership; that the result is not only to secure to the chartered bodies a monopoly in their own towns, but in the non-privileged towns also; and that this has acted prejudicially, and in a manner which the Sovereign in making the grants did not contemplate, to the interests of qualified public accountants outside Edinburgh, Glasgow and Aberdeen.

The editorial does not come down strongly on either side of the argument but does comment that 'a system of chartering the accountants of a single city is altogether out of date and indefensible. It is simply waste of breath to argue that Edinburgh, Glasgow or Aberdeen, or all of them, have any or the least right to privileges which other towns have not; and in the end the anomaly is bound to be rectified.'

Discussions on the subject of the petition obviously took a

long time since on 24 February 1890 the Glasgow Institute's Council again met to report on a meeting that had been held in Edinburgh between representatives of the three Chartered societies as to their continuing efforts to thwart the petition.

> It was agreed that the most strenuous and determined opposition should be offered to the granting of the proposed Charter and particularly under the proposed Title of 'The Incorporated Society of Accountants in Scotland' - same being held to be a complete misnomer as the Society proposed to be so designated would embrace in its membership a mere fraction of the Accountants of Scotland and not a single one of the leading members of the profession in Edinburgh, Aberdeen or Glasgow, while a considerable number of its members are not in any proper sense of the term 'Accountants' but occupy such positions as City Chamberlain, Bookkeepers, etc, while others are in business as House Agents, Factors, etc.

Further efforts to block the petition came in April 1890 when a circular was sent to all Scottish Members of Parliament asking them to support the Chartered Societies' opposition to the Charter for the Scottish Institute of Accountants. The hearing for the petition was fixed for 19 May 1890 and a deputation travelled to London to represent the Chartered Bodies. Part of the petition submitted by the Glasgow Institute stated that 'the present Institute of Accountants and Actuaries in Glasgow, incorporated by Royal Charter, is a body of gentlemen enjoying the complete confidence of the public of Glasgow and the West of Scotland, and to express our opinion that while securing complete freedom to all professional Accountants it is not necessary or desirable in the public interest that special powers should be granted to any other body that would interfere with or override the privilege of the said Institute.'

Having heard the evidence, the Privy Council, in a letter dated 1 July 1890, refused the application by the Scottish Institute, and it is probable that the strong opposition of the three existing Chartered Bodies played a significant part in this. The costs to the Chartered Bodies of mounting their opposition totalled £1377 5*s* 8*d*, to be shared among the three Societies.

However unsuccessful the application by the Scottish Institute of Accountants for a Charter had been, it did have repercussions which were of value to some of its members. Rule eight of the Glasgow Institute gave it power to admit members who had not fulfilled a four year apprenticeship as a clerk or apprentice with a member of that Institute or some other Institute or Society of Accountants or Actuaries. In special cases, accountants who were in practice might be admitted without serving an articled apprenticeship and without the requirement that they should be practising in Glasgow.

The Aberdeen Society discussed their attitude to this move at a Special General Meeting on 8 December 1890 and resolved to reserve the right to admit practising accountants who had been in business on their own or in partnership for at least five years and who held a respectable position as a businessman, and regardless of whether they worked in Aberdeen. Specific mention was made of the positions of Chamberlains of cities or towns, and Peter Cran, Chamberlain of Aberdeen, was admitted to membership of the Aberdeen Society as from 1 January 1891.

The Council of the Edinburgh Society discussed the actions of the Glasgow and Aberdeen societies at a meeting on 10 December 1890 and presumed that this move was in order to attract members of the Scottish Institute of Accountants and so weaken that body. Their response to this relaxation of the entry requirements was to fall into line with the other two societies, but with slightly stricter control in that a minority of one-fourth of Members present at a meeting could refuse an application for membership. They also agreed that the Edinburgh Society would not entertain applications from Glasgow or Aberdeen since they already had a society.

By the end of 1890, all of the Chartered Bodies had taken action to admit to membership, without completion of a regular apprenticeship and without passing the prescribed examinations, certain practising accountants. Without exception, the Dundee accountants who took advantage of this relaxation in the rules, applied for admission to the Glasgow Institute.

Unfortunately the membership records of the Scottish Institute of Accountants have not survived but the *Accountant* of 28 December 1889, carrying a report on the Annual General Meeting of the Scottish Institute held in Glasgow on 20 December 1889, listed the office bearers of the Institute and an examination of the admission records of the Chartered societies shows that most of them joined the Chartered Bodies when the admission rules were relaxed. The President, David Myles of Dundee, and one of the Vice-Presidents, E. Simpson Macharg, Glasgow, were both admitted to the Glasgow Institute in 1891 and 1892 respectively. Of the six Glasgow members of the General Council of the Scottish Institute, Thomson McLintock and Robert Tosh were both admitted to the Glasgow Institute in 1892 and James Drummond was admitted in 1898. McLintock was already a member of the English Institute having been admitted in 1880.[9] Although at that time he was in practice in Glasgow, he had received part of his training in the office of James L. Selkirk, Secretary and Treasurer of the Scottish Institute, also a member of the English Institute. James Davies, snr, was also a member of the English Institute and both Selkirk and he had sons who were admitted to the Glasgow Institute under the normal terms in 1896. D.G. Hoey had been admitted to the Glasgow Institute in 1870 but resigned his membership in 1873. He requested reinstatement in 1879, but the Council refused his request. Of the Glasgow members on the General Council only W.G. Lindsay and Vice-President Campbell from Greenock had no known connection with either the Glasgow or English Institute. All three Dundee members of the General Council, R.B. Ritchie, D. McIntyre and Alex. Tosh, were admitted to the Glasgow Institute in 1891, but none of the three Edinburgh General Council members were admitted to the Edinburgh Society, nor was the Edinburgh Vice-President, Robert Adam, accountant and chamberlain of the City of Edinburgh.

Despite this latest defeat in their quest to achieve incorporation through a Royal Charter, the Scottish Institute of Accountants did not give up the struggle, although their tactics did change. The minute of the Council of the Glasgow Institute's meeting on 6 January 1891 includes a letter from the legal advisers, Bannatyne and Co., calling attention to the fact that the Scottish Institute was applying to the Board of Trade for a licence under Section 23 of the Companies Act 1867 to be registered without the use of the word 'limited' and proposing that they be called 'The Incorporated Society of Accountants in Scotland.' It was agreed that representatives of the Glasgow Institute should confer with representatives of the Edinburgh

Society before opposing such an incorporation. Opposition to this proposal of the Scottish Institute seemed to take a different approach, since the Glasgow Institute stated no objection to such an incorporation: 'but they do most emphatically object to the title proposed, indicative as it is of the non-existence of any other Society of Accountants in Scotland, and they have pointed out that Sir Horace Davey in his speech at the hearing, suggested that 'they might call themselves . . . The Provincial Society or Institute of Accountants in Scotland. To the incorporation of the applicants under such a title, this Institute can have no objections.'

In April 1891, the Council Minutes show that a licence was likely to be granted under the title 'The Provincial Society of Accountants in Scotland', but by May the proposed title had been changed to 'The North British Institute of Accountants.' While the Glasgow Institute had no objection to the former proposed title, they did object to the latter on the grounds that 'The title proposed was considered quite as objectionable as that originally asked, and it was agreed that when the proper time came, objections should be taken thereto, in conjunction with the Edinburgh Society.' No further mention of this application appears in the Minute books and it would appear to have lapsed.

However, the Scottish Institute of Accountants did not give up their attempts to achieve a Charter. Writing in the *Accountant* of 3 December 1892, James Selkirk, the Secretary of the Scottish Institute, alluded to the way in which the Chartered Societies amended their rules in 1890 saying that this:

> looked remarkably like an admission that there was at least a measure of reasonableness in the application of the Scottish Institute; and it seemed strongly to suggest a greater desire to weaken, if possible, the position of a sister institution, called originally into existence through the narrow and indefensible exclusiveness of the Chartered Societies, and having similar aims and objects, than to promote the interests of the profession, which, with all respect to these Societies, are of higher importance to the community than are those of special bodies, however select.

Selkirk described the members as being 'men of as sound professional qualifications and as wide liberal culture as are to be found in any body of accountants. The aim of the Institute is to ensure that its members all possess the necessary qualifications and do honour to the profession. Beyond that it seeks, alike in the interests of the public and of individual accountants, that there shall be no monopoly or privilege, but that merit alone shall be the passport to status and public confidence and recognition.'

In March 1893 the Scottish Institute once more intimated its intention to apply for a Royal Charter of Incorporation but progress seems to have been slow, since James Selkirk is not reported as communicating again with the Chartered Bodies on this topic until November 1894, when he suggested that 'the scope and terms of the proposed Charter might be widened provided this Institute and the Edinburgh and Aberdeen Societies were prepared to enter into a joint scheme for the regulation of the whole profession in Scotland.' It appears that the Chartered Bodies were still strenuously opposed to the granting of a Charter to the Scottish Institute but were willing 'to consider favourably any reasonable proposal which the Scottish Institute should make for the regulation of the profession in any other way than by Royal Charter.'

Perhaps because of this continuing threat from the Scottish Institute, the Chartered Bodies instructed the drafting of the Accountants (Scotland) Bill to 'organise the profession of accountants in Scotland on lines similar to those on which the professions of law agents and solicitors, medical practitioners, and others have been organised, the governing bodies of which professions possess powers for ascertaining the qualifications of intending practitioners.' This Bill provided for registration for all members of the three Chartered Bodies and for all persons in professional practice as accountants in Scotland at the date of passing of the Act, on production of satisfactory evidence,[10] and would thus have included many members of the Scottish Institute. However, the Bill suffered the same fate as all of its predecessors.

The Scottish Institute's Charter petition was heard in May 1896 for incorporation as the 'Scottish Provincial Institute of Accountants' at which time it had a membership of 143. Despite the presentation of a strong case the application was refused and the costs incurred by the Chartered Bodies in opposing this petition amounted to £1100 8*s* 3*d*.

The catalyst which had sparked this latest Charter application by the Scottish Institute seems to have been the development of Scottish local government. An anonymous letter in the *Accountant* stated:

> The fees payable under indenture, and to the existing societies on admission, give them a monopoly which should be removed, in like fairness to accountants and the public. With the spread of local government in Scotland, as elsewhere, a great field has been opened to the profession, and particularly in the provinces, which was not dreamt of before, and now is the time to recognise the just claims of provincial accountants for a charter of their own.[11]

This opinion was echoing one which had been expressed in an editorial in the *Accountant* in the previous month:

> We understand that the present effort is made on account of the fact that during recent years the Legislature has largely extended the compulsory professional audit of the accounts of Scottish local authorities: the nomination of auditors rests with the Sheriff, and the appointments have hitherto been confirmed to chartered accountants. It is felt this is an injustice to local accountants, and a source of unnecessary expense to the authorities whose accounts are to be audited.[12]

The Scottish Institute of Accountants made no further efforts to gain incorporation through the granting of a Royal Charter or by any other means and in 1899 it was absorbed by the Society of Accountants and Auditors (Incorporated), which had been formed in England in 1885, effectively becoming its Scottish Branch while still retaining its identity as the Scottish Institute.[13] Ironically, in view of all that had gone before, the Incorporated Society integrated with the Chartered Bodies on 2 November 1957 and the members of the Scottish Branch, the late Scottish Institute of Accountants, were admitted to membership of the Institute of Chartered Accountants of Scotland.[14]

(*c*) *Corporation of Accountants*

One might have thought that the existence in Scotland, by 1880, of four accounting bodies would have been sufficient to satisfy the needs of those desiring to practise the discipline, but this seems not to have been the case. Although all four societies reserved the right to admit members on the grounds of relevant experience, the normal method of admittance was through apprenticeship and examination thereby excluding from membership men who could not afford such a pathway. The only differences in the admission policies of the Scottish Institute of Accountants were to admit to examination candidates who had been trained in offices other than those of a public accountant, and to admit to membership non-public accountants such as city treasurers.

> Once again, therefore, a growing number of capable men found themselves excluded from the existing organisations. And once again they were forced to the same remedy as their predecessors, which they applied in a yet more liberal way; so that the younger man who could afford neither the luxury of articles nor the long time service which the Incorporated Society required in lieu could still obtain a qualification, provided he had the ability and experience.[15]

This proved Stacey's point that: 'Immediately a new society of accountants became *comme il faut*, entry to it became restricted and still newer bodies were formed to take care of the rapidly growing marginal cases ineligible for entry into the existing associations.'[16]

This second wave of new bodies began in 1891 in Scotland with the formation of the Corporation of Accountants (Limited).[17] Its main characteristic was to be the first accounting body to declare that articled pupilage was not essential in order to become a qualified accountant, and it continued to retain, until 1928, the right to admit to membership in certain circumstances, accountants with a long record in practice or employed in other responsible positions.[18] The *Accountant* states that some of the founder members of the Corporation of Accountants were members of the Scottish Institute of Accountants.[19] Thus, since the Corporation was formed after the Glasgow Society had already altered its Rules so as to widen its admission policy, one might conclude that the founder members of the Corporation were either still ineligible for admission to the Glasgow Society or had become weary of the Scottish Institute's continuing failure to achieve incorporation by Royal Charter and decided to take action themselves.

Acknowledgement of the existence of this new body was noted in the minutes of the Edinburgh Society of Chartered Accountants on 20 November 1891 and at a meeting of the Council of the Institute of Accountants and Actuaries in Glasgow on 30 November 1891, called expressly to discuss this latest development in the profession. The Glasgow minute book contains a cutting from the *Herald* of 14 November 1891 which outlined the aims and objects of the Corporation of Accountants as being:

> to provide a special organisation for accountants and auditors, and to do all such things as from time to time may be necessary to elevate the status and advance the interests of the profession; to separate the profession of accountant from the business of stockbroking, and to provide for the supply of thoroughly-educated professional men by a system of examinations; . . . to apply for an Act of Parliament, Royal Charter, or other authority with a view to the attainment of the foregoing objects.

An editorial in the *Accountant* reveals the main concern of the established bodies to be that 'if those admitted do not pass an examination, how, without this test, are they to be known as competent?'[20] The Institute of Chartered Accountants in England and Wales had been formed as recently as 1880 and English CAs had, since then, seen the formation of the Society of Accountants and Auditors (Incorporated) in 1885, so it is perhaps easy to understand the concern that existing bodies felt about the launching of another, apparently inferior, accounting body. However, in Scotland, the

Chartered Bodies' attitude to the newly formed Corporation of Accountants was definitely coloured by the clause in the company's objects which stated that: 'The association shall consist of two classes, members and associates, and the former shall be entitled to designate themselves 'corporate accountants', or any initials or abbreviation of this term.'[21] The obvious abbreviation of the term was CA, which was at that time used exclusively by members of the Chartered Bodies.

The founder members of the Corporation of Accountants who signed the Memorandum of Association were James Martin, John Meikle, G.C. Dempster, C. Yule, J.L. Addie, and R.J. Kelso, accountants in Glasgow; and J. Miller, accountant in Greenock. With the exception of Miller, all of those named were involved in sequestration work at that time and perhaps felt that the formation of a company would protect this and other areas of work in which they were engaged.

In order that joint action might be taken against the possibility of members of the Corporation being mistaken for members of the Chartered Bodies, a joint meeting between representatives of the Glasgow and Edinburgh Chartered Societies was held in Edinburgh and Counsel's opinion was taken on the matter. Counsel was not clear about the right of the Chartered Bodies to insist that the Corporation's name be altered but was of the opinion that interdicts could be brought against individuals to prevent them from using the initials 'CA'.[22] There were at that time certain members of the Corporation who were advertising themselves with the designation CA after their name and the Glasgow Institute had instructed their agents to write to them and ask them to desist from so doing on the grounds that they were not members of any of the Chartered Bodies. In reply, the offending gentlemen stated that they had no intention of dropping the designation since it indicated that they were 'Corporate Accountants'.[23] This response left the Chartered Societies no option other than to attempt to enforce their legal right to the exclusive use of the designatory letters CA through raising a summons of Declarator and Interdict against the members of the Corporation in the Court of Session.

Interestingly, the Scottish Institute of Accountants were also unhappy about the formation of the Corporation of Accountants as correspondence reprinted in the *Accountant* shows: 'the Scottish

Institute were dead opposed to any such method of incorporation being resorted to.'[24] Also, at that time, the English Institute decided to reintroduce, in the House of Commons, the Chartered Accounts Bill, the Memorandum of which stated:

> Cases have recently occurred of persons describing themselves professionally as 'Chartered Accountants', although they are not members of any society or body incorporated by Royal Charter. This practice, if unchecked, being likely to mislead, it is proposed by this Bill, following the precedents of the Dentists Act, 1878 (41 & 42 Vict C 33), and of the Veterinary Surgeons Act, 1881 (44 & 45 Vict 6 62), to prohibit the use by any person of any name, title, or description, stating or implying that he is a member of a chartered institute or society of accountants, unless he is in fact such a member.

The Bill provided that it was forbidden to use the title CA unless the person was a member of an Institute or Society incorporated by Royal Charter and that accountants operating outwith the geographical limits of their charter must add their local designation.[25]

The Bill was blocked in the House of Commons, much opposition having come from Scotland over the provision to add local designation when operating outwith the limits of their charter. The English Institute subsequently agreed to drop this requirement but also decided that it was advisable to withdraw the Bill.[26]

The action that the Chartered Societies raised against the Corporation of Accountants was heard in the Court of Session on 12 January 1893. In his judgment, Lord Kyllachy stated that although there was no provision in any of the three Charters or in the by-laws of the Chartered Societies prescribing any particular designation to be used by the members, they had, from about the dates of their Charters, been accustomed to designate themselves Chartered Accountants and to use the letters CA.[27] In fact, an examination of sequestration records held in the Scottish Records Office shows that it was not until the late 1870s that such designation was generally used. Prior to that it was much more usual to find members of the Chartered bodies being described simply as 'accountant', but by 1891 it was unusual to find a chartered accountant not being specifically designated as such.

Lord Kyllachy found for the Chartered Bodies and granted them 'interdict against the defenders using for a professional purpose or professional designation the letters CA, or any other letters or words calculated to lead the public to believe that they are members of one or other of the three bodies of accountants in Scotland incorporated by Royal Charter.' The Corporation of Accountants appealed against the finding and the appeal was heard in the Court of Session on 31 May 1893. In giving judgment for the Society of Accountants in Edinburgh and others the Lord Justice-Clerk stated that he was 'satisfied that the only intention and purpose of those persons in using these initials is that they may appear to be, and pass themselves off as, members of one or other of the chartered societies. I cannot see any other purpose, and indeed no other purpose has been suggested.'

This legal protection of the letters CA came immediately after two Bills had been introduced into Parliament to attempt, primarily, to gain statutory protection of the title Chartered Accountant.[28] Both Bills had failed but these attempts, together with the granting of the interdict against the Corporation of Accountants, prompted a strongly-worded circular from James Martin, Secretary of the Corporation of Accountants on 23 June 1893. Martin stated that the Chartered Societies manifestly felt that they could no longer 'maintain their monopoly against the constantly increasing number of Accountants outside their Bodies, unless they can obtain from Parliament greater powers than have been granted in their Charters.' He further asserted that, in the promotion of these protectionist Bills 'the status of the profession and the protection of the public were entirely ignored and the evident purpose of the promoters was to magnify themselves at the expense of the whole profession, and by contrast to degrade, in the public estimation, all Accountants who are not members of their Societies.'

Martin made it quite clear that in his opinion the Chartered Societies were concerned only with their own members and not with the image of the accountancy profession as a whole:

> Their one object is to protect and extend their own monopoly, and so long as they can secure that object they care not what class of men may enter the

> profession from the outside, or what qualifications or character, or want of both, they may possess. Against such persons the Chartered Societies refuse to protect the profession and the public . . . Nothing could be more unworthy of any honourable profession than such an attitude. The public are entitled to rely that every person practising the profession and calling himself an Accountant shall be a person in whose hand their interests are safe.[29]

The circular went on to encourage accountants who were not already members of one of the existing Societies in Scotland, to join the Corporation of Accountants for an entrance fee and an annual subscription both of one guinea.

In the issue of the following week the editorial in the *Accountant* urged caution in the reading of this circular and showed its position in the matter quite clearly:

> it may be desirable that accountants who are unable to qualify for admission as chartered accountants should be able to enjoy the numerous benefits arising from co-operation, but we wish to emphasise the fact that no good can come of the mere multiplication of outside societies, and, further, that - if numerical majority and public esteem go for anything - the terms 'Chartered Accountants' and 'the Accountancy profession' are practically synonymous.[30]

In spite of the fact that the Corporation of Accountants continued to pursue an open door policy, to some extent, until 1928, it never became large enough to pose any real threat to the other Scottish Bodies. Stacey considered that there were two probable reasons for this. First, because the Corporation was based in Scotland it was perhaps less attractive to English accountants. Secondly 'and the less immediate reason, was the lack of real need in those days for an accountant to belong to any accounting body; the privileges and opportunities of those who belonged to one body and of those who belonged to none were not essentially disparate . . . In the halcyon days of all professions experience equated qualification and, at first, passing examinations was just another way of qualifying.'[31] Perhaps Stacey's second observation was more true in England than in Scotland and certainly, by the end of the nineteenth century, there were some areas of practice such as bankruptcy which were, almost exclusively, the domain of the Chartered Societies in Scotland.

The Corporation of Accountants did not, however, give up easily and a report in the Second *Annual Report* of the Council of the Corporation to the members showed that they felt that they had been unfairly treated by the Courts in their argument with the Chartered Bodies and continued to insist that they were right:

> The whole case against us therefore has broken down, as neither fact nor law is against us. We have infringed no legal right of theirs, although we have been mulcted in heavy expenses on the equivocal phrase 'calculated to lead the public to believe', a quibble invented for the occasion, and which is, in its present use, calculated to lead the public to believe that the decision founded on it is an attempt to give our opponents a monopoly which they have never possessed in law, and which they have sought and hitherto failed to obtain from Parliament.[32]

In early 1894, the Corporation of Accountants again attempted to boost their membership numbers by issuing another circular to members of the accounting profession who were not members of any of the Chartered Societies. This circular encouraged membership of the Corporation on the grounds that it was looking towards the real future of accountancy.[33] By the end of 1894, the Corporation had grown to 115 members and the relationship between it and the Chartered Bodies appeared to be no warmer than before. To be fair to the Chartered Bodies it must be said that the aggravation seemed to come almost exclusively from the Corporation of Accountants through the medium of its secretary, James Martin. The annual report of 1895 shows membership of the Corporation standing at 138 and the attitude of the Corporation to the Chartered Bodies unchanged. In its comment on this report, the *Accountant* refers to the Corporation as 'an association of clerks and bookkeepers, at least for the most part' and points out that: 'it is not the desire of professional accountants to promote any legislation that will interfere with clerks or bookkeepers pursuing their legitimate occupation; but if these gentlemen assume the name and business of accountants with their eyes open, they have only themselves to thank if they eventually discover that Parliament has passed a measure that is calculated to keep them in their proper place.'[34]

The Corporation certainly maintained a very active role in Scotland if that can be judged by the statements produced by James Martin in his role as Secretary. They issued a statement showing clear objections to the attempt by the Chartered Bodies to achieve registration in 1898, in which they point out that the Scottish Institute of Accountants was also excluded from the proposed legislation. One of the allegations in the statement gives an interesting insight into the business undertaken by accountants at that time: 'There is no provision for the separation of the business of accountant and stockbroker. In Glasgow, most of the leading chartered accountants are also stockbrokers, many in Edinburgh are so, and there are a few in Aberdeen, and the same men who are auditors of public companies also deal in the shares of such companies on the Stock Exchange.'[35]

Interestingly, in the following year when the Scottish Institute of Accountants was absorbed by the Society of Accountants and Auditors (Incorporated), James Martin was admitted as a Fellow of the Society while still retaining his post as Secretary and Treasurer of the Corporation of Accountants. He had been admitted to the Incorporated Society through his membership of the Scottish Institute of Accountants.[36]

The Corporation continued to be obsessed by the matter of designation and at a general meeting on 21 November 1900 the council issued a recommendation that the members should adopt the initials MCA - Member of the Corporation of Accountants - and use them in all professional matters.[37] This move was resented by the Chartered Bodies who felt that MCA was too close for comfort to CA and when they threatened to interdict certain members of the Corporation for so doing, the Corporation sought to have the legal right to the designation awarded by the Courts.

In 1903 the Corporation raised an action in the Court of Session against the three Chartered Bodies to seek declarator that they were entitled to use the letters MCA and that the Chartered Bodies should be interdicted from interfering with this.[38] At that time the Corporation was reported as having 276 members of whom only about forty-three resided in Scotland.[39] Counsel was heard by Lord Kincairney in Edinburgh on 3 November 1903 and his judgment given on 17 November 1903 in which he found for the Chartered Societies thus debarring members of the Corporation from using the letters MCA. The Corporation continued to press for registration for the profession but were no more successful in this than were any of the other societies. Membership continued to grow and in 1939, when it totalled 2100, the Corporation amalgamated with the London Association of Certified Accountants to form the Association of Certified and Corporate Accountants.[40]

2. Further Protection of Title

Millerson listed two of the secondary functions of professional organisation as being the raising of professional status and the protection of the profession and the public,[41] two objectives that are frequently mentioned throughout the first fifty years of accountancy's professionalization in Scotland, most particularly during the period from 1880 to 1900 when various attempts were made to secure registration for the profession. One of the ways in which professional status could be rendered easily recognisable by the public was in the use of designatory letters of title limited to members of a specific organisation. There can be no doubt that the members of the Chartered Societies sought to achieve monopolistic advantage in certain areas of work and this: 'is thought to be more easily attained if the association can secure legal protection of title for its members.'[42]

Shortly after the granting of their Charter the members of the Edinburgh Society of Accountants agreed to adopt the designation 'Chartered Accountant' and to use the designatory letters 'CA'.[43] This decision was intimated in the 1855 edition of *Index Juridicus, The Scottish Law List and Legal Directory*. Similarly in Glasgow the first discussion as to the propriety of all members adopting the title 'Chartered Accountant' or the initials 'CA' was in October 1855 and a resolution to this end was agreed at the Annual General Meeting held on 29 January 1856, with the proviso that adoption of the preferred styling should not be compulsory.

The more relaxed approach adopted by the Glasgow Institute was somewhat short-lived, apparently because of the concern of Glasgow members as to the effect that non-designation might have when compared with the practice adopted by Edinburgh members. This concern is clearly reflected in the minute books in 1858 where 'It was stated that the Character CA had been unanimously adopted by the Members of the Society of Accountants in Edinburgh and was now recognised by the Court of Session, and adopted in all remits made by them. After a discussion of the matter it was resolved by the meeting that it was expedient for the Institute to adopt a distinctive appellation.' As a result of this a letter was sent out to all members of the Glasgow Institute on 6 November 1858 recommending members 'generally to adopt the initial character CA or Chartered Accountant, after their names, in their official Accounts and Announcements.'

In the *Edinburgh and Leith Post Office Directory*, chartered accountants were separately listed from the 1855-6 edition onwards although in the advertisements for Insurance Companies in the same edition there was no use of the title CA by those entitled to it. Brown commented that it took some time before the new name became familiar to the public and indeed to the members 'but ere long it acquired a definite signification throughout Scotland.'[44]

Sequestration records show that from January 1857, some, but not all, of the Edinburgh chartered accountants involved in this sort of work designated themselves CA, but not consistently so. For example J.H. Balgarnie appears in January 1857 firstly as CA, then as Accountant and again, in February 1857 as CA, although it must be admitted that the Edinburgh CAs appear to have been more consistent in the use of designatory letters than were their Glasgow counterparts. The first instance of a Glasgow CA using the letters did not occur until February 1859 and the second not until July 1860, hardly indicative of a committed usage of the designation.

The first attempt to have legislative recognition of the designation Chartered Accountant came in 1863 during the discussion of the draft 'Court of Session Bill'. Clause 125 of the Bill gave powers to the Courts to remit any matters connected with accounts to 'Accountants or other qualified persons' and the Council of the Edinburgh Society agreed that they ought to attempt to have first refusal of this work by drawing the attention of the Lord Advocate to the expertise of Members of the Chartered Societies and, more specifically, by requesting the Lord Advocate to insert the word 'Chartered' before 'accountant'.[45] At this stage the Lord Advocate had no objection to such a suggestion but did not promise to make the requested alteration.

There seems to have been little further concern over the adoption and usage of the title until the Institute of Chartered Accountants in England and Wales was formed and included in paragraph seventeen of its Charter of Incorporation the use of the letters FCA and ACA to represent Fellow of the Chartered Accountants and Associate of the Chartered Accountants respectively.[46] Since the Charter did not apply in Scotland and Ireland by implication it limited the use of the title, in England and Wales, to members of the English Institute.[47] What did happen was that some accountants in Glasgow, who were debarred from membership of the Scottish Chartered Bodies on various grounds, were admitted to membership of the English Institute and began referring to themselves as 'Chartered Accountants'. This action seems to have incensed members of the Glasgow Society since they devoted much of their Council meetings from July 1880 to July 1881 discussing how to cope with this irritation. Although the problem appears to have arisen only in Glasgow, the members of the Edinburgh Society were consulted about its solution at a joint meeting in early 1881. The Aberdeen Society was also consulted and, typically, agreed to support any action taken by the other societies.

In an attempt to stop this practice, Wyllie Guild, the President of the Glasgow Institute, communicated with William Turquand, President of the English Institute, on 6 July 1880 stating that Turquand was 'no doubt aware that we obtained the Charter at our Institution about twenty-six years ago and are entitled to use the term CA or Chartered Accountant, and it occurs to me that if you admit parties practising here who are not eligible as members for our body a good deal of confusion may arise.' The implication here would seem to be that the English Institute was admitting accountants who were not suitably qualified to become members of the Glasgow Institute, but what was more interesting was that, although the Charter of the English Institute only extended to England and Wales, the Institute was prepared to admit accountants who practised outwith the geographical confines of the Charter at the date of their admission. This was completely different from the Scottish Chartered Bodies, which at that time imposed geographical limits most strictly.

Turquand did not deign to reply personally to Guild, but Howgrave, the Secretary of the English Institute, sent an immediate reply to the effect that the designatory letters of the English Institute were either ACA or FCA and this should not cause confusion in Scotland where the letters were simply CA. Guild was not quite satisfied with this, so he requested a list of English Institute members practising in Scotland. This was sent, again by return, with a note pointing out that these members could only be Associates of the English Institute since they were not practising in England or Wales. Obviously this was not the reaction that the Glasgow Institute wanted, since at this point they decided to take legal advice on the matter.

The first opinion they received was not encouraging, since it doubted their power to interfere with the right of members of the English Institute to use the title 'Chartered Accountant' in Scotland. At this stage the members of the Glasgow Institute decided to consult again with the Edinburgh Society to ask for their co-operation in order to create a larger pressure group.[48] Legal advice was requested by the Glasgow Institute and this time was much more specific, while still advising strongly against further pursuit of the matter. Two grounds were given in support of the advice. First, that, since the Charter of the Glasgow Institute contained no power of restraint against the use of the designation, it was clear that any legal opinion would be against them. This was unlike the Charter of the English Institute which did contain the right to use the designation ACA and FCA. Secondly, it was argued that, if such legal decision against the Glasgow Institute were to be published, then this would encourage other non-members to use the letters CA. To circumvent this problem the Glasgow members were advised to drop the initials 'CA' and to substitute in full 'Member of the Institute of Accountants and Actuaries in Glasgow' - rather a cumbersome solution to the problem![49]

This intelligence was communicated to the Edinburgh Society and was not well received, so the two groups decided to confer further on the matter and arranged to meet in Edinburgh. It is noticeable at this point that on any matter requiring to be discussed at a meeting, the Glasgow contingent always travelled to Edinburgh and the Edinburgh contingent never went to Glasgow. The Edinburgh Society agreed to take fresh legal advice on the matter from the Solicitor-

General and were no doubt delighted with the response, which was to the effect that members of the English Institute had no right to call themselves chartered accountants in areas outwith the scope of their Charter and that there was a reasonable chance that the Scottish Chartered Bodies would be found to have the exclusive right to the title Chartered Accountant in Scotland.[50]

At this stage, the problem assumed a new dimension in the form of the embryonic Scottish Institute of Accountants whose founder members included at least three Scottish members of the English Institute, i.e., Thomson McLintock, J.M. Davies and J. Selkirk. If their application for a Charter was successful, then they might have, or expect, the right to call themselves chartered accountants and it would also be unrealistic to expect the aforementioned members of the English Institute to drop the title willingly when they held dual membership of two bodies. James Meston, Secretary of the Aberdeen Society, then voiced his opinion on the matter. Having been to see James Howden, the Edinburgh Society secretary and having discussed the continuing problem with him, he was interested in hearing the feelings of the Glasgow Institute on the subject.

From the reports of their joint meetings it can be seen that the Edinburgh Society and the Glasgow Institute failed to agree completely on how to tackle the problem of designation. The Council of the Edinburgh Society resolved to instruct their law agent to write to any members of the English Institute practising in Edinburgh, requesting them to drop the designation 'Chartered Accountant' or the designatory letters 'CA' and threatening legal proceedings if this request was ignored.[51] In Glasgow, the Council, having again taken opinion from their legal advisers, resolved on 11 April 1881 that it would be inexpedient to take any action. They agreed, however, that it might be useful to seek a second opinion from the Lord Advocate and on 29 July 1881 on receipt of this opinion they confirmed their earlier decision of 29 April 1881 that no action should be taken.

In April 1883 when the Glasgow Institute had instructed its legal advisers to oppose the application for a Charter of the Scottish Institute of Accountants, the matter was again referred to:

> a number of Accountants here who are not members of its Corporation, [ie, the Glasgow Institute] have

> adopted their initials of 'CA' and thus hold themselves out to the public as chartered accountants, but, a considerable time ago, when this practice was commenced, we advised our clients that they could not prevent the adoption of these initials. Now, however, these same parties, it is said, are about to apply for a Charter incorporating the Accountants of Scotland, and it has been resolved by the incorporated bodies of both Edinburgh and Glasgow, to oppose this application if and when made.

From this point onwards, the Scottish Chartered Bodies changed their tactics and abandoned their campaign to restrict the usage of the designation 'Chartered Accountant' and successfully concentrated their efforts on attempts to prevent the Scottish Institute of Accountants from being given a Charter of Incorporation.

The other Chartered Accountancy bodies were similarly concerned to protect their title. When the Institute of Chartered Accountants in Ireland was chartered in 1888, included in the Charter was the provision that 'any person, while being a member of the Institute, may use after his name, in the case of a Fellow, the initials FCA, representing the words, Fellow of the Chartered Accountants, and in the case of an Associate the initials ACA, representing the words, Associate of the Chartered Accountants.'[52] Although the Charter did not specifically debar non-members from using the designation 'Chartered Accountant' there can be little doubt that protection of the designatory letters was intended.

Similarly, a Bill to amend the laws relating to chartered accountants, was promoted by the Institute of Chartered Accountants in England and Wales and introduced into the House of Lords in 1891. Although the Bill passed through its three readings in the House of Lords, it was blocked in the House of Commons and so failed. It attempted to restrict the usage of the title 'Chartered Accountant' and the letters CA to those who had a legitimate claim to them and stated that in future these should only be used by a fellow, member, or associate of an Institute or Society possessing a charter. Effectively this would have meant the restriction of the usage of the title CA to members of the five chartered bodies in existence at that time, i.e., the Institutes of Chartered Accountants in England and

Wales, Ireland and Scotland. The Bill, however, went further than this and suggested that chartered accountants should not designate themselves as such outwith their own country without making it clear that this was the case, so that an Edinburgh chartered accountant practising in London would be designated CA Edinburgh so that there was no belief that he might be an English chartered accountant.[53]

The inclusion of this provision might have been in retaliation for the way in which the Scottish chartered bodies attempted in 1881 to restrain members of the English Institute from calling themselves chartered accountant in Scotland or it may have been an expression of their concern at the amount of work being undertaken by non-English chartered accountants in England, particularly in London. Whatever the reason, the Council of the Edinburgh Society of Accountants, when considering the draft bill in 1891, moved that Edinburgh chartered accountants practising outside Edinburgh be designated CA Edinburgh.

In 1892 a second attempt was made by the English Institute to restrict the usage of the title Chartered Accountant. This would appear to have been stimulated by the formation of the Institute of Chartered Accountants of the Isle of Man which opened its membership to anyone in the United Kingdom and its colonies without requiring them to have achieved any level of general education or having passed any professional examinations.[54] Not unnaturally the English Institute was concerned that the performance of these less well qualified, self-styled chartered accountants would reflect badly on them. The Bill was, however, vigorously opposed by the Society of Accountants and Auditors and failed to reach the statute books.[55]

In November 1891 thc Corporation of Accountants Limited was registered as a Public Company and by December 1891 its existence was causing problems for the Scottish Chartered Bodies. As already explained, problems arose because of the provision in the Memorandum of Association of the Corporation that members should be entitled to designate themselves Corporate Accountants or any initials or abbreviations of this term. In spite of the fact that he must have known that his actions would create a serious altercation, James Martin, Secretary of the Corporation of Accountants, placed an advertisement referring to a Trust Estate with the initials 'CA' appended to his name.[56] The Glasgow Institute promptly wrote to

Martin asking him 'by what authority he used the name, and to require him to undertake to refrain from doing so in future, otherwise proceedings would be adopted in Court to restrain him.'[57] Martin refused to comply with this request on the grounds that his entitlement to describe himself as a 'Corporate Accountant' meant that his designatory letters were obviously 'CA' and he continued to use this designation until prevented from doing so by the Courts in 1893.[58]

Shortly after this victory for the Chartered Bodies, concern was expressed in the Glasgow Institute over firms being described as 'Chartered Accountants' when not all of the partners were members of the Institute and it was resolved by the Council of the Institute that this be forbidden unless either the majority of partners were chartered accountants or all partners named in the partnership name were chartered accountants.[59]

Before circulating this resolution to their members, the advice of their legal retainers was sought with a view to pursuing opinion from a QC if necessary. Once again, Bannatynes urged caution pointing out that the practice now being criticised had been going on for some years and 'we think it is very doubtful whether you can prevent a firm in which there is only one chartered accountant making use of the designation.' They also drew an interesting parallel between accounting and legal practices: 'In Edinburgh, firms in which only one of the partners is a WS or SSC adopt the designation of WS or SSC without complaint. The point appears to us to be so doubtful that we think your Institute would not be wise to raise it until further advice has been taken. To raise it unsuccessfully would impair greatly the value of the Judgment obtained some months ago.' It was suggested that the more tactful way to deal with this was to write to all members pointing out that firms who followed such a practice materially impaired the value of the recent judgment and they would probably then desist. The advice was interesting, considering that the English Institute specifically forbade the description of a firm as FCA or ACA unless all of the partners were members of the Institute.[60]

The Chartered Bodies seemed to have maintained a constant vigil over the use of designatory letters, since in January 1896 there is mention of correspondence having passed between the Glasgow Institute and one James L. Stewart, a member of the Corporation of Accountants who had appended the initials CA to his name in a docquet to the accounts of the Wishaw and District Economic Building Society. On investigation it was revealed that the letters had apparently been appended by Stewart's clerk in error and without his knowledge and Stewart undertook to see that this would not occur again.

The only other incidence of such behaviour which appears in the Minute Books at this period is, with hindsight, rather amusing. It concerned the discussion in April 1897 by the Council of the Glasgow Institute of an advertisement which appeared from time-to-time in the *Glasgow Herald* in which James Marwick, Chartered Accountant, 36 Wall Street, New York, invited correspondence in the areas of investigation of corporation and private accounts, acting as agent for trustees and supervising investments. Marwick, although born in Edinburgh and educated at Fettes, had been apprenticed to Wyllie Guild and admitted to the Glasgow Institute in 1886, his father being Town Clerk of Glasgow from 1883 to 1903. In 1897 he began to practise in New York with S. Roger Mitchell under the name of Marwick, Mitchell and Co. and was eventually to amalgamate with W.B. Peat and Co. to form Messrs Peat, Marwick and Co.[61] Marwick probably saw nothing unethical in advertising for business in Glasgow, since he was a member of the Glasgow Institute and the Council of the Institute agreed to take no action over this matter on the grounds that they had at that time no rule against members advertising for business.

Also, in 1897 William Mudie, a member of the Glasgow Institute who had been struck off in 1894 for non-payment of his subscription, was discovered to be continuing to style himself 'Chartered Accountant' in the Glasgow Directory and to be soliciting for business as a chartered accountant. This was considered to be serious enough to have the Glasgow Institute's law agent write to Mudie asking him to desist from this and to cause the President and Secretary to follow this up by calling on Mudie and getting his agreement to stop referring to himself as CA and to have these letters removed from his name plate.

Strenuous efforts were made in 1897 to protect the use of the designation chartered accountant as a means of protecting the public from less able accountants and sequentially to limit the performance of certain functions to those so designated. In particular, the passing of such legislation would have reserved the auditing of public companies, receivership, appearing as an expert witness, acting as liquidator of a company or as trustee on an estate to accountants registered as chartered accountants.[62] This particular effort never progressed any further than being a draft Bill but indicated the direction in which some parties wished to move.

However, opinion on this was not unanimous, as can be seen from a report on a Special General Meeting of the English Institute held on 13 January 1897 to discuss the draft Bill and at which Frederick Whinney stated that it was impossible to restrict public accountancy to chartered accountants on the grounds that it would be unfair to do so. Whinney, however, was strongly in favour of registration and warned the meeting that if the English Institute did not agree among themselves as to how this should be achieved there was a serious possibility that other parties might overtake them and threaten the privileges enjoyed by the Chartered Bodies. He revealed his lack of faith in Parliament when he referred to it as being despotic and as doing a great many things which did not conform to his ideas of justice. In Whinney's opinion, restrictive legislation was necessary so that the profession could be elevated and the public assured of a certain level of professional ability.

Ernest Cooper spoke against the need for restrictive legislation, one of the grounds for his opinion being, somewhat naively, that if someone used the designation of chartered accountant without being entitled to do so when he was a liar and a fraud and could not possibly benefit from his actions. Cooper felt that, in the sixteen years of their existence, the members of the English Institute had proved to the public, without shadow of doubt, the superiority of a chartered accountant and that such reputation was sufficient to continue to obtain for them the largest share of accounting work.[63]

The reprint of an article which had appeared in the *Financial Times* of 12 January 1897 cast serious doubt on the debate as to whether or not the chartered accountants would be prepared to countenance 'such a large extension of the number of persons who are entitled to use the mystic letters 'CA' after their names' and pointed out that the public did have an interest in the outcome of this debate since 'reliance is placed on the initials "CA" in prospectuses and Balance Sheets.' Since the *Financial Times*, at that period, was most likely to present an English viewpoint, it can be observed that the English Institute had done well to have achieved such acceptability for its members in the relatively short time since its formation in 1880.

The arguments as to whether or not registration should be sought and as to extension of the title of chartered accountant and the perceived benefits of such designation occupied many column inches in the *Accountant* during 1897 and 1898. Although much of the correspondence was from accountants with a vested interest, even the editorials tended to be against registration which would have placed all accountants on the same level, on the grounds that the title Chartered Accountant carried with it some guarantee of ability and respectability and a standard of professional competence which was not universally obtainable.

In 1903, certain members of the Corporation of Accountants again attempted to affix the initials 'MCA' to their names to indicate membership of the Corporation. The Chartered Bodies made representation to the Corporate Accountants requesting them to discontinue this practice, since they felt that the public would mistake such Corporate Accountants for members of the Chartered Bodies. In response, the Corporate Accountants raised an action of declarator and interdict in the Court of Session against the three Scottish Chartered Bodies to establish their right to the initials and to restrain the Chartered Bodies from interfering with this right. Judgment went to the Chartered Bodies following the earlier case raised by them against the Corporation and this seemed to settle the question of designation, in Scotland at least.[64]

3. Attempts to Provide for Registration

Attempts to achieve a legal status for accountants began in 1891 and continued unsuccessfully into the twentieth century. Throughout this period the various professional accounting bodies so involved insisted that registration was necessary in order to protect the unsuspecting public from the dangers of unqualified accountants. While this was undoubtedly partly true, it is probably more accurate to say that these attempts to achieve a system of registration were veiled attempts to secure a monopoly of certain types of accountancy work.

Ironically, it was the members of the new accounting bodies who first proposed registration, presumably in the hope that this would give them equivalent status to chartered accountants. Subsequently the chartered bodies saw registration as a method of securing control over the use of the title 'Chartered Accountant'. Eventually, however, their members felt that the possible loss of control to a government agency over entrance to the profession was too high a price to pay for statutory rights to their title. In any case, they had managed to safeguard their control over the use of their title through the courts without recourse to statute.

Registration was first attempted in a Bill brought before Parliament in 1892: 'To Amend the Law relating to Accountants practising in Scotland.' Garrett stated that the Incorporated Society first minuted the subject of registration in 1892:

> The idea was to set up a first register of all practising accountants and to limit future additions to persons with prescribed qualifications. Accountancy would become a definite profession recognized by statute, so relieving the Institute and the Society of continually recurring problems. The Institute entertained similar ideas, it may be with rather less conviction and on a more restricted basis than the Society considered necessary to deal with the situation.[65]

Perhaps on the basis of this information, Robinson attributed the 1892 Bill to the Incorporated Society.[66] However, he was mistaken in this, since the Incorporated Society would have been most unlikely to promote a Bill relating only to Scotland. The responsibility for the Bill must have rested with one of the bodies mentioned in it, i.e. the three Scottish Chartered Bodies, the Scottish Institute of Accountants (absorbed by the Incorporated Accountants in 1899) and the Corporation of Accountants Limited. The Minute Books of the Chartered Bodies make no mention of such action being taken; the Scottish Institute of Accountants specifically disclaim any involvement in a letter from their Secretary, James Selkirk,[67] which leads to the conclusion that the Bill was promoted by the Corporation of Accountants. This conclusion is further strengthened by the proposition in Section 7 of the Bill that all persons admitted to practise in Scotland under this Act should be designated Certificated Accountants and be permitted to use the initials CA and by the fact that the Corporation of Accountants were later involved in a lawsuit with the three Scottish Chartered Bodies who objected, successfully, to the Corporation of Accountants recommending that its members use the designatory letters CA.

The Bill proposed that admission to the profession would be through apprenticeship, examination and licensing, the licence to practise being renewable every year. However, it only progressed as far as its first reading. Reasons for the failure are listed in a leading article in the *Accountant*, which argued that the Chartered Bodies would receive no advantage from the Bill and would be unlikely to support it. In particular, it made the point that the Bill made no attempt to limit the practice of accountancy to licensed members of the new bodies, therefore no monopoly of work would be created. Among the disadvantages were listed the fact that accountants also practising as stockbrokers would be debarred from membership since the Bill insisted on members following only one career. The chartered accountants would have had to remit their funds to the new body and also share potential income and existing positions with men whom they probably considered to be both their professional and social inferiors. In addition, the Bill would have admitted women to the profession, a topic on which the profession, generally, had very strong views.[68] At the AGM of the Incorporated Society in 1891 a leading member of the Society maintained that 'accountancy was amongst those professions which required for their proper fulfilment those masculine qualities and experience of the world and intellectual capacity and courage which were very rarely to be found in members of the weaker sex.'[69] Similar views were expressed in an editorial in the *Accountant* in 1894: 'For our own part, we venture to think that there are few occupations more unsuitable to women, or - for that matter - even to the New Woman.'[70] Women were not admitted to membership of any of the British accounting bodies until after the passing of the Sex (Disqualification) Act 1919.[71]

Another factor which must have acted against the Bill's chances of becoming law was that the promoting body, the Corporation of Accountants consisted, at that time, of about twenty members in comparison with approximately 150 members of the Scottish Institute of Accountants and approximately 500 members of the three Scottish Chartered Societies.

In early 1893, the Society of Accountants and Auditors

(Incorporated) was responsible for promoting the Public Accountants Bill (No.1): 'To regulate the Profession of Accountancy, and to provide for the registration and control of persons acting as Public Accountants.' This Bill applied to the five Chartered Bodies, the Scottish Institute of Accountants and the promoting body, the Incorporated Accountants, and was extremely straightforward, stating that:

> no person shall describe himself as a professional accountant, or as a public accountant, or use any name, title, addition, or description, or letters indicating that he is a public or professional accountant, whether by advertisement, by description in, or at, his place of business or residence, by any document or otherwise, unless he is registered as a public accountant in pursuance of this Act.[72]

The Act would not have changed the structure of the Bodies to which it would apply, so that each would have retained its own system of examination and membership. Indeed, the only difference would have been the additional necessity to register as a public accountant with the Board of Trade. One of the most surprising things about this Bill was the apparent lack of consultation between the Bodies to be affected by it, indicated by the fact that the Minute Books of the Scottish Chartered Bodies make no mention of the Bill and the English Institute immediately launched the Public Accountants Bill (No.2): 'To Amend the Law Relating to Public Accountants.'[73] This only applied to the English Institute and the Society of Accountants and Auditors (Incorporated) and would have involved the maintenance, by the English Institute, of a register of accountants entitled to practise.

The fact that the Bill did not extend to Scotland or Ireland had two repercussions. It prohibited Scottish and Irish Chartered Accountants from styling themselves such in England and Wales and, more importantly, it debarred them from practising in England and Wales. However, for a very short transitional period, persons who were not members of either of the Bodies mentioned in it but who had been in practice as Public Accountants in England or Wales during the two years immediately preceding the first day of January 1893, would be admitted to registration.

From a leading article in the *Accountant* it would appear that a move of this kind was acceptable only because it was considered necessary:

> during the last eight or ten years, the solidarity of accountants outside the Institute has so increased as to seriously hinder the movements of chartered accountants in the advancement of their professional interests. In such cases of dead-lock there are but two courses open to the combatants: either to fight to the death, or to amalgamate. The former course would certainly benefit no practitioner of the present generation, and could hardly be said to advance the interests of the community; but the latter may readily suggest a *modus vivendi* which would eventually more than compensate all parties concerned for any temporary sacrifices that will be necessary.[74]

Not surprisingly, the members of the Scottish Chartered Bodies were not enamoured of this Bill and promptly despatched the Secretaries of the Edinburgh and Glasgow bodies to London to discuss the matter with Members of Parliament.[75] Members of the Irish Institute insisted that the Bill be altered to make it applicable to Ireland also.[76] Although the bodies involved did negotiate, the ultimate result was stalemate and both the No.1 and No. 2 Bills were discharged.

Robinson was perhaps correct in his conclusion that: 'This bill was, in effect, a take-over bid by the English Institute and may well have been intended merely to block the Society's bill rather than to obtain registration.' Although the Bills were discharged, the English Institute subsequently had a special meeting on 25 May 1893 to discuss the desirability of registration.

> The resolutions affirmed the desirability of legislation to restrict public accountancy to existing and future chartered accountants, and, with that purpose, of making arrangements with other existing bodies. But in the absence of such restrictions, the title 'Chartered

> Accountants' should be protected by legislation. There was some apprehension, undoubtedly shared by the Society, at the encroachment of 'officialism', particularly (a) by district auditors in the audit of local authorities' accounts, and (b) in regard to insolvencies.[77]

In 1894 the Society of Accountants and Auditors (Incorporated) introduced a Bill 'to regulate the Profession of Accountants, and to provide for the Registration and Control of Persons acting as Public Accountants.' Entitlement to registration by the Board of Trade was to be available to all members of the five Chartered Bodies, the Incorporated Society and the Scottish Institute of Accountants, the Bill seeking to limit the use of the description accountant to those so registered.[78]

An article in the *Financial News*, reprinted in the *Accountant*, welcomed the idea of registration, but felt that this particular Bill did not go far enough. The reservations expressed in the article are perfectly reasonable and make it clear that the preparers and sponsors of the Bill thought no further than making accountancy a closed profession.[79] Perhaps various attempts would have been more successful had they proceeded further along the lines suggested in the *Financial News*.

> If the public are to be limited to a set of men selected by the accountants' societies, and placed on the Board of Trade register, it is necessary that some lines should be laid down as to what does or does not constitute a faithful discharge of duty. If this Act were passed, one result would be that all audits would be carried out by gentlemen virtually practising under the authority of the Board of Trade. Does it not follow from this that some definition should be tacked on to the Bill as to what an audit is?

The response of the English Institute to this Bill, was to introduce, in early 1895, the Chartered Accountants Bill.[80] This was very similar to the Bill which they had attempted to have introduced in 1893, the main difference being that the new Bill excluded from registration members of the Society of Accountants and Auditors (Incorporated) but included members of the Institute of Chartered Accountants in Ireland. The Bill was designed, primarily, to protect the usage of the designation 'Chartered Accountant' and to provide for registration of chartered accountants. It did not extend to members of the three Scottish Chartered Bodies but they had already established at law their exclusive right to the use of the designation in Scotland: 'the unanimous view seems to be that the present situation affords them entire satisfaction, that they have nothing to complain of, and consequently no desire for any change.'[81] Once more, however, these attempts were doomed to failure largely because of a lack of co-operation and communication between the various interested bodies of accountants.

Towards the end of 1895 a series of three leading articles on 'The Accountancy Profession' appeared in the *Accountant*,[82] suggesting that:

> It is at times like the present, when there is in power a strong Ministry, supported by a powerful majority in both Houses of Parliament, that one is especially encouraged to hope for legislation of such a nature as that which the accountancy profession has been waiting for for so many years past . . . when there is every prospect of the continuance of the present Parliament and the present Ministry for another five years at least, there seems to be reason to hope that the legitimate claims of so deserving a body as the accountancy profession will receive due attention;

Whether or not these articles were the main casual factor is impossible to ascertain, but in 1896 there were no less than three Bills in Parliament dealing with the subject of registration.

The Society of Accountants and Auditors (Incorporated) promoted The Public Accountants' Bill - 'A Bill to Amend the Law Relating to Accountants' which would provide registration for their own members, those of the five Chartered Bodies and of the Scottish Institute of Accountants. In additional, the Bill prohibited the use of the description accountant or public accountant by anyone ineligible for registration.[83]

The English Institute promoted the Accountants (No.2) Bill - 'A Bill to complete the organisation of the Profession of Accountants throughout the United Kingdom.' Of the Bills introduced to date, this was perhaps the one which suggested an organisational structure most similar to that which was already in operation for the legal and medical professions. Registration was to be limited to members of the five Chartered bodies, the Society of Accountants and Auditors (Incorporated) and the Scottish Institute of Accountants and for a twelve month period after the passing of the Act, the Board of Trade would have the authority to admit other persons whom they deemed to be qualified for registration. A General Council of Accountants, consisting of representatives of the constituent bodies and of the non-affiliated accountants, was to be solely responsible for the examination of candidates who would be examined in the general rudiments of practice in the United Kingdom and in detail the law and practice of England and Wales, Scotland and Ireland. This recognized the fact that practice did vary geographically because some legislation, in particular that relating to bankruptcy, did not apply to the whole of the United Kingdom. Although this might have been seen as an attempt to limit accountants to practise within their own country, this was not the case since the Bill then made it clear that 'a candidate could offer himself for examination in law and practice for any part of the United Kingdom.' Having said that, there is little doubt that the English Institute were more concerned about Scottish accountants practising in London than were the Scottish bodies about English accountants practising in Edinburgh and Glasgow.

The final Bill to appear in 1896 was the Accountants (Scotland) Bill promoted by the three Scottish Chartered Bodies, the main provision being to restrain the misuse of the appellation 'Accountant'.

This series of attempts to provide legislation and the various leading articles in the journal, gave rise to a rush of letters to the Editor of the *Accountant*,[84] largely from anonymous sources. Given the allegations made in some of these letters it is not surprising that most of the writers preferred to remain anonymous. Sadly, little that was constructive emerged but many accusations were made of sharp practice, misconduct and inferior practice by various groups of accountants. The general tone of the letters was quite clearly that members of the Chartered Bodies were undoubtedly superior to all others and had no desire to be treated in the same way as members of the other accounting bodies. For example, by implication, a letter of 21 November 1896 refers to Incorporated Accountants as 'common accountants' and goes on to say: 'if we go on as we are, we shall, say in another sixteen years, be composed entirely of thoroughly competent men; we shall probably have all the business worth having, and a person who is not a chartered accountant, but styles himself an accountant, will be known to deal chiefly with the collection of debts and rents, the letting of public-houses, etc.'

In spite of all this correspondence the English Institute realised that co-operation was essential before any progress could be made and invited the Incorporated Society to confer with them in discussions which led to the preparation of a draft Bill - 'The Chartered Accountants Bill.'[85] Garrett described the scheme proposed in the Bill as being 'somewhat elaborate and attempted to combine the rigid views of the Institute on qualification with the more flexible ideas of the Society.'[86] In effect, the Bill proposed the registration of all practising accountants and the absorption of the Incorporated Society by the English Institute. Scottish accountants were not mentioned at all in the Bill, but the Irish Chartered Accountants were to be maintained on a separate register. Like most previous Bills on the subject of registration, the Chartered Accountants Bill provided that, for an interim period, registration should be open to accountants who were not members of any accounting body but who had been in practice as public accountants, in this case for a continuous period of three years immediately preceding the date of the Bill. In addition, the Council of the new body, would have had, until 1 January 1908, the power to admit to membership any candidate who had, up to the date of his application, been continuously in practice as a public accountant in England and Wales or Ireland for not less than ten years. Members of the Incorporated Society who were not in public practice were only to be admitted to Honorary membership of the Institute but, by implication, it would appear that all members of the Institute would have been admitted to full membership of the new body, whether or not they were in public practice. This seems to have been a clear case of discrimination against members of the Society and it is not surprising to find Garrett reporting that, in the Society of Accountants and Auditors, 'the most serious opposition came from members who were corporate (municipal) treasurers: they objected to becoming Honorary Fellows and Honorary Associates of the Institute and considered they were entitled to be FCAs or ACAs.'[87]

The Bill gave rise to a considerable number of letters to the Editor of the *Accountant* raising various points of contention and opposing the draft Bill. The grounds for such opposition varied through insufficient discussion and loss of advantage currently held by chartered accountants to an assertion that the draft Bill was 'obnoxious and revolutionary.'[88] There was no specific opposition to the Institute but much concern about the admission of unqualified practising accountants.

At a special general meeting of the English Institute on 13 January, the draft Bill was rejected by a large majority. 'The meeting of the incorporated accountants to consider the draft bill was held on the same day as that of the English Institute but, word having reached that meeting of the decision at the Institute gathering, the meeting was adjourned.'[89] Thus the first attempt to produce legislation after consultation with two accounting bodies failed before it was even introduced to Parliament. In an attempt to salvage something from all this, the English Institute then reintroduced the Bill that it had promoted in 1896, again unsuccessfully.[90]

At this stage, the Scottish Chartered Bodies introduced the Scottish Chartered Societies Bill which was designed to prohibit in Scotland the use of the designation accountant by any unqualified persons and to keep a register of practising accountants in Scotland.[91] This Bill also failed to progress very far in Parliament. The *Accountant* was somewhat scathing in commenting on this particular Bill when it stated:

> We have no hesitation in saying that it is absolutely hopeless to attempt any legislation whatever upon these lines. In the first place, the term 'Accountant' has been so generally used for such a large number of years past that it is futile to attempt to import into it any special significance at the present time, and to enforce that signification by Act of Parliament. In the second place, it is absurd to suppose that any legislation which may be passed upon this subject will deal with Scotland alone.[92]

In 1898 the Scottish Chartered Bodies attempted to promote The Accountants (Scotland) Bill - to amend the laws relating to Accountants in Scotland, and to regulate their qualifications and provide for their registration. Registration was to be open to all members of the three Chartered Bodies and to non-members in professional practice in Scotland on the production of evidence of such practice. Towards the end of the Bill are found the clauses that would protect much accounting work for registered members. First, is the provision that only registered accountants would be allowed to hold themselves out as accountants. Second, is the protection of audit duties in the audit of 'any corporation, bank, public company, society, association, or institution, incorporated by Royal Charter, or by Act of Parliament, or under the Companies Acts 1862 to 1890.'[93] This Bill was quite clearly another attempt to reserve large sections of work for a specific group of people.

The Corporation of Accountants issued their objections to the Bill stating: 'Altogether, the Bill is designed to create in Scotland a stringent monopoly of the accountant profession in the hands of the three Chartered Societies, and to rear up a huge vested interest which may become inimical to the interests of the public.'[94] An article in the same edition of the *Accountant* also voiced the opinion - 'that the Bill . . . does not stand the remotest chance of becoming law.' It further described the Bill as 'containing all the disadvantages which have existed in previous measures, with a few additional ones thrown in, and few, if any, of the redeeming features.'[95] Not surprisingly, in the light of its parochial tone, this Bill failed to become law.

In 1899 the Incorporated Society prepared a draft Bill - The Accountants Bill - 'A Bill to complete the organisation of the Profession of Accountant throughout the United Kingdom.' The draft Bill extended to the five Chartered Bodies, the Society of Accountants and Auditors (Incorporated) and the Scottish Institute of Accountants and suggested that registration as 'public accountants' should be the criterion for future practising accountants.[96] After a period of consideration, the draft Bill was introduced to Parliament as The Professional Accountants Bill where it failed to become law.[97] It was opposed by the English Institute who felt that the proposed new body would undermine their current position. James Martin, in a letter to the *Accountant*, emphasised the point that 'legislation for the profession can be of little immediate advantage to present accountants. Whatever is done will be done for the future, and I suspect that is the cause of the lack of interest in legislation shown by those who are the leaders in the profession.'[98]

Although there were subsequent attempts until 1912 to provide legislation for the regulation of accountants, the flood of attempts really ended in 1900.

Over the twenty year period beginning in 1891 one of the most serious obstacles in the path of registration was the fact that there was not just one professional accounting body, but several, between which communication was sparse. In spite of the warning in 1874 that: 'it would be well for all the respectable members of the profession to bind themselves together and, avoiding small matters of difference, work with a will to obtain the ultimate formation of an acknowledged profession.' The various professional accounting bodies appeared to take great delight in the rivalry which existed amongst them.[99]

The pattern of attempted registration that appeared was one of the promotion by one or more of the societies of a Bill which was promptly criticised by the others - a sad waste of the energy and talent of the professional accounting bodies of that time.

In addition, commentators of the day reveal the extreme parochialism that existed within the profession in the late nineteenth century. The argument in England was between the English Institute and the Incorporated Society, both of which had a membership spread throughout England and Wales, although the Institute's members were more concentrated in London and the Incorporated Society's in the Provinces. Their primary difference lay in the fact that the Institute required compliance with the apprenticeship system and the restriction of membership to those in public practice, while the Incorporated Society retained the right to admit to membership without apprenticeship and without the intention of a career in public practice.

In Scotland the three Chartered Bodies originally only admitted members on completion of an apprenticeship and examined those who intended to enter public practice in the city in which the particular Society was founded. It was not at all surprising to find eventual competition in 1880 from the Scottish Institute of Accountants, formed principally for and by accountants who were geographically ineligible to join one of the Chartered Bodies. Even the changes in the rules of the three bodies which were intended to dispel this problem did not erase it completely and their admission policies led the *Accountant* to make scathing criticism of the Scottish Chartered Bodies in 1897 during the struggle for registration:

> So far as we are able to judge, there is a need for legislation in Scotland which does not exist in this country, in as much as the Scottish Chartered Societies have for many years past looked upon themselves as being associations for the protection of their own individual members, rather than for the benefit of the public, with the result that they have so restricted their membership as to prevent it being any longer possible to suggest that Scottish Chartered Accountants have any longer a monopoly of respectability and competence. Had they adopted a more forward policy years ago, and increased their membership as reasonable demands were made upon them by capable men, the present difficulty would never have arisen, and they might have kept within their own ranks - as they did in the earlier years of their Charters - all the able and respectable practitioners. Now, however, through their own exclusiveness and narrow-mindedness, this is no longer the case; and, moreover, it may be reasonably urged against them that they used the benefits given them in the Charters for their own advantage, rather than for the advantage of the public.[100]

IX

Accountancy as a Profession

1. Emergence of Professional Bodies in early to mid-1800s

By the end of the eighteenth century professional organisations were not strongly developed and only the Church, medicine and the law were firmly established as 'learned professions'.[1] However, the Industrial Revolution brought with it a revolution in knowledge and led to 'the most notable and spectacular development in the nineteenth century ... the rise of the qualifying professional associations'.[2] Although the new associations began to emerge in the earlier part of the nineteenth century they were mainly a Victorian creation to help serve the needs of an industrial society.[3] Some of the new professions such as civil engineering were directly related to changing technology, while others, such as the actuaries and accountants, had less direct links with industry.

The Scottish accounting societies were by no means the first of the new professional institutions which were formed and chartered in the nineteenth century, following, as they did, the Institute of Civil Engineers, chartered in 1828, the Institute of British Architects (1837), the Pharmaceutical Society (1844), and the Royal College of Veterinary Surgeons (1844). In addition to having local links with these models of chartered bodies, the Edinburgh accountants had very close connections with the Scottish legal profession, which was based in Edinburgh, as well as having links with members of the Institute of Actuaries which had been formed in 1848. They therefore had every opportunity to mould their Society in such a way as to fit in with the established Victorian idea of what a profession should be.

In 1857, Thomson stressed the importance of the professions and their members which, he said: 'form the head of the great English middle class, maintain its tone of independence, keep up to the mark its standards of morality, and direct its intelligence'.[4] This suggests that the responsibility of professional bodies extends beyond their members to society as a whole, although there is little doubt that one of the effects of professional organisations was the establishment of a social distance between the members of such organisations and other groups.

2. Towards a Definition of 'Profession'

Many writers have attempted to formulate a precise definition of the word 'profession' but have tended to conclude that this task is extremely difficult.[5] Instead, they have offered a list of general criteria which should be met before the title can justifiably be applied to an organisation. Some of the definitions are rather simplistic, for example: ' a profession may be defined as an occupation possessing a skilled intellectual technique, a voluntary association and a code of conduct',[6] and 'professional has become a descriptive term vaguely suggestive of such legitimate privilege, based on specialised knowledge and ethical behaviour, as can be made acceptable to a society committed to an egalitarian ideal'.[7] However, there are several more detailed definitions which depend in turn on the definition of various characteristics necessary for the existence of a profession.

One of the most comprehensive studies of the emergence of the new professions was that carried out by Carr-Saunders and Wilson, which was published in 1933. In this they claimed that a profession grew out of a formal association by practitioners in the same field of work. Since such an association would initially lack social prestige, one way to gain this was through successful application for a Charter. The efforts of the association would gradually change to the means of protecting the interests of its members, one way of doing this being to hallmark those who were competent to practise by applying some system of training and testing

- a system which had long been used in the guild system of trades and crafts. The characteristics were, therefore, social prestige through obtaining a charter, recognised training and examination as qualifications for membership and, ultimately, obtaining a monopoly of certain areas of work through the legal protection of title.[8]

Blau and Scott concentrated on the members of a profession rather than the profession as a whole and examined what they considered to be necessary characteristics for members, though still claiming that the identity of an organisation was independent of its founders or its members. The first requirement was the mastering of a certain body of knowledge during a period of specialised training. Having completed this, the professional would be 'a specialised expert qualified to deal with problems in a strictly limited area' and his status would depend on him gaining and keeping his clients' confidence in his abilities in those areas. Relationships with clients would be characterised by personal detachment which would enable the professional to exercise reasoned judgment and his professional status would only be achieved through the correct performance of his tasks and through acting in the interests of the client, rather than for his own sake. The only other important characteristic of the profession was its control of entrants and members, arising from the supervision of their training, ensuring that they had a certain body of knowledge and acquired an acceptable code of professional ethics, and from the surveillance of a member's work by his peer group, which would be prepared to impose sanctions on that member in order to protect the reputation of the profession as a whole.[9]

Wilensky examined the way in which professions develop from occupations and noted the characteristic of each stage of this development. He saw this as a five-stage development starting with a substantial number of people undertaking some activity on a full-time basis. The second stage would be the establishment of a training school, with the formation of a professional association not coming until the third stage. Then there would be moves to gain legal protection for the group through a charter or other means and finally, the development of a code of ethics for the profession.[10]

Millerson identified the immediate cause of the formation of professional organisations as being a search for status. He then divided a profession's functions into primary and secondary, primary functions being the ability to organise into a body, thus producing a group of qualified members; to continue to study the particular subject and to disseminate that information; to register competent professionals and to promote and preserve a high standard of professional conduct. The secondary functions were: the raising of professional status and the control of entry to the profession; the protection of the profession and the public; the ability to act as a group on behalf of the members; the encouragement of social activities and inter-professional co-operation and the provision of welfare benefits to members.[11]

Hall saw the emergence of a profession as being an inevitable development from the specialisation of some occupations. Members of the occupational group who became involved in specialist areas would become increasingly involved with fellow specialists and would ultimately form an informal group excluding those not active in the specialist area. At the same time, the existence of a specialised occupation would require more training of prospective members in order to qualify for membership and those who underwent the system of training would tend to develop a professional identity.[12]

Perhaps one of the best definitions of the attributes of a profession was that produced by Greenwood. His first requirement was the existence of a systematic theory which could be intellectual as well as practical. The second was professional authority, which means that since the profession dictates the requirements of the client, the practitioner is given authority by the client because of the belief that his expertise will enable a correct judgment to be made. In turn, the community, by giving the profession power to determine its own training process, gives informal sanction to the profession's powers and privileges. The profession must produce ethical statements or codes on the behaviour of its members and gradually it will also develop its own culture. This professional culture will include specialist languages and symbols and will be a means of differentiating between professionals and outsiders since only the former will understand the symbolic system.[13]

3. Accountancy as a Profession

Few definitions of the profession of accountancy have been made since the majority of writers assume that the profession has existed for many years, including those who drafted the petitions for the Charters of the three Scottish Chartered Societies.

One rather basic definition of a professional accountant was that given by Worthington which stated that: 'professional Accountants in the primary sense are those who have, or who pose as having, a superior expert knowledge of accounts, the benefits of which acquirement they are willing to dispense to those who may require them'.[14] Carr-Saunders and Wilson in their discussion on the organisation of professional accountancy seem to consider that the only significant factors were the formation of the early societies and the admission only of those deemed to be qualified and the subsequent training and examination of entrants by the Societies.[15]

Littleton, however, addressed himself more specifically to the question of whether public accounting was a business or a profession. He commented generally that:

> A profession starts as an occupation. By slow stages it advances to the point where it is widely accepted as being a profession. Most of the early steps are unplanned; change at first is individual and largely accidental. Only at long last do men enter upon activities and policies conscious of possible professional import.

More specifically, he identified three elements that were necessary before an activity could be classified as a profession. These were the existence of professional knowledge and appropriate skill; recognition by the public in a demand for services and in statutory recognition; moral and economic independence of members. He considered that accountancy was no different from other professional activities and that the same requirements ought to be made of it.[16]

Portwood and Fielding stated that accountancy is not a homogeneous profession since it consists of various professional bodies characterised by a hierarchy of prestige headed by the Institute of Chartered Accountants in England and Wales which, they claimed, achieved this status by modelling its organisation on the Inns of Court and retained it through resisting registration for accountants.[17] They also referred to the hierarchy of power within the professional bodies. As far as the characteristics of the profession are concerned, they were in no doubt that the main concerns of any profession were wealth, status and power and accountancy was rated as being interested in all of these and deserving of classification as a profession. Reader differed in his identification of the concerns of the English Institute on its formation in 1880 stating that they were the usual objects of professional associations' 'proper qualifications, standards of conduct, lobbying in the profession's interest'.[18] Nisot saw that in some countries it is impossible to have any clear definition of the accountancy profession because there is often nothing to prevent any person from adopting the title 'accountant'.[19] In Britain, although there is protection for the title 'chartered accountant' there is none for 'accountant' and it is therefore difficult to define the profession precisely.

None of the definitions agrees completely with any other on what constitutes a profession, but there are several requirements that appear in most of them. Those are the development of a specialist area of work, the formation of a professional association, control of entry to the group, development of training and a code of ethics. Some writers disagree strongly with one or other of the criteria. Marshall, for example, considered that the emphasis on ethics was 'a mere camouflage to disguise the purely selfish desire to create an artificial scarcity and to win the material and immaterial advantages which scarcity can confer'.[20]

Several writers on the professions have claimed that without a legal monopoly on certain areas of work or legal protection through registration, a profession cannot be said to exist.

At no time during the nineteenth century did accountants achieve a legal monopoly over any area of work, although some legislation appeared to favour the professional accountant rather than the non-professional. Section 14 of The Limited Liability Act (1855) required that at least one of the auditors of a company be approved by the Board of Trade but did not state the qualifications required for this approval. The 1855 Act was repealed in 1856 when the Joint Stock Companies Act removed compulsory auditing but included model regulations which although not compulsory, introduced the concept that auditors need not be shareholders in the company, a change that could be seen as opening the way for the position of auditor to be filled by professional accountants.

Compulsory audit was not reintroduced for ordinary

registered companies until the Companies Act (1900) implemented the findings of the Davey Committee by providing for the compulsory election of auditors, but again there was no requirement that the auditor be a professional accountant. The Warmington Committee on Company Law Amendment (1906)[21] again failed to recommend professional audit but the Bill introduced into Parliament as a result of this Committee recommended that, in the case of companies with authorised capital of fifty thousand pounds, at least one of the auditors should be a public accountant.[22] The degree of influence of the accounting bodies on Parliament can be judged from the fact that this clause was deleted by the Standing Committee of the House of Commons.[23]

In 1918 the Wrenbury Committee on Company Law Amendment stated: 'We have made enquiry into the question whether the law should be amended by requiring that the auditors must have some and what professional qualification. We do not make any recommendation to that effect. We have not traced any mischief which requires remedy in the matter'.[24] Further discussions on this topic took place in 1925 in the Greene Committee on Amendments to the Companies Acts. Although some witnesses recommended that auditors should possess professional qualifications this was insufficient to convince the committee which stated: 'Cases in which auditors fall below the level of their duty are few and far between',[25]

It was not until the Cohen Committee on Company Law Amendment was appointed in 1942 that changes in the auditing requirements were recommended.[26] The requirement that the auditor be a member of a body designated by the Board of Trade as qualifying its members to audit the accounts of companies was first included in the Companies Act 1947 and consolidated into the Companies Act 1948.[27] Even then the Chartered Societies did not get a monopoly since Board of Trade recognition was also given to the Association of Certified and Corporate Accountants.

However, it is conceivable that this apparent lack of interest in securing a monopoly of the audit of registered companies during the second half of the nineteenth century is not as significant as it might first appear. An indication of the comparative importance of these companies can be judged from interpreting the figures for the nominal values of securities quoted on the London Stock Exchange at ten yearly intervals from 1853 onwards. (Table 9.1).

TABLE 9.1

Composition of nominal values of UK financial, commercial and industrial securities quoted on the London Stock Exchange 1853-1903

	1853 %	**1863** %	**1873** %	**1883** %	**1893** %	**1903** %
UK Railways	74.3	74.3	65.7	71.0	60.7	44.5
Banks and Discount Companies	2.3	5.3	18.3	5.9	4.7	8.2
Insurance	2.3	2.4	0.4	1.6	0.9	2.5
Total	78.9	82.0	84.4	78.5	66.3	55.2
Others	21.1	18.0	15.6	21.5	33.7	44.8
Total UK Financial, Commerical and Industrial	100.0	100.0	100.0	100.0	100.0	100.0

Source: E.V. Morgan & W.A. Thomas, *The Stock Exchange* (London, 1962) Table V.

This indicates that it was not until 1903 that registered companies, other than those categorised, amounted to a significant proportion of the total and that throughout the second half of the nineteenth century they were possibly not of sufficient importance to lead any of the chartered bodies to attempt to achieve a legal monopoly over this area of audit. Perhaps, also, the effort required to obtain a legal monopoly was deemed unnecessary since, by 1881, Pixley was commenting that: 'nearly all the prospectuses of new Companies now include among their officers the names of professional Accountants as their Auditors, while the older Companies are gradually replacing the Shareholder Auditor by a professional one'.[28]

The first society of professional accountants to submit testimony to a committee appointed to consider amendments to the

Companies Act was the Society of Accountants and Auditors in 1906. The Scottish chartered accountants did respond to the Greene Committee on Amendments to the Companies Acts in 1925, in the form of a memorandum from the Joint Committee of Councils of Chartered Accountants of Scotland which recommended that auditors should possess professional qualifications.[29] This recommendation was supported by both the English Institute and the Incorporated Society but failed to be included in legislation at that time.[30]

4. Scottish Accountancy as a Profession

The first accounting society, the Edinburgh Society of Chartered Accountants was founded by a group of men who were involved in the specialist area of bankruptcy work and could be said to have developed out of the legal profession in Edinburgh. The hierarchical structure which was adopted consisted of a President, Treasurer, Secretary and a Council, along with a Committee of Examinators which was convened as required. From the outset, the Society stated its opinion that an attempt should be made to limit certain areas of work to members; a formal admission procedure for prospective members was agreed and the desirability of having a Royal Charter was discussed.[31] Standardised forms for indentures and certificates of qualification were drawn up within two years and the first examinations for admission held in March 1855.[32] So, the Edinburgh Society very quickly had a structure, rules, a Charter, entry procedures and examinations.

The Glasgow Institute followed along similar lines, although it initially had a Committee of Elder Members as well as the Council. It also formed a Bankruptcy Committee at an early stage to discuss the proposed changes in bankruptcy legislation that were responsible for the formation of the Institute. There was no special examiners' committee, instead all members of Council were designated examinators. The first example of the role of the Societies in regulating the professional conduct of members was in October 1855 when James McClelland, President of the Glasgow Institute, was authorised to write to members who had not yet made their sequestration returns for 1850 to 1853, requesting them 'to do so without delay, as it was of importance to have these returns completed, and as the Edinburgh Accountants had promptly complied with the request, it was not creditable to any Member of the Glasgow body to hold back'.[33]

Both of the groups had specialist knowledge and voluntary association and within a short period, they had both received Charters and had Rules and Constitutions. Neither of them had written codes of ethics, but perhaps could argue that these were unnecessary since they only admitted people who had high ethical standards. Although both had examination systems, these were initially rather informal and certainly unwritten. In addition, the Glasgow Institute continued to admit people to membership on the grounds of experience and without completion of articles. Since the societies had no legal monopoly over any area of work, it is doubtful that, at formation, they complied with a sufficient number of the prerequisites to qualify for designation as a profession, in spite of their claims to the contrary in their Charter application.

In the early years of their existence, the two Scottish societies took several steps to strengthen their position as a profession. Both formed committees to discuss the impact of changing bankruptcy legislation on their members and acted as a pressure group in this respect. The requirement that apprentices attend law classes identified skill in the specialist area of bankruptcy and this was reinforced by the gradual build up of a near monopoly in certain areas of work such as bankruptcy and the audit of railway companies, banks, insurance companies and local government which all served to identify the chartered accountant as having special skills, a requirement emphasised in most studies on professionalization.

Training continued to be by the system of apprenticeship with first a suggestion in 1865 that law classes be attended by Edinburgh apprentices,[34] followed by a compulsion so to do in 1874.[35] In addition, it was agreed in 1864 by the Edinburgh Society, that in the future, examinations ought to be in writing as well as viva voce.[36] In these respects, the Glasgow Institute was different in that it continued for a much longer period to admit members who had not completed the traditional apprenticeship and although examinations were introduced in 1855 and odd references made to the preparation of certain examination papers,[37] it would seem that Glasgow did not have a completely formal examination system until the introduction of the Central Board of Examiners in 1892, which effectively introduced standardised examinations for all Scottish apprentices. This meant that the Scottish chartered accountant was hallmarked with a recognised standard of professional competence and also helped to establish a professional identity for the group.

As far as protection of title was concerned, there is no doubt that by the end of the nineteenth century the designation 'Chartered Accountant' had been limited to members of the three Scottish bodies and the English and Irish Institutes. This helped to strengthen the professional identity of the group and, in certain areas, created a demand for the chartered accountant in preference to other accountants.

The one area where no obvious advances were made during the period of study was in the provision of a code of conduct, which is claimed by some to be the main distinguishing mark of the professions.[38] However, the absence of a written code of conduct cannot be accepted as evidence that no code of conduct existed, since various incidents referred to in the Minute Books prove that all three Societies reacted very severely to what they considered to be the professional or social misconduct of members.

This is amply illustrated by the treatment of a former President of the Aberdeen Society who having practised in Surrey had returned to Aberdeen in 1894 and apparently fallen on hard times. His presence in Aberdeen caused such embarrassment to his fellow members that they indicated their willingness to expend £20 to £25 to assist him to emigrate on condition that he resigned his membership of the Society. He refused this offer and in 1896 was struck off for being four years in arrears at which time it was agreed that the Council should have the power to spend up to £42 for his benefit, this being the amount of the entry money he had paid to the Society.[39]

Although no legal monopoly of audit existed, by the end of the nineteenth century, Scottish chartered accountants had built up a virtual monopoly of the audit of Scottish railways, banks and insurance companies, which would appear to have constituted the most significant proportion of available audit. In addition, they quickly built up a monopoly of the new area of audit made available by the reorganisation of Scottish local authorities. It is therefore conceivable that, in Scotland, chartered accountants saw no need to expend their Societies' resources in pressing for a legal monopoly in areas where they already had a virtual monopoly and the absence of a legal monopoly cannot, in this case, be seen as an indication that the Scottish chartered accountants should not be regarded as a profession.

As far as proving professional existence through the legal protection of registration is concerned, accountancy can again be seen to be different. The fact that the profession developed as a system of different accounting bodies made it difficult to have productive discussions and reach any kind of agreement on the subject of registration. Although various attempts were made towards the end of the nineteenth century to introduce registration, the pressure came, initially from the non-chartered bodies who wished to share in what they saw as the more prestigious and lucrative areas of accounting that had gradually been dominated by the Chartered bodies. The Chartered bodies only entered the registration debate in order to protect themselves from the possibility that members of other accounting bodies might obtain a legal right to some areas of work, currently carried out almost exclusively by chartered accountants. The latter had no need of registration since they had succeeded in convincing the public that they were superior practitioners and therefore the most obvious choice for certain areas of work. So again, it would be wrong to say that a lack of registration indicated the non-existence of a profession.

By the end of the nineteenth century, the Scottish chartered accounting societies clearly had all the characteristics of a professional body, and through the emigration of a significant proportion of their members, had contributed to the formation of other accounting societies throughout the colonies. Much of the development of the profession and the expansion of its horizons came as a result of steady work by individuals or groups of members rather than the bodies themselves and the late nineteenth century was a period where accountants transferred their energies from being primarily interested in bankruptcy to the inclusion of auditing, financial accounting and taxation.

These developments could almost be compared with the present day scene, where the profession is dominated by a few large accounting firms showing renewed aggression in moving into areas which were never envisaged by their professional bodies, such as counting votes and identifying multiple applications for share issues, but where the professional bodies then support them through maintaining the professional image of chartered accountancy.

The continuing pattern of amalgamation of firms of chartered accountants throughout the United Kingdom has resulted in the loss of many of the partnerships which were formed in the early days of Scottish chartered accountancy and removed many of the superficial differences between members of the Scottish and English Institutes. The digress areas of pseudo-accounting work now undertaken by accounting firms have necessitated the employment of an increasing proportion of non-accountant specialists so that an outsider might be forgiven for mistaking the accounting profession for the accounting industry.

In 1951, almost one hundred years after the formation of the Edinburgh and Glasgow societies, the three Scottish societies amalgamated to form the Institute of Chartered Accountants of Scotland which should mean theoretically that 'there will, in future, be but one class of Chartered Accountants in Scotland'.[40] Although a uniform apprenticeship and training system has done much to ensure that to be the case, it is doubtful that the character differences of the various geographical areas of Scotland could have been overcome by mere legislation. However, such parochial differences are relegated to a secondary position in times of extreme need. In 1989 the Councils of the English and Scottish Institutes of Chartered Accountants recommended to their members that they vote for the establishment of a British Institute. The English Institute vote was strongly in favour but the Scots, who perhaps viewed the move as a takeover rather than a merger, voted very firmly to retain their own Scottish Institute, with its unique collegiate training system, proving conclusively that in Scotland, at least, loyalty to 'the firm' is secondary to loyalty to 'The Institute'. This demonstrates the continuing existence of a professional *esprit de corps* which, together with the educational and training system, imminent right of registration under the 1989 Co.'s Act and a near monopoly of audit and insolvency work, provides strong evidence of the claim that Scottish chartered accountancy is a profession. Lingering doubts remain over the growing influence and aggression of the ICAEW in Scotland together with the propensity of the large accounting firms to expand into areas of work for which the profession provides no training.

Sources

1. Manuscript:

Society of Accountants in Aberdeen:

Council Minute Books, 1867-1904.
General Meeting Minute Books, 1867-1904.

Society of Accountants in Edinburgh:

Council Sederunt and Minute Books, 1853-1904.
General Meeting Minute Books, 1854-1904.
Register of Indentures, 1855-1904.
Register of Members, 1855-1904.

Institute of Accountants in Glasgow:

Members Admission Books Vol. 1-4.
Minute Books, 1853-1904.

General Register Office for Scotland:

Census Returns for Scotland, 1841-91.
Statutory Registers of Births, Marriages and Deaths for Scotland, 1855-1980.
Old Parochial Records of Baptism, Banns and Burials.
Records of Sequestration Awards, 1856-1904.
Annual Reports by the Accountant of Bankruptcy in Scotland to the Court of Session, 1857-1904.

2. Periodicals:

Accountant
Accountants' Magazine
Baillie
Banking Almanac
Glasgow Herald

Herapath's Railway Journal
Incorporated Accountant's Journal
Scotsman
Scots Law Times

3. Directories:

Annual *Post Office Directories* for: Aberdeen, Dundee, Edinburgh and Leith, Glasgow and London.
Bradshaw's Railway Almanac, Directory, Shareholders' Guide and Manual.
Scottish Chartered Accountants, *Official Directory.*
Society of Incorporated Accountants and Auditors, *List of Members etc.*

4. Parliamentary Acts, Bills, etc:

Parliamentary Acts:

1641 V, 6466 Scottish Education Act.

1696 c.26, X, 63, Scottish Education Act.

1719 6 Geo.1, c.18, Bubble Act.

1811 51 Geo.3, c.133, Incorporation of Company with power to construct a Railway from Spittal to Kelso.

1814 54 Geo.3, c.137, For Rendering the Payment of Creditors more equal and expeditious in Scotland.

1825 6 Geo.4, C.91, To Repeal 6 Geo.1, c.18 and to confer Additional Powers upon His Majesty, with Respect to the Granting of Charters of Incorporation to Trading and Other Companies.

1831 1 & 2 Wm 4, c.56, To Establish a Court in Bankruptcy.

1835 5 & 6 Wm 4, c.76, To Provide for the Regulation of Municipal Corporations in England and Wales.

1836 6 & 7 Wm 4, c.32, For Making and Maintaining a Railway from the Royal Burgh of Dundee in the County of Forfar to the Royal Burgh of Arbroath in the Same County.

1838 1 & 2 Vict. c.58, For Making and Maintaining a Railway between the Royal Burgh of Arbroath in the County of Forfar and the Royal Burgh of Forfar in the same County.

1839 2 & 3 Vict. c.41, For Regulating the Sequestration of the Estates of Bankrupts in Scotland.

1844 7 & 8 Vict. c.66, For Making a Railway from the City of Edinburgh to the Town of Berwick-upon-Tweed, with a Branch to the Town of Haddington.

1844 7 & 8 Vict. c.85, To attach Certain Conditions to the Construction of Future Railways.

1844 7 & 8 Vict. c.110, For the Registration, Incorporation, Index and Regulation of Joint Stock Companies.

1844 7 & 8 Vict. c.113, To Regulate Joint Stock Banks in England.

1845 8 & 9 Vict. c.16, Companies Clauses Consolidation.

1845 8 & 9 Vict. c.17. Companies Clauses Consolidation (Scotland).

1845 8 & 9 Vict. c.20, Railways Clauses Consolidation.

1845 8 & 9 Vict. c.162, For Making a Railway from Carlisle to Edinburgh and Glasgow and the North of Scotland.

1846 9 & 10 Vict. c.75, Joint Stock Banking (Scotland).

1846 9 & 10 Vict. c.158, For Making a Railway from Ferryhill near Aberdeen to Aboyne.

1847 10 & 11 Vict. c.34, Scottish Union Insurance Company.

1847 10 & 11 Vict. c.35, Incorporating Scottish Equitable Life Assurance Society.

1851 14 & 15 Vict. c.134, Caledonian Railway Arrangements Act.

1853 16 & 17 Vict. c.53, To Amend the Laws Relating to Bankruptcy in Scotland.

1855 18 & 19 Vict. c.133, For Limiting the Liability of Members of Certain Joint Stock Companies.

1856 19 & 20 Vict. c.133, Joint Stock Companies.

1856 19 & 20 Vict. c.79, To Consolidate and Amend the Laws Relating to Bankruptcy in Scotland.

1859 22 & 23 Vict. c.49, Incorporating the National Fire and Life Insurance Company of Scotland by the Name of The Scottish National Insurance Company.

1862 25 & 26 Vict. c.89, Joint Stock Companies.

1867 30 & 31 Vict. c.126, To Amend the Laws Relating to Railway Companies in Scotland.

1868 31 & 32 Vict. c.119, To Amend the Laws Relating to Railways.

1869 32 & 33 Vict. c.71, To Consolidate and Amend the Laws of Bankruptcy.

1870 33 & 34 Vict. c.61, To Amend the Law Relating to Life Assurance Companies.

1878 41 & 42 Vict. c.53, Amalgamating the Scottish Union Insurance Company and the Scottish National Insurance Company and for Incorporating the Amalgamated Companies by the Name of 'The Scottish Union and National Insurance Company'.

1879 42 & 43 Vict. c.76, To Amend the Law with Respect to the Liability of Members of Banking and Other Joint Stock Companies.

1882 45 & 46 Vict. c.50, For Consolidating, with Amendments, Enactments Relating to Municipal Corporations in England and Wales.

1888 51 & 52 Vict. c.41, To Amend the Laws Relating to Local Government in England and Wales.

1889 52 & 53 Vict. c.39, To Amend and Extend the Law Relating to Judicial Factors and Others in Scotland and to Unite the Offices of the Accountant of The Court of Session and the Accountant in Bankruptcy in Scotland.

1889 52 & 53 Vict. c.50, To Amend the Laws Relating to Local Government in Scotland.

1889 52 & 53 Vict. c.116, West Bromwich Corporation (Consolidation of Loans).

1892 55 & 56 Vict. c.55, For Regulating the Police and Sanitary Administration of Towns and Populous Places, and for Facilitating the Union of Police and Municipal Administration in Burghs in Scotland.

1900 63 & 64 Vict. c.48, To Amend the Companies Act.

1900 63 & 64 Vict. c.49, To Consolidate and Amend the Law

Relating to the Election and Proceedings of Town Councils in Scotland.

1919 9 & 10 Geo.5 c.71, To Amend the Law with Respect to Disqualifications on Account of Sex.

1947 10 & 11 Geo.6, c.47, To Amend the Law Relating to Companies and Unit Trusts and to Dealing in Securities, and in Connection therewith to Amend the Law Relating to the Registration of Business Names.

1948 11 & 12 Geo.6, c.38, To Consolidate the Companies Act 1929 and 1947.

Parliamentary Bills:

1852-3 (441) i, To Amend the Laws Relating to Bankruptcy in Scotland.

1854-5 (120) iii, To Consolidate and Amend The Laws of Scotland Regarding Insolvency and Bankruptcy.

1856 (54) i, To Consolidate and Amend The Law Relating to Bankruptcy in Scotland.

1878-9 (58) iii, For the Better Auditing of the Books and Accounts of the Chartered and Other Joint Stock Banks in Scotland.

1890-1 (431) i, To Amend the Law Relating to Chartered Accountants.

1892 (255) ii, To Amend the Law Relating to Accountants Practising in Scotland.

1893-4 (65) vii, To Regulate the Profession of Accountancy, and To Provide For the Registration and Control of Persons Acting as Public Accountants.

1893-4 (248) vii, To Amend the Law Relating to Public Accountants.

1893-4 (261) v, To Amend the Local Government (Scotland) Act, 1889.

1894 (291) i, To Regulate the Profession of Accountants, and to Provide for the Registration and Control of Persons Acting as Public Accountants.

1895 (41 - Sess. 1) i, To Amend the Law Relating to Chartered Accountants.

1896 (114) i, To Amend the Law Relating to Accountants.

1896 (137) i, To Amend the Law Relating to Accountants in Scotland, and To Regulate Their Qualifications and Provide For Their Registration.

1896 (318) i, To Complete the Organization of the Profession of Accountants throughout the United Kingdom.

1897 (94) i, To Amend the Law Relating to Accountants in Scotland, and To Regulate Their Qualifications and Provide for Their Registration.

1897 (163) i, To Complete the Organization of the Profession of Accountants throughout the United Kingdom.

1898 (201) i, To amend the Laws Relating to Accountants in Scotland.

1900 (112) iv, To Provide for the Better Organisation of Professional Accountants.

Commission, Reports of:

1867-8 Vol. xxviii, To Inquire into the Education given in Schools in England.

Select Committees:

Secret Committee:

1836 (591) ix, To inquire into the Operation of the Act Geo.4, c.46, permitting the establishment of Joint Stock Banks, and whether it be expedient to make any alteration in that Act.

Secret Committee:

1837 (531) xiv, To inquire into the Operation of the Acts permitting the establishment of Joint Stock Banks in England and Ireland, and whether it is expedient to make any amendment in those Acts.

Secret Committee:

1837-8 (626) vii, To inquire into the Operation of the Acts permitting the establishment of Joint Stock Banks in England and Ireland, and whether it is expedient to make any amendment in those Acts.

1843 (523) xi, To inquire into the State of the Laws respecting Joint Stock Companies (except for Banking), with a view to the Greater Security of the Public.

1844 (119) vii, To inquire into the State of the Laws respecting Joint Stock Companies (except for Banking), with a view to the Greater Security of the Public.

1849 (371) x, (421) x, First and Second Reports from the Select Committee of the House of Lords on Audit of Railway Accounts.

1857 (220) x, To inquire into the operations of the Bank Act of 1844, and of the Bank Acts of Scotland and Ireland of 1845.

1857-8 (441) xvi, To inquire into the Acts relating to Savings Banks and the operation thereof.

1867 (329) x, To inquire into the operation of the Limited Liability Acts.

1906 Cd 3052, xcvii, Company Law Amendment Committee.

1906 Cd 3053, xcvii, Appendix to Cd 3052.

1918 Cd 9138, vii, Company Law Amendment Committee.

1926 Cmd 2657, ix, Company Law Amendment Committee.

1945 Cmd 6659, iv, Company Law Amendment Committee.

Bibliography

Alexander, E.R. *The Historical Relationship between Accountants and Actuaries*, Dissertation, Strathclyde University (1974).

Alphabetical Compendium of Scotch Mercantile Squestrations 1851 (London, 1851).

Anderson, R.D. *Education and Opportunity in Victorian Scotland* (Oxford, 1938).

Bagwell, P.S. *The Railway Clearing House in the British Economy 1842-1922* (London 1968).

Blau, P.M. and Scott, W.R. *Formal Organizations: A Comparative Approach* (London, 1963).

Bone, T.R. (ed.) *Studies in the History of Scottish Education 1872-1939* (London, 1967).

Briston, R.J. and Kedslie, M.J.M. 'Professional Formation: The Case of Scottish Accountants. Some Correction and Some Further Thoughts', *British Journal of Sociology* (Mar., 1986).

Brown, R. (ed.) *A History of Accounting and Accountants* (Edinburgh, 1905).

Buckton, T.J. *Railway Audit really Independent* (London, 1850).

Byres, T.J. 'Entrepreneurship in the Scottish Heavy Industries 1870-1900', P.L. Payne (ed.) *Studies in Scottish Business History* (London, 1967).

Cairncross, A.K. 'The Social Origins of Chartered Accountants', *Accountant* (Sept., 1937).

Campbell, R.H. 'The Law and the Joint-Stock Company in Scotland' in P.L. Payne (ed.) *Studies in Scottish Business History* (London, 1967).

Caplow, T. *The Sociology of Work* (London, 1964).

Carr-Saunders, A.M. and Caradog Jones, D. *A Survey of the Social Structure of England and Wales*, 2nd ed. (Oxford, 1937).

Carr-Saunders, A.M. and Wilson, P.A. *The Professions* (Oxford, 1933).

Chatfield, M. (ed.) *Contemporary Studies in the Evolution of Accounting Thought* (New York, 1968).

Chatfield, M. (ed.) *The English View of Accountants' Duties and Responsibilities 1881-1902* (New York, 1978).

Checkland, O. *Philanthropy in Victorian Scotland: Social Welfare and the Voluntary Principle* (Edinburgh, 1980).

Checkland, S. G. *Scottish Banking: A History 1695-1973* (Glasgow, 1975).

Cleveland-Stevens, E. *English Railways* (London, 1915).

Cook, T.G. (ed.) *Education and the Professions* (London, 1973).

Cottrell, P.L. *Industrial Finance 1830-1914* (London, 1980).

Couper, C.T. *Report of the Trial before the High Court of Justiciary. Her Majesty's Advocate against the Directors and the Manager of the City of Glasgow Bank* (Edinburgh, 1879; repr. New York, 1984).

Crew, A. 'The Characteristics and Functions of a Professional Accountant', *Accountants' Magazine* (Dec.1938, Feb. 1939, Mar. 1939).

Daiches, D. *Glasgow* (London, 1977).

Davidson, A.R. *The Faculty of Actuaries in Scotland 1856-1956* (Edinburgh, 1956).

Deane, P. *The First Industrial Revolution* (Cambridge, 1965).

Dent, J. *Crisis in Finance* (Newton Abbot, 1973).

De Salis, H.R. *Bradshaw's Canals and Navigable Rivers of England and Wales* (London, 1904).

Dicksee, L.R. *Auditing*, 11th ed. (London, 1919).

Dobie, T.B. 'The Scottish leaving Certificate 1888-1908', in T.R. Bone (ed.) *Studies in the History of Scottish Education 1872-1939* (London, 1967).

Edcy, H.C. 'Company Accounting in the Nineteenth and Twentieth Centures' in M. Chatfield (ed.) *Contemporary Studies in the Evolution of Accounting Thought* (California, 1968).

Edey, H.C. and Panitpakdi, P. 'British Company Accounting and the Law 1844-1900', in A.C. Littleton & B.S. Yamey (eds) *Studies in the History of Accounting* (London, 1956).

Edwards, J.D. *History of Public Accounting in the United States* (Alabama, 1978).

Edwards, J.R. *British Company Legislation and Company Accounts 1844-1976* (New York, 1980).

Edwards, J.R. *Company Legislation and Changing Patterns of Disclosure in British Company Accounts 1900-1940* (London, 1981).

Eldridge, H.J. *The Evolution of the Science of Book-keeping* (London, 1954).

Emden, P.H. *Quakers in Commerce* (London, 1939).

Evans, D.M. *The History of the Commercial Crisis 1857-58 and the Stock Exchange Panic of 1859* (London, 1859).

Fifty Years. The Story of the Association of Certified and Corporate Accountants 1904-54 (London, 1954).

Forrester, D.A.R. 'The Great Canal that linked Edinburgh, Glasgow and London', *Issues in Accountability* (Mar., 1979).

Forster, P.G. *T. Cullen Young; Missionary and Anthropologist* (Hull, 1989).

Garrett, A.A. — *History of the Society of Incorporated Accountants 1885-1957* (Oxford, 1961).

Gibb, Sir A. — *The Story of Telford: The Rise of Civil Engineering* (Edinburgh, 1935).

Glass, D.V. (ed.) — *Social Mobility in Britain* (London, 1954).

Glass, D.V. and Hall, J.R. — 'Social Mobility in Great Britain: A Study of Inter-Generation Changes in Status', in D.V. Glass (ed.) *Social Mobility in Britain* (London, 1954).

Gordon, R.A. and Howell, J.E. — *Higher Education for Business* (New York, 1959).

Graham, A.W. — *The First Fifty Years 1909-1959* (New Zealand, 1960).

Gray, M. — *The Highland Economy 1750-1850* (Edinburgh 1957).

Gray, R.Q. — *The Labour Aristocracy in Victorian Edinburgh* (Oxford, 1976),

Gray, W.F. — *One Hundred Years: A Brief Chronicle of the Scottish Union and National Insurance Company 1824-1924* (Edinburgh, 1924).

Green, W.L. — *History and Survey of Accountancy* (New York, 1930).

Greenwood, E. — 'Attributes of a Profession', *Social Work* (July, 1957).

Hadfield, C. — *The Canal Age* (London, 1971).

Hadfield, C. — 'Sources for the History of British Canals', *Journal of Transport History* (Nov. 1955).

Hall, R.H. *Occupations and the Social Structure* (London, 1969).

Hamilton, H. *The Industrial Revolution in Scotland* (London, 1966).

Haskins, C.W. *Business Education and Accountancy* (New York, 1978).

Hein, L.W. *The British Companies Acts and the Practice of Accountancy 1844-1962* (New York, 1978).

Heiton, J. *'The Castes of Edinburgh'* (Edinburgh, 1861).

Hibbert, C. *The Illustrated London News Social History of Victorian Britain* (London, 1975).

Historical Sketch of the Glasgow Society of the Sons of Ministers of the Church of Scotland: Instituted 1790 (Glasgow, 1931).

History of The Chartered Accountants of Scotland (Edinburgh, 1954).

History of the Institute of Chartered Accountants in England and Wales 1880-1965 and of its Founder Accountancy Bodies 1870-1880 (London, 1966).

History of the Scottish Amicable Life Assurance Society 1826-1976 Salas 150 (Edinburgh, 1976).

Hoe, A.M. *The First Hundred Years* (Liverpool, 1977).

Hopkins, L. *The Hundredth Year* (London, 1980).

Hunt, B.C. *The Development of the Business Corporation in England 1800-1867* (New York, 1969).

Hyam, R. *Britain's Imperial Century 1815-1914* (London, 1976).

Institute of Municipal Treasurers & Accountants: A Short History 1885-1960 (London, 1960).

Interim Account ... of a Going Concern (Glasgow, 1967).

Jackson, W.T. *The Enterprising Scot* (Edinburgh, 1968).

Johnson, T. 'The Professions in the Class Structure', in R. Scase (ed.) *Industrial Society: Class, Cleavage and Control* (London, 1977).

Johnson, T.L. and Caygill, M. 'The Development of Accountancy Links in the Commonwealth', *Accounting and Business Research* (Spring, 1971).

Jones, E. *Accountancy and the British Economy 1840-1980* (London, 1981).

Kaye, B. *The Development of the Architectural Profession in Britain* (London, 1960).

Kedslie, M.J.M. 'Accountants in Old Aberdeen', *Accountants' Magazine* (Dec. 1977).

Keith, A. *The North of Scotland Bank Limited 1836-1936* (Aberdeen, 1936).

Kelsall, R.K. 'Self-recruitment in Four Professions', in D.V. Glass (ed.) *Social Mobility in Britain* (London, 1954).

Kerr, A.W. *History of Banking in Scotland* (London, 1926).

Kerr, A.W. *Scottish Banking during the Period of Published Accounts* (London, 1898).

Kitchen, J. — *Accounting: A Century of Development* (Hull, 1978).

Kitchen, J. and Parker, R.H. — *Accounting Thought and Education: Six English Pioneers* (London, 1980).

Knowles, L.C.A. — *The Industrial and Commercial Revolution in Great Britain during the Nineteenth Century* (London, 1921).

Laird, T.P. — 'The Development of Accountancy in Relation to Commerce', *Accountants' Magazine* (Nov. 1919).

Lardner, D. — *Railway Economy; A treatise on the New Art of Transport, its Management, Prospects and Relations etc.*, (London, 1850; repr. New York, 1968).

Larson, M.S. — *The Rise of Professionalism: A Sociological Analysis* (California, 1977).

Lawson, W.R. — *British Railways: A Financial and Commercial Survey* (London, 1913).

Lee, G.A. — 'The Concept of Profit in British Accounting', *Business History Review* (1975).

Lee, T.A. — 'A Brief History of Company Audits 1840-1940', *Accountants' Magazine* (Aug. 1970).

Lee, T.A. — *Company Financial Reporting: Issues & Analysis* (London, 1976.

Lenman, B. — *An Economic History of Modern Scotland 1660-1976* (London, 1977).

Lenski, G.E. — *Power and Privilege: A Theory of Social Stratification* (London, 1966).

Lewin, H.G. — *The Railway Mania and its Aftermath 1845-1852* (London, 1936; repr. New York, 1968).

Lewis, R. and Maude, A. — *Professional People* (1952).

Lindsay, J. — *The Canals of Scotland* (Newton Abbot, 1968).

Lisle, G. — *Accounting in Theory and Practice* (Edinburgh & London, 1906).

Littleton, A.C. — *Accounting Evolution to 1900* (New York, 1933).

Littleton, A.C. — *Essays on Accountancy* (Illinois, 1961).

Littleton, A.C. and Yamey, B.S. (eds) — *Studies in the History of Accounting* (London, 1956).

McCorkindale, W. (preparer) — *The Insurance and Actuarial Society of Glasgow 1881-1981* (Glasgow, 1981).

MacDonald, K.M. — 'Professional Formation: The Case of Scottish Accountants', *British Journal of Sociology* (June, 1984).

MacKinnon, J. — *The Social and Industrial History of Scotland* (London, 1921).

MacLaren, A.A. (ed.) — *Social Class in Scotland: Past & Present* (Edinburgh, 1976).

Malcolm, C.A. — *The History of the British Linen Bank* (Edinburgh, 1950).

Mann, Sir J. — 'Glimpses of Early Accountancy in Glasgow', *Accountants' Magazine* (June, 1954).

Marshall, T.H. — 'The Recent History of Professionalism in Relation to Social Structure and Social Policy', *Canadian Journal of Economics and Political Science* (1939).

Marwick, W.H. — *Economic Developments in Victorian Scotland* (London, 1936).

Michie, R.C. — *Money, Mania and Markets* (Edinburgh, 1981).

Millerson, G. — 'Education in the Professions', in T.G. Cook (ed.) *Education and the Professions* (London, 1973).

Millerson, G. — *The Qualifying Associations* (London, 1964).

Moir, F.L.M. — *After Livingstone* (London, 1923; repr. Malawi, 1986).

Morgan, E.V. and Thomas, W.A. — *The Stock Exchange* (London, 1962).

Moser, C.A. and Hall, J.R. — 'The Social Grading of Occupations', in D.V. Glass (ed.) *Social Mobility in Britain* (London, 1954).

Moss, M. — 'Forgotten Ledgers', *Issues in Accountability,* (Apr. 1983).

Munn, C.W. — *The Scottish Provincial Banking Companies 1747-1864* (Edinburgh, 1981).

Munro, N. — *The History of the Royal Bank of Scotland 1727-1927* (Edinburgh, 1928).

Murray, D. — *Chapters in the History of Bookkeeping, Accountancy & Commercial Arithmetic* (Glasgow, 1930).

Nisot, M.T. 'The Protection of Professional Titles II' *International Labour Review* (Feb. 1940).

Oakley, C.A. *Second City* (Edinburgh & Glasgow, 1947).

Our Bank: The Story of the Commercial Bank of Scotland Ltd. 1810-1941(London, 1941).

Parnell, Sir H. *On Financial Reform* (London, 1831).

Parkin, F. 'Strategies of Social Closure in Class Formation', in F. Parkin (ed.) *The Social Analysis of Class Structure* (London, 1974).

Parris, H. *Government and the Railways in Nineteenth-Century Britain* (London, 1965).

Payne, P.L. *The Early Scottish Limited Companies 1856-1895* (Edinburgh, 1980).

Payne, P.L. (ed.) *The Law and the Joint-Stock Company in Scotland* (London, 1967).

Payne, P.L. 'The Savings Bank of Glasgow 1836-1914', in P.L. Payne (ed.) *Studies in Scottish Business History* (London, 1967).

Pixley, F.W. *Accountancy* (London, 1980).

Pixley, F.W. *Auditors: Their Duties & Responsibilities* (London, 1881).

Pixley, F.W. *The Profession of a Chartered Accountant* (London, 1897; repr. New York, 1978).

Pollard, S. *The Genesis of Modern Management* (Harmondsworth, 1968).

Pollins, H. 'Aspects of Railway Accounting before 1868', in A.C. Littleton & B.S. Yamey (eds) *Studies in the History of Accounting* (London, 1956).

Portwood, D. and Fielding, A. 'Privilege and the Professions', *Sociological Review* (1981).

Prandy, K. *Professional Employees: A Study of Scientists and Engineers* (London, 1965).

Rait, R.S. *The History of the Union Bank of Scotland* (Glasgow, 1930).

Reader, W.J. *Professional Men* (London, 1966).

Reader, W.J. *Victorian England* (London, 1973).

Records of the Glasgow Stock Exchange Association 1844-1926 (Glasgow, 1927).

Reed, M.C. *Investment in Railways in Britain 1820-1844* (Oxford, 1975).

Reed, M.C. 'Railways and the Growth of the Capital Market' in M.C. Reed (ed.) *Railways in the Victorian Economy* (Newton Abbot, 1969).

Reed, M.C. (ed.) *Railways in the Victorian Economy* (Newton Abbot, 1969).

Reid, J. *A Manual of the Scottish Stocks and British Funds with a List of the Joint Stock Companies in Scotland* (Edinburgh, 1841).

Reid, J.M. *The History of the Clydesdale Bank 1838-1938* (Glasgow, 1938).

Richards, A.B. *Touche Ross & Co. 1899-1981* (London, 1981).

Robertson, C.J.A. — *The Origins of the Scottish Railway System 1722-1844* (Edinburgh, 1983).

Robinson, H.W. — *A History of Accountants in Ireland* (Dublin, 1964).

Royal Bank of Scotland 1727-1977 (Edinburgh, 1977).

Rubinstein, W.D. — 'The Victorian Middle Classes: Wealth, Occupation and Geography', *Economic History Review* (1977).

Schooling, Sir W. — *The Standard Life Assurance Company 1825-1925* (Edinburgh, 1925).

Scott, J. and Hughes, M. — *The Anatomy of Scottish Capital* (London, 1980).

Scott, J. and Hughes, M. — 'The Scottish Ruling Class: Problems of Analysis and Data' in A.A. MacLaren (ed.) *Social Class in Scotland: Past & Present* (Edinburgh, 1976).

Scratchley, A. — *Scratchley on Associations for Provident Investment* (London, 1860).

Simpson, I.J. — *Education in Aberdeenshire before 1872* (London, 1949).

Simpson, M.A. — 'The West End of Glasgow 1830-1914' in M.A. Simpson & T.H. Lloyd (eds) *Middle Class Housing in Britain* (Newton Abbot, 1977).

Simpson, M.A. and Lloyd, T.H. (eds) — *Middle Class Housing in Britain* (Newton Abbot, 1977).

Slaven, A. — *The Development of the West of Scotland 1750-1960* (London, 1975).

Smout, T.C. *A Century of the Scottish People 1830-1950* (London, 1986).

Smout, T.C. *A History of the Scottish People 1560-1830* (London, 1969).

Stacey, N.A.H. *English Accountancy 1800-1954* (London, 1954).

Steuart, M.D. *The Scottish Provident Institution 1837-1937* (Edinburgh, 1937).

Stewart, J.C. *Pioneers of a Profession* (Edinburgh, 1977).

Stewart, J.C. 'Qualification for Membership A Hundred Years Ago', *Accountants' Magazine* (July, 1974).

Thomas, J. *The North British Railway: Volume One* (Newton Abbot, 1969).

Thomas, J. *A Regional History of the Railways of Great Britain, Vol.VI, Scotland: The Lowlands and the Borders* (Newton Abbot, 1971).

Thomas, W.A. *The Provincial Stock Exchanges* (London, 1973).

Thompson, F.L.M. *Chartered Surveyors: The Growth of a Profession* (London, 1968).

Thompson, F.L.M. *English Landed Society in the Nineteenth Century* (London, 1963).

Thomson, H.B. *The Choice of a Profession* (London, 1857).

Tyson, R.E. 'The Failure of the City of Glasgow Bank and the Rise of Independent Auditing', *Accountants' Magazine* (Apr. 1974).

Vamplew, W. 'The Railways and the Iron Industry: A Study of Their Relationship in Scotland', in M.C. Reed (ed.) *Railways in the Victorian Economy* (Newton Abbot, 1969).

Vamplew, W. 'Railways and the Scottish Transport System in the Nineteenth Century', *Journal of Transport History* (Feb. 1972).

View of the Merchant House of Glasgow (Glasgow, 1866).

Walker, S.P. *The Society of Accountants in Edinburgh 1854-1914* (New York, 1988).

Webster, N.E. (compiler) *The American Association of Public Accountants: its First Twenty Years 1886-1906* (New York, 1954).

Webster, W. *Essays on Book-keeping ... To Which is Added a Large Appendix Containing a Variety of Specimens in Company Accounts* (Glasgow, 1758).

Notes

Notes for pages 1 - 4

I Introduction

1. B. Worthington, *Professional Accountants: An Historical Sketch* (London, 1895) p. 42; and J.C. Stewart, *Pioneers of a Profession* (Edinburgh, 1977) p. 6.
2. N.A.H. Stacey, *English Accountancy 1800-1954* (London, 1954).
3. Worthington, p. 42.
4. A.H. Woolf, *A Short History of Accountants and Accountancy* (London, 1912) pp. 174-5.
5. 1 & 2 Wm 4, c. 56 (1831).
6. G.A. Lee, 'The Concept of Profit in British Accounting 1760-1900', *Business History Review* (1975) 13.
7. E. Jones, *Accountancy and the British Economy 1840-1980 - The Evolution of Ernst & Whinney* (London, 1981) p. 19.
8. *A History of the Chartered Accountants of Scotland* (Edinburgh, 1954) p. 13.
9. W.H. Marwick, *Economic Developments in Victorian Scotland* (London, 1936) p. 71.
10. 6 Geo. 1, c. 18 (1719).
11. 7 & 8 Vict., c. 113 (1844).
12. 7 & 8 Vict., c. 110 (1844).
13. T.A. Lee, *Company Financial Reporting: Issues and Analysis* (London, 1976) p. 23.
14. H. Pollins, 'Aspects of Railway Accounting before 1868', in A.C. Littleton and B.S. Yamey (eds) *Studies in the History of Accounting* (London, 1956) p. 336.
15. 8 & 9 Vict., c. 20 (1845).
16. Stacey, p. 36.
17. 8 & 9 Vict., c. 16 (1845).
18. F.W. Pixley, *Auditors: Their Duties and Responsibilities* (London, 1881) p. 15.
19. 18 & 19 Vict., c. 133 (1855).
20. 19 & 20 Vict., c. 47 (1856).

Notes for pages 4 - 7

21. R.H. Campbell, 'The Law and the Joint-Stock Company in Scotland', in P.L. Payne (ed.) *Studies in Scottish Business History* (London, 1967) p. 139.
22. H.C. Edey and P. Panitpakdi, 'British Company Accounting and the Law 1844-1900', in Littleton and Yamey p. 361.
23. 25 & 26 Vict., c. 89 (1862).
24. Worthington, p. 4.
25. 32 & 33 Vict., c. 71 (1869).
26. Stacey, p. 37.
27. A.M. Carr-Saunders and P.A. Wilson, *The Professions* (Oxford, 1933) p. 210.
28. R. Brown (ed.) *A History of Accounting and Accountants* (Edinburgh, 1905) p. 318.
29. Jones, p. 47.
30. *History of The Institute of Chartered Accountants in England and Wales 1880-1965 and of its Founder Accountancy Bodies 1870-1880* (London, 1966) pp. 4-5.
31. F.W. Pixley, *Accountancy* (London, 1908) p. 27.
32. W.L. Green, *History and Survey of Accountancy* (New York, 1903) p. 49.
33. Jones, p. 84.
34. Carr-Saunders and Wilson, p. 209.
35. R. Lewis and A. Maude, *Professional People* (London, 1952) p. 30.
36. F.M.L. Thompson, *English Landed Society in the Nineteenth Century* (London, 1963) pp. 158-9.
37. *Accountant* (1874) 6.
38. Brown, p. 182.
39. Stacey, pp. 18, 20.
40. Stewart, p. 8.
41. S. Pollard, *The Genesis of Modern Management* (Harmondsworth, 1968) p. 40.
42. P. 4.
43. G. Millerson, *The Qualifying Associations: A Study in Professionalization* (London, 1964) p. 183.
44. *Accountant* (1937) 526.
45. Stacey, p. 20.

Notes for pages 7 - 14

46. P. 98.
47. Pollard, p. 250.
48. Sir J. Mann, KBE, CA, 'Glimpses of Early Accountancy in Glasgow', *Accountants' Magazine* (1954) 297-306.
49. Lewis and Maude, p. 8.
50. Millerson, pp. 52, 54.
51. W.J. Reader, *Professional Men: The Rise of the Professional Classes in Nineteenth-Century England* (London, 1966) p. 120.
52. Carr-Saunders and Wilson, p. 303.
53. 'Report of the Committee appointed at the General Meeting of the Society of Writers to Her Majesty's Signet, to consider the Details and Report upon a Bill brought into Parliament for the Appointment of an Accountant-General in the Court of Session', preamble p. 2.
54. *Accountants' Magazine* (1897) 496.
55. J. Heiton, *The Castes of Edinburgh* (Edinburgh, 1861) p. 6.
56. Heiton, pp. 159, 160.
57. *Bailie*, no. 43 (13 Aug. 1873) Comment on Peter White.
58. Ibid., no. 319 (27 Nov. 1878).
59. Stacey, p. 19.
60. *Accountant* (1883) 12.
61. Reader, pp. 148-9.
62. Millerson, p. 30.
63. P. 1.
64. See Chapter 6.
65. *Accountants' Magazine* (1929) 91.
66. T.L. Johnson and M. Caygill, 'The Development of Accountancy Links in the Commonwealth', in R.H. Parker (ed.) *Readings in Accounting and Business Research* (London, 1978) 154.
67. Institute of Accountants, Sederunt Book, Council Minutes, No. 1 (19 Apr. 1854) 31.
68. Ibid. (15 July 1859) 95.

Notes for pages 15 - 19

II The Work of Accountants in the Mid-Nineteenth Century

1. Brown, p. 177.
2. Ibid., p. 233.
3. BPP 1849 ((371) x, p. 181.
4. Brown, p. 183.
5. A.W. Kerr, *History of Banking in Scotland* (London, 1926) p. 60.
6. D. Murray, *Chapters in the History of Bookkeeping Accountancy & Commercial Arithmetic* (Glasgow, 1930) p. 20.
7. J. Thomas, *A Regional History of the Railways of Great Britain, Vol VI, Scotland: The Lowlands and the Borders* (Newton Abbot, 1971) p. 16.
8. Murray, p. 34.
9. W. Webster, *Essays on Book-keeping* (Glasgow, 1758).
10. Pollard, p. 248.
11. Ibid., p. 256.
12. Murray, pp. 106-13.
13. Stewart, p. 3.
14. B.S. Yamey, 'Scientific Bookkeeping and the Rise of Capitalism', *Economic History Review* (1949) 101.
15. M. Moss, 'Forgotten Ledgers', *Issues in Accountability* (1983) 21.
16. Pollard, p. 109.
17. Sir A. Gibb, *The Story of Telford: The Rise of Civil Engineering* (1935) pp. 186-7.
18. H.R. De Salis (Comp.) *Bradshaw's Canals and Navigable Rivers of England and Wales* (London, 1904) p. vii.
19. P. Deane, *The First Industrial Revolution* (Cambridge, 1965) p. 79.
20. C. Hadfield, *The Canal Age* (London, 1971) pp. 22-5.
21. Ibid., p. 95.
22. D.A.R. Forrester, 'The Great Canal that Linked Edinburgh, Glasgow and London, *Issues in Accountability* (1979) 1.
23. C. Hadfield, 'Sources for the History of British Canals', *Journal of Transport History* (1955) 84.

Notes for pages 19 - 23

24. *Issues in Accountability*, op. cit., pp. 8-11.
25. J. Lindsay, *The Canals of Scotland* (Newton Abbot, 1968) pp. 210-13.
26. W. Vamplew, 'Railways and the Scottish Transport System in the Nineteenth Century', *Journal of Transport History* (1972) 137.
27. Hadfield, p. 84-5.
28. Ibid., p. 129.
29. *Bradshaw's Railway Almanac, Directory, Shareholders' Guide and Manual for 1848* (London, 1848) p. 19.
30. Marwick, p. 73.
31. J. Mackinnon, *The Social and Industrial History of Scotland* (London, 1921) p. 153.
32. L.C.A. Knowles, *The Industrial and Commercial Revolution in Great Britain during the Nineteenth Century* (London, 1921) p. 114.
33. Stacey, p. 13.
34. P.S. Bagwell, *The Railway Clearing House in the British Economy 1842-1922* (London, 1968) p. 41.
35. D. Lardner, *Railway Economy: A Treatise on the New Art of Transport, its Management, Prospects, and Relations, etc., London (1850)* reprinted (New York, 1968) p. 150.
36. Bagwell, p. 135.
37. 31 & 32 Vict., c. 119 (1868).
38. Worthington, p. 42.
39. BPP 1849 (371) x, BPP 1849 (421) x.
40. BPP 1849 (371) x, p. 214.
41. Ibid., p. 184.
42. *Herapaths Railway Journal*, (1850) 880.
43. C.J.A. Robertson, *The Origins of the Scottish Railway System 1722-1844* (Edinburgh 1983) p. 168.
44. De Salis, p. viii.
45. 51 Geo. 3, c. 133 (1811) s. xlix.
46. Eg. 6 & 7 Wm 4, c. 34 (1836) Arbroath and Forfar Railway Act, s. lxxvi.
47. 1 & 2 Vict., c. 58 (1838) s. lxvii.
48. Ibid., s. clxvi.

Notes for pages 23 - 30

49. 7 & 8 Vict., c. 66 (1844) ss. cx, cxiv, xciv, xcv, xcix.
50. *Bradshaw's* (1848) p. 125.
51. 7 & 8 Vict., c. 66 (1844) ss. lxxvii, iii.
52. *Bradshaw's* (1854) p. 261.
53. 9 & 10 Vict., c. 158 (1846) s. xxi.
54. 14 & 15 Vict., c. 134 (1851) s. lvi.
55. Mackinnon, p. 153.
56. B. Lenman, *An Economic History of Modern Scotland 1660-1976* (London, 1971) p. 167.
57. *Banking Almanac* (1847) 43.
58. *Accountant* (1887) 387.
59. W.J. Reader, *Victorian England* (London, 1973) p. 149.
60. Ibid., p. 102.
61. Ibid., p. 176.
62. *Aberdeen Post Office Directory* (1854-5) p. 167.
63. Stewart, pp. 48, 91, 107.
64. 7 & 8 Vict., c. 66 (1844) ss. iii, lxxvii.
65. 8 & 9 Vict., c. 162 (1845) ss. vi, xi.
66. *Bradshaw's* (1851) p. 219, (1854) pp. 52, 120, 243, (1856) p. 33.
67. Stewart, p. 122.
68. *Bradshaw's* (1854) p. 244.
69. N. Munro, *The History of the Royal Bank of Scotland 1727-1927* (Edinburgh, 1928) p. 44.
70. R.S. Rait, *The History of the Union Bank of Scotland* (Glasgow, 1930) p. 4.
71. Kerr, p. 60.
72. J.M. Reid, *The History of The Clydesdale Bank, 1838-1938* (1938) p. 15.
73. S.G. Checkland, *Scottish Banking: A History 1695-1973* (Glasgow, 1975) p. 199.
74. C.A. Malcolm, *The History of the British Linen Bank* (Edinburgh, 1950) p. 86.
75. Ibid., p. 89.
76. Reid, p. 69.
77. S.G. Checkland, p. 371.
78. Ibid., p. 326.

Notes for pages 30 - 35

79. Kerr, p. 71.
80. S.G. Checkland, p. 337.
81. Op. cit., p. 73.
82. Op. cit., p. 390.
83. BPP 1837 (531) xiv, para. 4200.
84. BPP 1837 (531) ix, para. 653.
85. BPP 1836 (591) ix para. 849.
86. *Accountant* (1886).
87. BPP 1836 (591) ix, para. 2148, p. 130.
88. BPP 1837 (531) xiv, para. 1825.
89. Ibid., para. 3545.
90. BPP 1837-38 (626) vii, para. 66.
91. 9 & 10 Vict., c. 75 (1846) s. iv.
92. P. 160.
93. P. 167.
94. Pp. 7-8.
95. Pp. 505-6.
96. Pp. 20, 35.
97. *Aberdeen Directory.*
98. P. 167.
99. Pp. 316-17.
100. Brown.
101. Rait, p. 61.
102. Pollard, p. 245.
103. Thompson, *English Landed Society,* p. 153.
104. Brown, p. 72.
105. Stewart, p. 26.
106. Pollard, p. 40.
107. Sir H. Parnell, *On Financial Reform* (London, 1831) p. 160.
108. 5 & 6 Wm 4, c. 76 (1835).
109. Stacey, p. 45.
110. T.C. Smout, *A Century of the Scottish People 1830-1950* (London, 1986) p. 41.
111. Brown, p. 186.
112. Ibid., p. 194.
113. Lenman, p. 152.
114. Op. cit., p. 18.

Notes for pages 35 - 39

115. Op. cit., p. 195.
116. Pp. xlii-lxxii.
117. P. 1.
118. Pp. 557-61.
119. *Accountant* (1901) 169.
120. A.R. Davidson, *The Faculty of Actuaries in Scotland 1856-1956* (Edinburgh, 1956) Preface.
121. W. McCorkindale (preparer) *The Insurance and Actuarial Society of Glasgow 1881-1981* (Glasgow, 1981) p. 3.
122. Institute of Accountants in Glasgow, Minute Book No. 1, p. 48.
123. Glasgow Post Office Directory (1853-4) pp. 495-6, 557-62, 595.
124. Scottish Records Office, C 2/255.
125. Pp. 778-80, 891-7, 971-4.
126. W.F. Gray, *One Hundred Years: A Brief Chronicle of the Scottish Union & National Insurance Company, 1824-1924* (Edinburgh, 1924) p. 159.
127. R.C. Michie, *Money, Mania and Markets* (Edinburgh, 1981) p. 17.
128. M.C. Reed, 'Railways and the Growth of the Capital Market', in M.C. Reed (ed.) *Railways in the Victorian Economy* (Newton Abbot, 1969) p. 172.
129. Michie, pp. 103-4.
130. Stewart, p. 24.
131. Michie, p. 43.
132. *Records of the Glasgow Stock Exchange Association 1844-1926* (Glasgow, 1927) Appendix 1.
133. Worthington, p. 13.
134. Marwick, p. 71.
135. Murray, p. 85.
136. Ibid., p. 92.
137. Stewart, p. 4.
138. T.P. Laird, 'The Development of Accountancy in Relation to Commerce', *Accountants' Magazine* (1919) 461.
139. BPP 1843 (523) xi, 283.
140. *A History of the Chartered Accountants of Scotland*, p. 11.

Notes for pages 40 - 53

141. Murray, p. 107.
142. Ibid., p. 113.
143. Green, p. 49.
144. Stewart, p. 26.
145. 2 & 3 Vict., c. 41 (1839) para. lxiii.
146. *The Alphabetical Compendium of Scotch Mercantile Sequestrations 1851* (London, 1852).
147. Op. cit.
148. R.H. Hall, *Occupations and the Social Structure* (1969) p. 70.

III Scottish Bankruptcy Legislation and the Formation of Professional Accounting Bodies in Scotland

1. 54 Geo. III, c. 137 (1814).
2. Ibid., ss. xvi, xxiii, xxxiv, xlv, xlvi.
3. Ibid., ss. xiii, lvi, lvii.
4. BPP, 1852-3, Vol. I, p. 89, para. 1.
5. Ibid., p. 97.
6. 16 & 17 Vict., c. 53 (1853) An Act to Amend the Laws Relating to Bankruptcy in Scotland, s. 1.
7. Ibid., ss. ii, xvii.
8. BPP, 1854-5, Vol. III.
9. BPP, 1854-5, Vol. III, p. 241; BPP, 1855-6, Vol. I, pp. 85, 159.
10. 19 & 20 Vict., c. 79 (1856).
11. Ibid., s. 75.
12. Ibid., s. 46.
13. Ibid., s. 84.
14. BPP, 1854-5, Vol. III, p. 217, para. cxxxviii.
15. Op. cit., s. 85.
16. Scottish Records Office, CS 322/1-30.
17. Ibid., CS 322/31-33.
18. 52 & 53 Vict., c. 39 (1889).
19. Op. cit., CS 322/34.
20. Op. cit., CS 322/1 etc.
21. Institute of Accountants, Sederunt Book No. 1, Council Minutes, p. 1.

Notes for pages 54 - 63

22. Brown, pp. 212-13.
23. Institute of Accountants, op. cit., p. 1.
24. Brown, p. 203.
25. Institute of Accountants, op. cit., p. 1.
26. Pp. 314-15.
27. Reader, *Professional Men*, p. 164.
28. Carr-Saunders and Wilson, p. 298.
29. Lewis and Maude, p. 9.
30. Brown, p. 204.
31. Institute of Accountants, op. cit., p. 4.
32. Stewart, p. 8.
33. Ibid., p. 54.
34. Institute of Accountants, op. cit., p. 6.
35. Millerson, p. 54.
36. Institute of Accountants, op. cit., p. 6.
37. Brown, p. 205.
38. Institute of Accountants, op. cit., p. 6.
39. Ibid., p. 49.
40. Ibid., p. 18.
41. Ibid., pp. 20-1.
42. BPP, 1852-3, Vol. I, p. 89.
43. Institute of Accountants, op. cit., p. 21.
44. Ibid., p. 20.
45. Stewart, p. 14.
46. BPP, 1852-3, Vol. I, p. 97.
47. Institute of Accountants, op. cit., pp. 30-1.
48. Brown, pp. 206-7.
49. *Edinburgh and Leith Post Office Directory* (1854-5) pp. 316-17.
50. *Accountants' Magazine* (1919) 461.
51. Brown, p. 208.
52. Institute of Accountants, op. cit., p. 50.
53. Society of Accountants in Edinburgh, General Minutes, Book 1, p. 2.
54. Institute of Accountants, op. cit., p. 55.
55. Society of Accountants in Edinburgh, op. cit., p. 13.
56. Institute of Accountants, op. cit., p. 138-40.

Notes for pages 63 - 72

57. Ibid., p. 167-74.
58. Ibid., p. 207.
59. Ibid., p. 218.
60. Ibid., paras 2, 6, 12.
61. Stewart, pp. 106, 115.
62. Pp. 557-61.
63. *Records of the Glasgow Stock Exchange Association 1844-1926.*
64. Institute of Accountants in Glasgow, Minute Book No. 1, p. 37.
65. Ibid., p. 1.
66. Ibid.
67. Ibid., p. 2.
68. Stewart, p. 83.
69. Ibid., p. 125.
70. p. 495-6.
71. Institute of Accountants in Glasgow, op. cit., p. 4.
72. Ibid., pp. 11-12.
73. Ibid., p. 15.
74. Ibid., p. 23.
75. Institute of Accountants, op. cit., p. 160.
76. Brown, p. 324.
77. Institute of Accountants in Glasgow, op. cit., p. 30.
78. Ibid., p. 31.
79. Ibid.
80. Institute of Accountants in Glasgow, op. cit., p. 33.
81. *View of the Merchant House of Glasgow* (Glasgow, 1866) p. 476.
82. Ibid., p. 478.
83. Ibid., p. 479-80.
84. Institute of Accountants in Glasgow, op. cit., p. 37.
85. Ibid., p. 42.
86. Brown, p. 208.
87. Ibid., p. 210.
88. Ibid.
89. Ibid.
90. Institute of Accountants in Glasgow, Admission Book, Vol. 1, p. 3.

Notes for pages 73 - 84

91. Brown, p. 211.
92. Institute of Accountants in Glasgow, op. cit., pp. 56-7.
93. Ibid., p. 79.
94. Ibid., p. 126.
95. Mann, 297-309.
96. *Accountants' Magazine* (1919) 462.
97. Stewart, p. 10.
98. Society of Accountants in Aberdeen, General Minutes, Book 1, pp. 1-2.
99. Brown, pp. 397, 399, 400.
100. Society of Accountants in Aberdeen, op. cit., pp. 18-19.
101. Institute of Accountants, op. cit., p. 159-160.
102. Brown, p. 211.
103. F.M.L. Thompson, *Chartered Surveyors: The Growth of a Profession* (London, 1968) p. 173.
104. Millerson, p. 50.

IV Social Background

1. Brown, pp. 207, 210.
2. Reader, *Professional Men*, p. 23.
3. Carr-Saunders and Wilson, p. 23.
4. Lewis and Maude, p. 48.
5. Millerson, p. 20.
6. Lewis and Maude, p. 49.
7. D.V. Glass and J.R. Hall, 'Social Mobility in Great Britain: A Study of Inter-Generation Changes in Status', in D.V. Glass (ed.) *Social Mobility in Britain* (London, 1954) p. 178.
8. Institute of Accountants, Sederunt Book, Council Minutes, No. 1, p. 1.
9. *Edinburgh and Leith Post Office Directory* (1852-3) p. 313.
10. Stewart, p. 143.
11. T.C. Smout, *A History of the Scottish People 1560-1830* (London, 1969) p. 375.
12. Stacey, pp. 180-1.
13. *A Survey of the Social Structure of England & Wales* (Oxford, 1937) chaps V, VI, VII.

Notes for pages 85- 104

14. R.K. Kelsall, 'Self-Recruitment in Four Professions', in Glass (ed.) p. 308.
15. A.K. Cairncross, 'The Social Origins of Chartered Accountants', *Accountant* (1937) 373-4.
16. Stewart, p. 26.
17. Ibid., p. 109.
18. Reader, p. 12.
19. Smout, p. 382.
20. 1641 V, 6466.
21. 1696 c. 26, X, 63.
22. C.A. Oakley, *The Second City*, (Edinburgh & Glasgow, 1947) p. 84.
23. Murray, pp. 43-51.
24. Ibid., p. 316.
25. Oakley, p. 85.
26. Smout, p. 364.
27. Marwick, p. 141.
28. C. Hibbert, *The Illustrated London News Social History of Victorian Britain* (1975) p. 116.
29. R. Hyam, *Britain's Imperial Century 1815-1914* (London, 1976) p. 49.
30. Lenman, p. 203.
31. W.J. Reader, p. 115.
32. *Accountant* (1874) 6.
33. I.J. Simpson, *Education in Aberdeenshire before 1872* (London, 1949) p. 47.
34. BPP 1867-8, Vol. XXVIII, p. 21.
35. Ibid., pp. 104, 121, 131.
36. Ibid., Part 6, p. 193.
37. Ibid., Part 8, p. 65.
38. Stewart.
39. Ibid., p. 27.
40. Stacey, p. 21.
41. Institute of Accountants, op. cit., p. 120.
42. P. 211.
43. Institute of Accountants in Glasgow, Minute Book No. 1, p. 62.

Notes for pages 104 - 111

44. Ibid., p. 362.
45. Ibid., p. 416.
46. Society of Accountants in Aberdeen, Rule 34, Minute Book 1, p. 16.
47. Ibid., pp. 227-8; Institute of Accountants, op. cit., p. 232.
48. Institute of Accountants in Glasgow, Minute Book No. 3, p. 344.
49. Ibid., p. 508.
50. Institute of Accountants, Minute Book No. 2, p. 293.
51. *Accountants' Magazine* (1920) 48.
52. Reader, p. 142.
53. *Accountants' Magazine* (1952) 385.
54. Ibid. (1929) 290.
55. Ibid. (1976) 260.
56. Ibid. (1938) 535.
57. Ibid (1940) 83.
58. Ibid. (1940) 270.
59. Ibid (1921) 571.
60. Ibid. (1939) 284.
61. Ibid (1937) 429.
62. Ibid. (1919) 454.
63. Ibid. (1947) 117.
64. Ibid. (1919) 320.
65. Carr-Saunders and Wilson, pp. 317-18.
66. W.J. Reader, p. 117.
67. M.A. Simpson, 'The West End of Glasgow 1830-1914', in M.A. Simpson and T.H. Lloyd (eds) *Middle Class Housing in Britain* (Newton Abbott, 1977) p. 45.
68. *Accountants' Magazine* (1919) 404.
69. John Mann, Memoirs, Part 6; Social Experiments and Public Service (1952) pp. 3, 5.
70. *Accountants' Magazine* (1957) 686.
71. Ibid. (1917) 153.
72. Ibid. (1926) 510.
73. Ibid. (1948) 265.
74. Ibid. (1933) 8.
75. Ibid. (1959) 12.

Notes for pages 112 - 117

76. Ibid. (1934) 5.
77. Society of Accountants in Aberdeen, Minute Book No. 2, p. 367.
78. *The History of the Institute of Chartered Accountants in England and Wales 1880-1965*, p. 5.
79. *Accountants' Magazine* (1898) 399.
80. Ibid. (1947) 166.
81. Lenman, p. 107.
82. Smout, p. 364.
83. O. Checkland, *Philanthropy in Victorian Scotland* (Edinburgh, 1980) p. 312.

V Importance of Bankruptcy Work to the New Professional Bodies

1. Stewart, p. 14.
2. *A History of the Chartered Accountants of Scotland*, Edinburgh p. 40.
3. R. Winsbury, *Thomson McLintock and Co - The First Hundred Years* (London, 1977) p. 15.
4. A.B. Richards, *Touche Ross and Co 1899-1981: The Origins and Growth of the United Kingdom Firm* (1981) p. 77.
5. Ibid., p. 54.
6. *Accountant*, 1881.
7. Jones, p. 43.
8. Ibid., p. 47.
9. Brown, p. 326.
10. F.W. Pixley, *The Profession of a Chartered Accountant* (London, 1897) reprinted (New York, 1978) pp. 16-19.
11. *Accountant* (1897) 644.
12. D. Morier Evans, *The History of the Commercial Crisis 1857-58 and the Stock Exchange Panic of 1859* (London, 1859) p. 13.
13. Ibid., p. 46.
14. Oakley, p. 142.

Notes for pages 117 - 138

15. Kerr, p. 189.
16. S.G. Checkland, p. 468.
17. Scottish Records Office, CS 322/4, p. 3.
18. Stacey, p. 37.
19. Brown, p. 318.
20. Kerr, p. 233.
21. Lenman, p. 118.
22. P.H. Emden, *Quakers in Commerce* (London, 1939) pp. 113-14.
23. C.T. Couper, *Report of the Trial Before the High Court of Justiciary. Her Majesty's Advocate Against the Directors and the Manager of the City of Glasgow Bank* (Edinburgh, 1879), reprinted (New York, 1984) pp. 462-3.
24. Winsbury, p. 15.
25. Jones, p. 89.
26. *Interim Account of a Going Concern* (Glasgow, 1967) p. 24.
27. Institute of Accountants in Glasgow, Minute Book No. 1, p. 37.
28. Scottish Records Office, CS 322.
29. Table 5.1.

VI Development of Other Areas of Practice to 1900

1. 6 Geo. 4, c. 91 (1825).
2. Jones, p. 28.
3. BPP 1843 (523) XI, p. 217.
4. BPP 1844 (119) VII, p. 370.
5. Ibid., pp. 8, 64, 284.
6. Stacey, p. 36.
7. 8 & 9 Vict., c. 17 (1845).
8. Stacey, p. 37.
9. Brown (ed.) p. 318.
10. BPP 1867 (329) X, p. 393 and para. 871.
11. *Accountant* (1937) 524.
12. Ibid. (1881).
13. *Accountants' Magazine* (1954) 297-306.

Notes for pages 138 - 145

14. *Accountant* (1886).
15. Jones, p. 56.
16. *Accountant* (1891) 586.
17. Ibid. (1896) 975.
18. Ibid. (1897) 122.
19. Pixley, *The Profession*, p. 7.
20. BPP 1895 (c. 7779), lxxxviii.
21. 63 & 64 Vict., c. 48 (1900).
22. Stacey, p. 66.
23. H.C. Edey, 'Company Accounting in the Nineteenth and Twentieth Centuries', in M. Chatfield (ed.) *Contemporary Studies in the Evolution of Accounting Thought* (New York, 1968) p. 225.
24. 10 & 11 Geo. 6, c. 47 (1947) s. 23(1).
25. *Accountant* (1901) 40.
26. G. Lisle, *Accounting in Theory and Practice* (Edinburgh & London, 1906) p. 1.
27. Jones, p. 63.
28. 7 & 8 Vict., c. 110 (1844) s. IV.
29. BPP 1857 (220) X, para. 2422.
30. BPP 1857-8 (441) XVI, paras 1570, 1635, 1965, 2919, 2920, 2923.
31. Edey and Panitpakdi, p. 361.
32. A. Scratchley, *Scratchley on Associations for Provident Investment* (London, 1860) p. 81.
33. Ibid., pp. 83, 280.
34. R.E. Tyson, 'The Failure of the City of Glasgow Bank and the Rise of Independent Auditing', *Accountants' Magazine* (1974) 126.
35. Kerr, p. 270.
36. Tyson, p. 126.
37. S.G. Checkland, pp. 468, 470.
38. Kerr, p. 241.
39. BPP 1867-8, Vol. XXVIII, Part 8, p. 271.
40. Kerr, p. 244.
41. BPP 1878-9 (58) III, 453, ss. 4, 6.
42. 42 & 43 Vict., c. 76 (1879) ss. 7(1), (2), (5), (6).

Notes for pages 145 - 149

43. Malcolm, p. 135.
44. *The Royal Bank of Scotland 1727-1977* (Edinburgh, 1977).
45. A. Keith, *The North of Scotland Bank Limited, 1836-1936* (Aberdeen, 1936) p. 100.
46. Reid, p. 181.
47. Rait, pp. 314-15.
48. Malcolm, pp. 135-6.
49. Tyson, p. 131.
50. *Accountant* (1886).
51. Ibid. (1894) 649.
52. Ibid. (1897) 122.
53. H. Woodburn Kirby, *Accountancy as a Profession* (London, 1907) p. 57.
54. 45 & 46 Vict., c. 50 (1882).
55. 51 & 52 Vict., c. 41 (1888).
56. 52 & 53 Vict., c. 50 (1889) para. 69.
57. Jones, p. 90.
58. Stacey, p. 25.
59. A.A. Garrett, *History of the Society of Incorporated Accountants 1885-1957* (Oxford, 1961) p. 13.
60. 52 & 53 Vict., c. 116 (1889) s. 56(1).
61. *Fifty Years, The Story of the Association of Certified and Corporate Accountants 1904-1954* (London, 1954) p. 39.
62. *A History of the Chartered Accountants of Scotland*, p. 42.
63. Brown, p. 320.
64. Carr-Saunders and Wilson, p. 215.
65. *Accountant* (1894) 652.
66. BPP 1893-4 (261) V, 173.
67. *Incorporated Accountants' Journal*, Vol. XI (1900) 147.
68. 55 & 56 Vict., c. 55 (1892) s. 69.
69. 63 & 64 Vict., c. 49 (1900).
70. *Incorporated Accountants' Journal*, Vol. XI (1900) 113.
71. BPP 1844 (119) VII, paras 247, 1756, 1758, 1907-8.
72. 10 & 11 Vict., c. 34 (1847).
73. 10 & 11 Vict., c. 35 (1847).
74. 22 & 23 Vict., c. 49 (1859) para. 40.
75. Scratchley, Division III, p. xi.

Notes for pages 150 - 158

76. 33 & 34 Vict., c. 61 (1870) paras 3, 5, 7.
77. Edey, p. 224.
78. 41 & 42 Vict., c. 53 (1878) paras 66, 70.
79. Gray, pp. 106, 111.
80. Ibid., pp. 159, 187.
81. M.D. Steuart, *The Scottish Provident Institution 1837-1937* (Edinburgh, 1937) p. 8.
82. Brown, p. 195.
83. Jones, p. 86; Stewart, p. 18 etc.
84. McCorkindale (preparer) p. 3.
85. Pixley, *Auditors*, p. 14.
86. 8 August, p. 585, 30 January, p. 122.
87. Ibid. 21 July. p. 648.
88. Lenman, p. 166.
89. H. Hamilton, *The Industrial Revolution in Scotland* (London, 1966) p. 245.
90. A. Slaven, *The Development of the West of Scotland 1750-1960* (London, 1975) p. 42.
91. Hamilton, p. 246.
92. W. Vamplew, 'The Railways and the Iron Industry', in Reed (ed.) p. 50.
93. Lenman, pp. 172-3.
94. 51 Geo. 3, c. 133 (1811) para. xlix.
95. Op. cit., ss. xciv, xcx, lxxvii, iii, xcvi, xcix, cxiv.
96. 7 & 8 Vict., c. 85 (1844) s. v.
97. T.A. Lee, 'A Brief History of Company Audits 1840-1940', *Accountants' Magazine* (1970) 363.
98. Op. cit., s. cii.
99. *Accountant* (1937) 525.
100. P. 1052.
101. Pollins, p. 145.
102. BPP 1849 X (371) paras 1875, 1880, 1991, 1921, 1978, 1979.
103. Ibid., paras 2214, 2228-30, 2232, 2282, 2288.
104. Ibid., paras 1382, 2158, 2548, 2761.
105. BPP 1849 (421) X, pp. viii, xiii, xiv.
106. T.J. Buckton, *Railway Audit Really Independent* (London, 1850) pp. 9, 12.

Notes for pages 159 - 176

107. *Accountant* (1904) 504.
108. 30 & 31 Vict., c. 126, (1867) s. 30.
109. Op. cit., p. 393, 1824-7.
110. P.L. Cottrell, *Industrial Finance 1830-1914* (London, 1980) pp. 57, 61.
111. 31 & 32 Vict., c. 119 (1868) ss. 11, 12, 13.
112. Pixley, op. cit., pp. 78, 152.
113. *Accountant* (1882) 418.
114. L.R. Dicksee, *Auditing* (London, 1919) pp. 119, 299.
115. Lee, *Accountants' Magazine*, p. 365.
116. Brown, p. 318.
117. Stewart, p. 80.
118. Ibid., p. 150.
119. Brown. p. 399.
120. *Accountant* (1874) 6, 7.
121. Pixley, *Auditors*, p. 97.
122. *Accountant* (1894) pp. 646-7.
123. Jones, pp. 34, 62.
124. *Accountant* (1894) 646.
125. Brown, pp. 215, 332, 340.
126. *Incorporated Accountants' Journal*, Vol. VII. (1896) p. 103.
127. Brown, p. 335.
128. *Accountant* (1883) 8.
129. *Accountants' Magazine* (1909) 274.
130. Ibid. (1907) 2.
131. Ibid. (1903) 142.
132. Ibid. (1954) 740.
133. Ibid. (1943) 4.
134. Ibid. (1939) 490.
135. Brown, p. 265.
136. *Accountant* (1894) 1029.
137. Ibid. (1895) 215.
138. Garrett, pp. 56-7.
139. *Accountants' Magazine* (1903) 143.
140. Brown, p. 265.
141. Institute of Accountants in Edinburgh, Sederunt Book No. 2, p. 363.

Notes for pages 176 - 184

142. Garrett, p. 58.
143. Brown, pp. 266-7.
144. *Accountants' Magazine* (1948) 264.
145. Ibid. (1947) 371.
146. Ibid. (1952) 5.
147. Ibid. (1916) 411.
148. P.G. Forster, *T. Cullen Young: Missionary and Anthropologist* (Hull, 1989).
149. Brown, p. 253.
150. *Accountants' Magazine* (1926) 259.
151. Ibid. (1932) 204.
152. Ibid. (1917) 458.
153. Ibid. (1937) 120.
154. Brown, p. 332.
155. *Accountants' Magazine* (1920) 91.
156. Ibid. (1907) 87.

VII The Establishment of Entry Standards

1. Lewis and Maude, p. 30.
2. Ibid., pp. 29-30.
3. Ibid., p. 31.
4. Carr-Saunders and Wilson, p. 307.
5. Reader, *Professional Men*, p. 117.
6. Institute of Accountants, Sederunt Book, Council Minutes, No. 1, p. 4.
7. Ibid., pp. 18, 52.
8. *Index Juridicus: The Scottish Law List and Legal Directory, 1853* (Edinburgh, 1853) preface pp. x-xii.
9. Constitution and Objects, para. 2.
10. Constitution and Laws, para. 7.
11. Brown, p. 207.
12. A. Crew, 'The Characteristics and Functions of a Professional Accountant', *Accountants' Magazine* (1938) 611.
13. Society of Accountants in Edinburgh, General Minutes, Book 1, p. 16.

Notes for pages 186 - 196

14. Institute of Accountants, op. cit., p. 232, Sederunt Book, Council Minutes, No. 1.
15. Ibid., pp. 66, 73, 87.
16. Table 7.1.
17. Register of Indentures Recorded, Book 1, p. 1 (No. 1).
18. Ibid., Indentures No. 4, 9, 11-15.
19. Institute of Accountants, op. cit., p. 210.
20. Pixley, *The Profession of a Chartered Accountant,* p. 3.
21. J. Kitchen and R.H. Parker, *Accounting Thought and Education: Six English Pioneers* (London, 1980) p. 26.
22. Institute of Accountants, op. cit., Book 3, p. 5.
23. *Official Directory of the Chartered Accountants of Scotland* (1903).
24. Institute of Accountants, op. cit., Book 2, p. 347.
25. F.L.M. Moir, *After Livingstone* (Blantyre, 1986) p. 3.
26. S.P. Walker, *The Society of Accountants in Edinburgh, 1854-1914* (New York, 1988).
27. Institute of Accountants, op. cit., Book 1, p. 61.
28. Ibid., p. 67.
29. Ibid., p. 70.
30. Ibid., pp. 134-5, pp. 149-52.
31. E.R. Alexander, *The Historial Relationship between Accountants and Actuaries*, BA Dissertation, Strathclyde University, 1973-4, p. 7(a).
32. Pp. 6-7.
33. Society of Accountants in Edinburgh, General Minutes, Book 1, p. 131.
34. Institute of Accountants, Sederunt Book, Council Minutes, No. 1, p. 188.
35. Brown, p. 211.
36. Institute of Accountants, op. cit., p. 203.
37. Ibid., pp. 215-16.
38. Bye-laws, Rules and Regulations, 1874, para. 38, p. 12.
39. Bye-law 38.
40. J.C. Stewart, 'Qualification for Membership a Hundred Years Ago', *Accountants' Magazine* (1974) 264.
41. Ibid. (1974) p. 324.

Notes for pages 197 - 213

42. T.B. Dobie, 'The Scottish Leaving Certificate 1888-1908', in T.R. Bone (ed.) *Studies in the History of Scottish Education 1872-1939* (London, 1967) 137-9.
43. G. Millerson, 'Education in the Professions' in T.G. Cook (ed.) *Education and the Professions* (London, 1973) p. 7.
44. Glasgow Admission Book, Vol. 1, p. 4, Rule 5.
45. Reader, op. cit., p. 47.
46. Glasgow Admission Book, op. cit., Rule 7.
47. *Accountant* (1901) 169.
48. Davidson, preface.
49. Institute of Accountants in Glasgow, Minute Book No. 1, p. 7.
50. Ibid., p. 23.
51. Mann, p. 302.
52. Accountant (1974) 6-7.
53. *Interim Account*, p. 22.
54. Table 7.1.
55. *Interim Accountant*, p. 27.
56. Winsbury, p. 11.
57. Institute of Accountants in Glasgow, Minute Book No. 2, p. 362.
58. Ibid., p. 391.
59. Institute of Accountants in Glasgow, op. cit., p. 532.
60. 4 February 1893, p. 101.
61. M.J.M. Kedslie, 'Accountants in Old Aberdeen', *Accountants' Magazine* (1977) 514.
62. Society of Accountants in Aberdeen Minute Book, No. 1, p. 517.
63. *Accountant* (1889) 703.
64. Institute of Accountants in Glasgow, Minute Book No. 2, pp. 471-2.
65. Institute of Accountants in Edinburgh, Sederunt Book No. 2, p. 128.
66. Society of Accountants in Aberdeen, Minute Book No. 1, p. 487, Institute of Accountants in Glasgow, Minute Book No. 3, p. 62.
67. Pp. 280-1.

Notes for pages 213 - 233

68. 7 January 1893, p. 4.
69. Pp. 101-3.
70. 18 February 1893, pp. 150-1.
71. *Accountant* (1893) 101.
72. Ibid. (1893) 281.
73. Ibid. (1894) 233-5.
74. Ibid. (1896) 7.
75. Ibid. (1898) 916.
76. B. Worthington, pp. 96-7.

VIII Attempts to Maintain a Monopoly over Professional Work

1. *Accountant* (1885) 5.
2. Society of Accountants in Edinburgh, General Minutes, Book 1, p. 3.
3. op. cit., p. 6.
4. H.W. Robinson, *A History of Accountants in Ireland* (1964) p. 78.
5. Stacey, pp. 27-8.
6. Lewis and Maude, p. 20.
7. *Fifty Years*, p. 3.
8. 9 February, 1884, p. 3.
9. Winsbury, p. 11.
10. BPP, 1896 (137), I, 19.
11. 8 June 1895, p. 514.
12. 11 May 1895, p. 450.
13. Garrett, p. 24.
14. Ibid. p. 330.
15. *Fifty Years*, p. 4.
16. Stacey, p. 72.
17. *Fifty Years*.
18. Stacey, p. 67-8.
19. 15 July 1893, p. 633.
20. 12 December 1891, p. 867.
21. Institute of Accountants in Glasgow, op. cit., Minute Book No. 3, p. 55.
22. Institute of Accountants in Glasgow, op. cit., p. 58.

Notes for pages 233 - 245

23. *Accountant* (1892) 122.
24. 13 February 1892, p. 140.
25. S2, S3.
26. Institute of Accountants in Glasgow, op. cit., pp. 83, 85.
27. Session Cases, 1893, 20 R, p. 750, The Society of Accountants in Edinburgh and Others versus The Corporation of Accountants, Limited, and Others.
28. BPP 1890-1891 (431) 1, 315, Bill to Amend the Law Relating to Chartered Accountants. BPP 1892 (255) 11, 35-8, op. cit.
29. *Accountant* (1893) 631.
30. 15 July 1893, p. 634.
31. Stacey, p. 68.
32. *Accountant* (1893) 1010.
33. Ibid. (1894) 101.
34. Ibid. (1895) 956.
35. Ibid. (1898) 526.
36. Ibid. (1907) 661.
37. Ibid. (1903) 1475.
38. Ibid. (1903) 1433.
39. Ibid. (1903) 104.
40. Stacey, p. 33-4.
41. Millerson, pp. 30-1.
42. Carr-Saunders and Wilson, p. 539.
43. Stewart, *Pioneers* p. 10.
44. Brown, p. 212.
45. Institute of Accountants, op. cit., Book 1, pp. 138, 140.
46. Institute of Chartered Accountants in England and Wales, Charter of Incorporation and Bye-Laws (1880), pp. 17-18.
47. *The History of The Institute of Chartered Accountants in England and Wales 1880-1965*, p. 23.
48. Ibid. pp. 125-6, 129.
49. Institute of Accountants in Glasgow, op. cit., p. 131.
50. Institute of Accountants, op. cit., p. 291.
51. Institute of Accountants in Glasgow, op. cit., pp. 153-4.
52. Robinson, p. 362.
53. BPP 1890-1 (431) I, 315.
54. Institute of Accountants in Glasgow, op. cit., p. 526.

Notes for pages 245 - 258

55. Garrett, p. 6.
56. Institute of Accountants, op. cit., Book 2, p. 133.
57. Institute of Accountants in Glasgow, op. cit., p. 58.
58. Session Cases 1893, 20 R, p. 750.
59. Institute of Accountants in Glasgow, op. cit., pp. 189-90.
60. ICAEW, op. cit., Bye-Law 52, p. 44.
61. *Accountants' Magazine* (1939) 90.
62. *Accountant* (1897) 49-52.
63. Ibid. (1897) 71-82.
64. Ibid. (1903) 217.
65. op. cit., p. 14.
66. Robinson, p. 129.
67. *Accountant* (1892) 924-5.
68. 26 November 1892, pp. 889-90.
69. Garrett, p. 7.
70. 6 October 1894, pp. 867-8.
71. 9 & 10 Geo. 5, c. 71 (1919).
72. BPP 1893-4 (65) VII, 119-120, S 1.
73. BPP 1893-4 (248) VII, 123.
74. *Accountant* (1893) 237-9.
75. Institute of Accountants, op. cit., Minute Book No. 2, p. 175.
76. Robinson, p. 129.
77. Garrett.
78. BPP 1894 (291) I, 1, S4.
79. 7 July 1894, pp. 605-6.
80. BPP 1895 (41-Sess I) I, 359.
81. *Accountant* (1895) 196.
82. 23 November, pp. 933-5; 30 November, pp. 955-6; 7 December, pp. 977-9.
83. BPP 1896 (114) I, 3.
84. BPP 1896 (318) I, 7.
85. e.g., 7 November 1896, pp. 918-19; 14 November, pp. 938-9; 21 November, pp. 956-8; 28 November, pp. 975, 977.
86. *Accountant* (1897) 49-52.
87. op. cit., p. 16.
88. Garrett, p. 19.
89. 9 January 1897, pp. 32-5; 16 January, pp. 64-7; 23 January, pp. 99-105; 6 February, pp. 151-4.

Notes for pages 258 - 266

90. Robinson, pp. 131-2.
91. BPP 1897 (163) I, 5.
92. BPP 1897 (94) I, 17.
93. 22 May 1897, p. 517.
94. BPP 1898 (201) I, 17.
95. *Accountant* (1898) 526.
96. Ibid. pp. 556-8.
97. *Accountant* (1899) 430-3.
98. BPP 1900 (112) IV, 191.
99. 31 March 1900, pp. 309-10.
100. *Accountant* (1874) 5.
101. Ibid. (1897) 518.

IX Accountancy as a Profession

1. M.S. Larson, *The Rise of Professionalism* (California, 1977) p. 19.
2. Millerson, *Qualifying Associations*, p. 23.
3. Reader, *Professional Men*, p. 2.
4. H.B. Thomson, *The Choice of a Profession* (London, 1857) p. 5.
5. G.E. Lenski, *Power and Privilege* (New York, 1966) p. 365.
6. K. Prandy, *Professional Employees* (London, 1965) p. 45.
7. Lewis and Maude, p. 53.
8. Carr-Saunders and Wilson, pp. 298, 302, 307, 359.
9. P.M. Blau and W.R. Scott, *Formal Organizations* (London, 1963) pp. 1, 60-1, 63.
10. H.L. Wilensky, 'The Professionalisation of Everyone', *American Journal of Sociology* (1964) 137-58.
11. Millerson, *Qualifying Associations*, pp. 28-32, 54.
12. Hall, p. 70.
13. E. Greenwood, 'Attributes of a Profession', *Social Work* (1957) pp. 45-55.
14. Worthington, p. 1.
15. Carr-Saunders and Wilson, p. 209.
16. A.C. Littleton, *Essays on Accountancy* (Urbana, 1961) pp. 461-4.

Notes for pages 266 - 274

17. D. Portwood and A. Fielding, 'Privilege and the Professions', *Sociological Review* (1981) 749-73.
18. Reader, *Professional Men*, p. 161.
19. M. Nisot, 'The Protection of Professional Titles II', *International Labour Review* (1940) 115-33.
20. T.H. Marshall, 'The Recent History of Professionalism in Relation to Social Structure and Social Policy', *The Canadian Journal of Economics and Political Science* (1939) 327.
21. BPP (1906) Cd 3053, XCVII, 249.
22. BPP (1907) (208) 1, 407, 521 (1).
23. BPP (1907) (321) 1, 441, 519 (1).
24. BPP (1918) (Cd 9138) VII, 727, para 58.
25. BPP (1926) (Cmd 2657) IX, 477, para 73.
26. BPP (1945) (Cmd 6659) IV, 793.
27. 11 & 12 Geo. 6, c. 38 (1948) s. 161.
28. Pixley, *Auditors*, p. 161.
29. Departmental Committee on Amendments to the Companies Acts, Minutes in Evidence, HMSO, London, (1925), Appendix V, para. 8.
30. Ibid., Appendix AA, para. 86, Appendix FF, para. 8d.
31. Institute of Accountants, Sederunt Book, Council Minutes, No. 1, p. 6.
32. Ibid., pp. 60-1.
33. Institute of Accountants in Glasgow, Minute Book No. 1, p. 81.
34. Society of Accountants in Edinburgh, Annual General Meetings, Minute Book, p. 131.
35. Ibid, Bye-laws, Rules and Regulations (1874) para. 38, p 12.
36. Institute of Accountants, op. cit., pp. 149-52, para. 5.
37. Institute of Accountants in Glasgow, Minute Book No. 2, p. 445.
38. B. Kaye, *The Development of the Architectural Profession in Britain* (London, 1960) p. 17.
39. Society of Accountants in Aberdeen, Minute Book No. 2, pp. 39, 68.
40. *Accountant* (1893) 4.

Name Index

Subject Index